RELIGION AND THE NEWS

In *Religion and the News* journalists and religious leaders reflect on their interactions with one another and their experiences of creating news. Through a series of original contributions, leading practitioners shed light on how religious stories emerge into the public domain. Experienced journalists and religious representatives from different faith traditions critically consider their role in a rapidly evolving communicative environment.

Aimed at journalists, faith representatives, religious leaders, academics and students this book offers a timely exploration of the current state of religious news coverage and makes an original contribution to the emerging media, religion and culture literature, as well to media and communication studies. *Religion and the News* presents insights from leading journalists and religious leaders, many well-known figures, writing openly about their experiences.

D0242600

Religion and the News

Edited by

JOLYON MITCHELL
Edinburgh University, UK

OWEN GOWER
Cumberland Lodge, UK

Routledge
Taylor & Francis Group

LONDON AND NEW YORK

First published 2012 by Ashgate Publishing

Published 2016 by Routledge
2 Park Square, Milton Park, Abingdon, Oxon OX14 4RN
711 Third Avenue, New York, NY 10017, USA

Routledge is an imprint of the Taylor & Francis Group, an informa business

British Library Cataloguing in Publication Data
Religion and the news.
   1. Religion and the press. 2. Mass media—Religious aspects. 3. Journalism, Religious.
   I. Mitchell, Jolyon P. II. Gower, Owen.
   070.4'492–dc23

Library of Congress Cataloging-in-Publication Data
Religion and the news / edited by Jolyon Mitchell and Owen Gower.
      p. cm.
   Includes bibliographical references (p.   ) and index.
   ISBN 978-1-4094-2018-7 (hardcover : alk. paper) – ISBN 978-1-4094-2019-4 (pbk. : alk. paper) 1. Religion and the press. 2. Journalism, Religious. I. Mitchell, Jolyon P. II. Gower, Owen.
   PN4756.R45 2012
   070.4'492–dc23

                                                                       2012012834

ISBN 9781409420187 (hbk)
ISBN 9781409420194 (pbk)

Contents

SECTION 3: REPRESENTING RELIGION AND THE NEWS

SECTION 4: CONTESTING RELIGION AND THE NEWS

List of Figures

Front Cover. *Montage*: Courtesy of Shutterstock and jannoon028 (hand touching flow of images), Korionov (man holding camera), Ryan Rodrick Beiler (a minaret of the King Hussein Mosque and the steeple of the Coptic Orthodox Church silhouetted on the Amman skyline) and (Jerusalem's Dome of the Rock and the Western Wall), Schmid Christophe (Christ, Corcovado in Rio de Janeiro, Brazil), kbrowne41 (woman in traditional middle eastern niqab veil), Micha Rosenwirth (planet earth), with thanks to David Wright and Brian Fischbacher.
Back cover. A group of photographers focusing down towards the viewer. Courtesy of Losevsky Pavel / Shutterstock.com

List of Contributors

Simon Barrow is co-director of the beliefs and values think-tank Ekklesia. He has worked both for denominational and ecumenical church structures, nationally and internationally, and for traditional and digital media as a news reporter, columnist and commentator. He acts as an adviser and consultant for religious bodies seeking to engage the media, and for media operators seeking to come to terms with religion.

Charlie Beckett is the founding director of Polis, the media and society think-tank at the London School of Economics. He is the author of *SuperMedia: Saving Journalism So It Can Save The World* (Blackwell 2008) and *WikiLeaks: News in the Networked Era* (Polity 2011). Before setting up Polis in 2006 he was an award-winning filmmaker and editor at LWT, BBC and ITN's Channel 4 News.

Andrew Brown is a journalist, writer and broadcaster. He most recently founded and edits the *Guardian's* belief site, which won a Webby award for the best religion site in the world after six months of operation. He has written two books of popular science, *The Darwin Wars* (2000), and *In the Beginning was the Worm* (2003), which was shortlisted for the Aventis prize for science writing; his book about Sweden, *Fishing in Utopia* (2008), won the Orwell prize in 2009.

Robin Gill held the Michael Ramsey Chair in Modern Theology at the University of Kent for twenty years having previously been the William Leech Professorial Fellow in Applied Theology at the University of Newcastle. He continues as Professor of Applied Theology at Kent. His most recent books are *Theology in a Social Context: Sociological Theology* Volume 1, 2012, *Theology Shaped by Society: Sociological Theology* Volume 2, September 2012 and *Society Shaped by Theology: Sociological Theology* Volume 3, Spring 2013, all published by Ashgate.

Ruth Gledhill has been at *The Times* since 1987 and has reported on every significant religious story and witnessed many dramatic changes in the field. She has also written many feature and comment pieces for *The Times*, has edited books of prayers and sermons, wrote the *At Your Service* column for eleven years and ran the Preacher of the Year Award. She has been quick to keep up with technical developments and her blog, *Articles of Faith*, is regularly listed on a number of sites as among the top ten newspaper and religion blogs. She has been nominated three times in the UK Press Awards and other nominations include the Andrew Cross Award for religious reporting.

Richard Harries was Bishop of Oxford from 1987–2006. On his retirement he was made a Life Peer and he continues to be active in the House of Lords as a Crossbencher. He is Gresham Professor of Divinity and an Honorary Professor of Theology at King's College, London. Professor Harries has published over twenty-five books and numerous articles, covering a wide range of interests, including *Faith in Politics? (2010), Questions of Life and Death* (2010), *The Re-enchantment of Morality* (2008), *The Passion in Art* (2004), *After the Evil: Christianity and Judaism in the Shadow of the Holocaust* (2003) and a collection of his contributions to *Thought for the Day* on BBC Radio 4's *Today* Programme to which he has been a regular contributor since 1972, *In the Gladness of Today* (2000).

Jonathan Heawood has been Director of English PEN since 2005. He was previously Editorial Director of the Fabian Society and Deputy Literary Editor of the *Observer*.

Mark Hill is in private practice at the Bar in London, Honorary Professor of Law at Cardiff University and a Fellow of its Centre for Law and Religion.

Monawar Hussain is the Muslim Tutor at Eton College. He studied theology at the University of Oxford, majoring in Islam and the West, and trained as an Imam under the guidance of the late Shaykh Dr Zaki Badawi KBE at the Muslim College, London.

Kim Knott is Professor of Religious Studies at Lancaster University and, from 2005 to 2010, was director of the Diasporas, Migration and Identities Programme for the Arts and Humanities Research Council (AHRC). In 2008 she returned to the subject of her first post-doctoral project, *Media portrayals of religion*, co-directing a new study with Elizabeth Poole and Teemu Taira, which will be the subject of their forthcoming book, *Media Portrayals of Religion and the Secular: Representation and Change* (Ashgate).

Christopher Landau studied theology to master's level at Cambridge University before undertaking a BBC News traineeship in 2002. In 2003 he began reporting for Radio 4's *Sunday* programme, later reporting for *World at One* and *PM*, before his appointment as religious affairs correspondent, based at the World Service, in 2008. In 2010 he left the BBC to resume academic study of theology at Oxford University, combined with training for ordination in the Church of England.

Catherine Pepinster has been editor of *The Tablet* for over seven years. She has been a journalist for all her working life and before joining *The Tablet* worked for the *Independent* and *Independent on Sunday*, where she worked as the executive editor.

Elizabeth Poole is a Senior Lecturer in Media Studies at Staffordshire University and Award Leader of the MA in Media Management. She has written widely in the area of the representation and reception of Muslims in the news and is author of *Reporting Islam: Media Representations of British Muslims* (I.B. Tauris) and editor, with John Richardson, of *Muslims and the News Media* (I.B. Tauris). With Kim Knott, she co-directed *Media portrayals of religion and the secular sacred*. Other research interests include ethnicity and the news, audiences and new media.

Jonathan Romain is rabbi of Maidenhead Synagogue. He has a PhD in Anglo-Jewish history. He writes regularly for *The Times* and *The Jewish Chronicle* and is frequently on radio. His many books include *The Jews of England* (1988) and *Reform Judaism and Modernity* (2004). He is a Fellow of St George's House, Windsor, and a member of the BBC's Standing Conference on Religion and Belief.

Roger Royle presented his own television show for Southern and Ulster Television, took part in various television panel games and became a regular presenter of *Songs of Praise*. On radio, he presented his regular Sunday morning show on Radio 2, *Good Morning Sunday*, and an occasional series called *Royle Tour*. He also presented *Sunday Half Hour* for sixteen years and was a regular contributor to *Pause for Thought* with Terry Wogan.

Ruth Scott is an Anglican priest, writer and broadcaster. She works in the fields of conflict transformation and interfaith relations. She is a well-known broadcaster and presenter of *Pause for Thought* on Radio 2's *Wake up to Wogan* show. She has recently written her third book, *Give a Boy a Gun: One Man's Journey from Killing to Peace-Making* (2009), with one of her colleagues, Alistair Little, an ex-Loyalist paramilitary.

Lord Indarjit Singh of Wimbledon, CBE, DL is a nationally recognised journalist and broadcaster. He edits the widely respected *Sikh Messenger* and is Director of the Network of Sikh Organisations, the premier body of Sikhs in the UK with more than 100 affiliates.

Teemu Taira is a researcher of religious studies at the University of Turku, Finland, and was a research fellow at the University of Leeds from 2008 to 2010, working on *Media portrayals of religion and the secular sacred*. He works in the fields of religious studies, cultural studies and the sociology of religion, and has published in both Finnish and English. His current projects are on discourse on religion and the secular in Finnish media and the new visibility of atheism.

Paul Woolley is Executive Director of Charity at the Bible Society. Until January 2011, he was Director of Theos, the public theology think-tank. Paul has two degrees in theology and a background in politics. In addition to working as a Parliamentary Researcher and directing a political unit, he has had extensive public affairs experience in the charity sector.

Acknowledgements

Religion and the News emerged from the conversations at a Cumberland Lodge Conference held in October 2009, with encouragement from the Conference Chairman, Lord Harries, and the Principal of Cumberland Lodge, Dr Alastair Niven. Some of the contributors to this volume were not present at the initial conversations, but the existence of this book owes much to the vibrant energy of those discussions. The editors are particularly grateful to Cumberland Lodge, the Rayne Trust, the Centre for Theology and Public Issues (CTPI) at the University of Edinburgh and the Binks Trust for supporting this publication. Tim Joss, at the Rayne Foundation, was instrumental in getting the conference off the ground and in pursuing the outcomes from it. Thanks to Ginny Felton and Janis Reeves for all their work on the conference. Sarah Lloyd, Abigail Fenton and Beatrice Beaup and Ann Allen at Ashgate deserve hearty thanks for their good-humoured support and encouragements. The royalties from the sale of this book are being given to The Estelle Trust, which provides education and training for orphans in Zambia, water aid to rural communities and vulnerable children, as well as support for microloans.

We are both hugely grateful to each of the contributors to this book for their fine chapters, for their patience and for their creative engagement with the topic of religion and the news. Thanks to Richard Harries, Christopher Landau and Andrew Brown for their initial enthusiasm and support for this project. Many scholars, broadcasters and journalists have provided direct or indirect support and advice. These include Nick Adams, Florian Amberg, Arun Arora, Andrew Barr, Bridget Cass, Rebecca Cato, Clifford Christians, Nick Couldry, Zaki Cooper, David Craig, Tim Dean, Frederick Dove, John Eldridge, Alison Elliot, Jo Elliot, David Fergusson, Mark Fackler, Bob Fortner, Hugh Goddard, Andrew Graystone, James Jones, Tim Joss, James Kidner, Kim Knott, Jane Leek, Alan Little, Knut Lundby, David Lyon, Gordon Lynch, Jake Lynch, Jim McDonnell, Colin Morris, Michael Northcott, Oliver O'Donovan, Greg Philo, Philip Plyming, John Pritchard, Ben Quash, Amy Richards, James Robbins, Scott Ross, Mona Siddiqui, the late Roger Silverstone, Jon Snow, Geoffrey Stevenson, Sam Thambusamy, Rachel Viney, David Winter, Michael Wakelin, George Wilkes, Alan Wilson, Diane Winston, Linda Woodhead, and Jenny Wright. Theodora Hawksley has been outstandingly helpful during the last few laps. Thankyou to each of the above and many other colleagues and friends.

We are grateful to members of *the International Study Commission in Media, Religion and Culture* for sharing their insights about news and religion in different parts of the world, through a series of international workshops and seminars. Thanks to Kwabena Asamoah-Gyadu, Lynn Schofield Clark, Roberto Goizueta,

Juan Carlos Henríquez, Mary Hess, Stewart Hoover, Peter Horsfield, Adán Medrano, David Morgan, Fabio Pasqualetti, Frances Forde Plude, Germán Rey, Siriwan Santisakultarm and Bob White, as well as each of the Porticus research fellows. Jolyon Mitchell is particularly grateful to Porticus for making this cross-cultural research and collaboration possible, and to the Binks Trust for their generous support of the *Peacebuilding through Media Arts* research project, hosted at CTPI in Edinburgh, which has also influenced the shape of this book.

On a personal note Owen Gower thanks his colleagues at Cumberland Lodge, particularly Alastair Niven, Amanda Fitzgerald, Annie Gosling and Faye Taylor. They, along with my students at Royal Holloway, have offered valuable reflections on the themes and arguments of this book. I also thank my wife, Jessie, for her support and understanding.

Jolyon Mitchell thanks Iona, John and Sarah Birchall, Pom and Kit Bowen, Katharine and Matthew Frost, Anna King, F. Ellis Leigh, Andrew and Judith Matheson, Fiona and Richard Parsons, and my mother Catharine Beck, and my father Peter Mitchell for so much encouragement. I remain indebted to Clare for so much, including her careful, critical and constructive reading, and to our children Sebastian, Jasmine and Xanthe, who regularly show that what is left outside the news frame are often the most interesting stories of all.

The Editors

Owen Gower is Director of the Cumberland Lodge Programme, where he works to promote cross-sector and interdisciplinary collaboration on matters affecting the development of society. His PhD in Philosophy is from the University of London, and his academic interests focus particularly on questions in epistemology and moral psychology. He teaches philosophy at King's College London and Royal Holloway, where he is an honorary research associate.

Jolyon Mitchell is Professor of Communications, Arts and Religion, Director of the Centre for Theology and Public Issues (CTPI), and Deputy Director of the Institute for Advanced Study in the Humanities (IASH), at the University of Edinburgh. Prior to this he worked as a producer and journalist with BBC World Service and Radio 4. His books include *Media Violence and Christian Ethics* (Cambridge University Press, 2007) and *Promoting Peace, Inciting Violence: the Role of Religion and Media* (Routledge, 2012).

Introduction

Owen Gower and Jolyon Mitchell

Over the last three decades the coverage of religious news in the media has radically changed: religion is no longer a 'soft' story. Religious issues pervade the reporting of many stories related to domestic politics and foreign affairs alike. Following the terrorist attacks in Western cities such as New York (11 September 2001), Madrid (11 March 2004) and London (7 July 2005), as well as the invasions of Afghanistan (from October 2001) and Iraq (from March 2003), religion has increasingly broken into mainstream Western news agendas. Some scholars suggest that this process began even earlier with the Iranian Revolution (1979), the global performances of a 'media friendly' Pope, John Paul II (1978–2005), and the rise of the 'religious right' in the USA (from the late 1970s).[1] The cumulative result is that religion is less commonly marginalised, and is sometimes used as an interpretative key for making sense of many news stories.

Even if a religious story seems self-contained, its ramifications often generate comment from unrelated parts of what is sometimes described as 'the secular press'. The visit of Pope Benedict XVI to the UK in 2010, for example, generated a huge amount of coverage from commentators and reporters not normally associated with religious news. Indeed, as we shall see (chapter 2), comparing the coverage of the papal visit in 1982 with the 2010 visit sheds light on the changing relationship between religion and the news: there is now more comment on the plurality of faith traditions in Britain (with a particular emphasis on Islam); the marginalisation of Christianity is a recurring theme; and the rise of 'aggressive secularism' has been especially notable. While it is more likely than ever before for religion to be *in* the news, it is also more likely for the coverage to focus on conflict, threat and scandal. Despite many religious leaders wanting to see their faiths represented as being harmonious, reconciliatory and profoundly ethical, many news stories pick up on disharmony or highlight failings. Why is there this contrast between what religious leaders want reported and what journalists feel is newsworthy about religions in the UK?

One frequent explanation is that what counts as newsworthy is driven by market forces. It is commonly claimed that celebrity, conflict, the outlandish and scandal is what we – the public – want to read and hear about, and therefore these are the kind of stories we will pay for. If the market partly defines what is newsworthy, then it also helps to shape journalism. As new technologies have entered the

---

[1]   Stewart Hoover, *Religion in the News: Faith and Journalism in American Public Discourse* (Thousand Oaks, CA, London and New Delhi: Sage Publications, 1998), pp. 1–17.

marketplace, journalism has become more instantaneous and increasingly open to amateur commentators. News and religion have gone digital. Information and comment are even harder to control than they were before the advent of the Internet and related technologies. While market pressures and digital communication may contribute to the frustration of religious leaders with religious news, the demands of the market and the widespread use of the new technologies may also be opening doors onto novel patterns of news production. Professional journalists and editors are no longer the gatekeepers of media messages in this increasingly networked world. Their authority has been reduced in many spheres over the last three decades, in a way not dissimilar to the loss of authority and respect experienced by many religious institutions over the last century. Changing economic, social and power relations have contributed to a radical series of transformations within Europe's communicative environment.

Irrespective of what has caused religious news to become increasingly critical, and there are various explanations in the chapters that follow, the upshot is that many religious representatives often feel misrepresented in the press. Likewise, many journalists believe that religious people do not appreciate how the media operates: it does not exist to provide free publicity or to evangelise. On the contrary, reporters investigate, uncover and analyse, and that often leads to the coverage of stories that embarrass members of faith traditions. Where does this leave the relationship between faith representatives and journalists? Is there an inevitable clash of values and priorities between the two groups? Or is there a recurring 'blind spot' when it comes to many journalists covering religion, and another 'blind spot' when many religious leaders attempt to engage with the news media?[2]

This book offers a rare opportunity for journalists and faith leaders to express, to explain and to analyse their frustrations with one another, and to offer their views on how to create a more engaged relationship between religious representatives and journalists. These perspectives are framed by analyses of the current state of reporting on religion in the UK, along with chapters on significant issues such as the law, blasphemy, violent conflict and the role of technology in shaping both beliefs and the news coverage of faith traditions.

Many of the contributions to this book are characterised by the personal experiences of the writers with the interaction between religion and the news. These reflections are sometimes marked by anger or disappointment and illustrated with examples of mistreatment by one side or another. There has been no attempt to downplay these personal sentiments or to try and develop a consistent analysis across the different voices in the book. We considered calling this book a 'reader', but in reflecting carefully on the range of contributions realised that it could also be called a 'listener'. Several of the authors write more commonly for the ear than for the eye, others write more regularly for general audiences rather than specialist readers. Their distinct voices, accents and styles have been intentionally preserved,

---

² See Paul Marshall, Lela Gilbert, and Roberta Green Ahmanson (eds), *Blind Spot: When Journalists Don't Get Religion* (New York and Oxford: Oxford University Press, 2009).

reflecting the multiplicity of ways that religion and the news are both interpreted and covered. Listening carefully to the different voices in this book will reveal fresh ways of reflecting on both old and new arguments. Some of the chapters that follow are grounded in empirical evidence and original research, while others are rooted in practical experience, which can result in the passionate expression of strongly held beliefs and deeply felt emotions. In the pages that follow, insights, criticisms and proposals are to be found embedded both in rational arguments and personal anecdotes. This range of voices, approaches and perspectives provides a rich resource for understanding the complex relations between religion and the news.

The different authors found in this book disagree about fundamental issues, such as the nature of free speech, the correlation between demographics and coverage, the role of truth in journalism, whether different religions require different treatment by the press, what is wrong with religious press and public relations departments, the 24-hour news cycle, the standard of religious education among journalists and so on. Seeing these fault-lines close-up provides a valuable insight into some of the difficulties faced by journalists as they attempt to cover news about religion and by religious leaders who are trying to articulate and to embody the beliefs and the practices of their own religious tradition. While tensions are certainly present, all contributors agree that the relationship between religion and the news can be improved. A constructive vision of the relationship between religion and the news does emerge from the contributions, but it emerges gradually, through an account of the mistakes and frustrations of the past as well as hope for a future where journalists and religious leaders have developed a clearer understanding of each other's crafts and callings.

SECTION 1
Understanding Religion and the News

Figure 1   *News and Religion.* Courtesy of Shutterstock.com and David Wright.

Introduction to Section 1: Understanding Religion and the News

What is the relationship between religion and the media in the UK today? In particular, what is the relationship between religion and the news?

All of the contributors to this volume engage with these central questions. Later on, we will hear media experts talk about their experience of engaging with religion (section 2), and religious representatives talk about their experience of engaging with different media (section 3). The purpose of this first section is to ground that later conversation by providing a broad overview of the relationship between religion and news media in the UK.

Jolyon Mitchell investigates the different approaches to religion and the news, through a study of how the St Paul's protests were covered. He argues that it is important to go beyond analysis of the evolving story, to consider the cultural, political and historical contexts in which the news emerges, as well as the roles of creative journalists and active audiences. Teemu Taira, Elizabeth Poole and Kim Knott provide a statistical picture of how religion is treated in British television and newspapers. A more detailed summary of their argument is provided at the start of their chapter. Brief summaries are also provided before all the remaining chapters. Robin Gill discusses what news coverage reveals about developing and differing perceptions of religion in the modern world. Paul Woolley closes the section by arguing that the relationship between religion and media is 'worth getting right', and making some constructive suggestions for how it could be improved.

The chapters in this section raise several important issues for the discussion that follows in sections two and three. These include questions relating to representation, authority and communication. First, representation, reporters covering religious stories in the news media face a tension between presenting the 'story' and presenting the religious community in a balanced way – a tension that often causes significant frustration for both religious leaders and reporters, as we shall see later on. The second issue concerns media authority, and the question of what makes religion reporting sufficiently informed and authoritative. Should correspondents covering religion have specific expertise comparable to that of many economic or business correspondents and academic qualifications in religious studies or theology? Should religion correspondents be people of faith themselves or should they at least have a sympathetic understanding of faith? Or should journalists remain reticent about their own world-views and beliefs? The third issue relates to communication. Why is it that some journalists and religious leaders appear often to misunderstand or to misrepresent each other? And what does evolving journalistic coverage communicate about perceptions of faith, belief and skepticism? These issues resonate through the interpretations, criticisms and suggestions of the contributions that follow.

Chapter 1

Religion and the News: Stories, Contexts, Journalists and Audiences

Jolyon Mitchell

Introduction

Many journalists observed in October 2011 that for the first time since London's Blitz during the Second World War, the doors of St Paul's Cathedral were closed to the public. It was noted that, by contrast, the flaps of the tents of the anti-capitalist protestors, camping in front of the cathedral, were left open to visitors. Numerous reporters visited the 'Occupy' camp, listened to speeches, recorded interviews and photographed the placards. This evolving story was covered not only by religion correspondents, programmes and papers, but also attracted news coverage from all over the world. For example, *The New York Times* claimed that the '"Occupy" Protest at St. Paul's Cathedral in London Divides Church' (30 October 2011). On several days in late October and early November 2011 news about St Paul's made the front pages of many papers, as well as being one of the lead items for broadcast and online news reports.

The St Paul's protest is a useful example for reflecting on different approaches to religion and the news. In this chapter I consider four approaches. They can be characterised by a distinct primary focal point: the story, the context, the journalist or the audience. At the outset it is important to underline that behind every newsworthy event, or series of events, there are multiple stories, contexts, journalists and audiences. These are not frozen in time, but dynamic elements within the making of news. This will become clearer as we examine evolving stories, contested contexts, creative journalists, and expressive audiences. There are a multiplicity of representations, reporters and receptions, emerging out of a range of settings. In order to develop a nuanced analysis of the relation between religion and the news it is useful to draw upon questions and methods from each of these four approaches.[1]

---

[1]   These are by no means watertight categories. As will become clear by listening to the different voices through this book, interpretations of religion and the news sometimes draw from more than one approach.

The vast majority of earlier studies on religion and the news have emerged in North America.[2] To varying degrees they draw upon each of these four approaches. By contrast, European books on news, by both academics and journalists, tend either to overlook religion altogether, or to deal with it only in a cursory fashion.[3] This is slowly changing in the UK, Europe and other parts of the world,[4] especially following the increased interest in the place of Islam in the news.[5] Both this chapter and the entire book contribute to these emerging global discussions. The aim here is to shed critical light on the coverage of religion by journalists, on religious leaders' engagement with the news media, and on several possible ways forward for reparative reflection and action.

Evolving stories

First, those who employ a *narrative-centred approach* tend to focus on the actual content of an individual news story or cluster of stories. Description of the evolving narrative combined with analysis of the language, the structure, and the images, as well as the use and choice of interviewees characterise this approach. In other

---

[2]   See, for example: Mark Silk, *Unsecular Media: Making News of Religion in America* (Urbana: University of Illinois Press, 1995); Stewart Hoover, *Religion in the News: Faith and Journalism in American Public Discourse* (London: Sage, 1998); Judith Buddenbaum, *Reporting News About Religion: An Introduction for Journalists* (Ames, Iowa: Iowa State University Press, 1998). See also: Diane Winston (ed.), *The Oxford Handbook on Religion and the American News Media* (Oxford: Oxford University Press, forthcoming 2012) and her *Heartland Religion: The American News Media and the Reagan Revolution* (Oxford: Oxford University Press, forthcoming 2013).

[3]   See, for example, Howard Tumber (ed.), *News: A Reader* (Oxford: Oxford University Press, 1999). It is striking how this extensive collection of major essays and articles on news lacks any sustained treatment of news and religion. The British journalist Andrew Marr's, *My Trade: A Short History of British Journalism* (London: Macmillan, 2004), is another example, from many autobiographically informed discussions of the British press, which overlooks consideration of the relation between religion and the news.

[4]   See, for example, Kim Knott and Jolyon Mitchell, 'The Changing Faces of Media and Religion', in Linda Woodhead and Rebecca Catto (eds), *Religion and Change in Modern Britain* (London and New York: Routledge, 2012), pp. 243–64. See also recent decent discussions of 'mediatization', such as Knut Lundby (ed.), *Mediatization, Concept, Changes, Consequences* (New York and Oxford: Peter Lang, 2009). See also Yoel Cohen, *God, Jews and the Media: Religion and Israel's Media* (London and New York: Routledge, 2012) and the following two chapters for further examples.

[5]   See, for example, K. Moore, P. Mason and J. Lewis, *Images of Islam in the UK: The Representation of British Muslims in the National Print News Media 2000–2008* (Cardiff: Cardiff University and Channel 4, 2008); and Jake Lynch, *Debates in Peace Journalism* (Sydney: Sydney University Press, 2008), especially chapter 8 on 'The "Islam Problem" in news journalism and scope for media activism', pp. 163–82.

words, how has a news story been covered? What makes up the story and what has been left out? How has it evolved, developed or fragmented? News stories are rarely static; they are constantly moving, adapting and evolving.

This can be seen in how the St Paul's protest and related stories were covered. The event in London began on *Facebook* on the 10 October 2011, with an online encouragement to follow in the footsteps of the *Occupy Wall Street* demonstrations in New York.[6] On 15 October demonstrators tried to occupy the privately owned property Paternoster Square outside the London Stock Exchange, but were prevented from doing so by the police, who were acting on a court order. The demonstration of around 2000 protestors relocated to outside St Paul's cathedral, with over 70 tents being used for overnight accommodation. The cathedral's Canon Chancellor, Giles Fraser, attracted both criticism (e.g. *Daily Mail*) and praise (e.g. the *Guardian*) for asking the police and not the protestors to move on, supporting their right to demonstrate. In the light of subsequent events, this was interpreted both as a warm welcome and tacit support for the protestors' endeavour. A more permanent encampment was established to the west of the cathedral by 17 October 2011, which would soon increase to around 200 tents, including a larger 'Tent City University', a bookshop, a kitchen and the *Occupied Times of London* newspaper. The majority of these would remain for over four months.

There then followed a pivotal moment in this evolving story. St Paul's, 'the capital's cathedral', was closed indefinitely on Friday 21 October due to 'health and safety' concerns. These were not elaborated upon until after the weekend. In an age of 24-hour news, where there is an insatiable hunger for rapid response, immediate justification and swift judgement this explanation was interpreted by several commentators as prevarication. How did different news media cover the closing of the cathedral? The next day on BBC Radio 4's *Today* programme, Rob Marshall, an experienced broadcaster and cleric based in Hull, represented St Paul's and tried to explain the decision to close its doors to the public. In the face of an unremitting 'grilling' by *Today* presenter John Humphries he was robust in defence of the Dean and Chapter's controversial decision.

On the same day the *Daily Mail* ran the headline: 'Surrender of St Paul's: Protest rabble force the cathedral to close, a feat that Hitler could barely manage' (22 October 2011). Their story was illustrated by the famous photograph by Herbert Mason from 29 December 1940 of St Paul's emerging out of the smoke during the Blitz.[7] Readers were reminded that the picture was taken from the roof

---

[6]   Many journalists reference the iconic poster, created by the Canadian magazine *Adbusters* in July 2011, as the starting point of the 'Occupy' movement. It shows a ballerina poised on the back of the huge 'Wall Street Bull' statue in Manhattan's Financial District. Above the figure is a question in red letters: 'What is our one demand?' The answer below is on three lines in white letters: 'OccupyWallStreet September 17th. Bring Tent'.

[7]   John Keegan, Philip Knightly, Sarah Jackson, Annabel Merullo and David Rowley, *The Eye of War: Words and Photographs from the Front Line* (London: Weidenfeld & Nicolson, 2003), pp. 136–7.

Figure 2   Occupy protest and camp outside St Paul's Cathedral, London,
                including one of many banners. 5 January, 2012. Courtesy of Alison
                Henley / Shutterstock.com

of the *Daily Mail*'s former offices, in Fleet Street. They were also told why St Paul's last closed: a time-delayed bomb 'hit' the cathedral on the 12 September 1940, which only reopened when the bomb, which could have done catastrophic damage, was removed and detonated safely. 'For the rest of the war, however, even as Luftwaffe bombs reduced much of the surrounding area to rubble, St Paul's remained open.'[8] The condemnation of the cathedral Dean and Chapter's decision on what were assumed to be 'spurious health and safety grounds' was widespread and unforgiving. Several television news reports used black and white footage from Reuters or Pathé of another bomb's damage in December 1940 to the interior and high altar. Few reports distinguished between the different attacks that the cathedral had survived during the Blitz. Some simply ignored the comparison between the closing of the cathedral doors in 1940 and in 2011.

Several television news reports included interviews with disappointed or frustrated tourists who were unable to visit or even worship at St Paul's. *The Times* highlighted how William Hill, the bookmakers, was offering odds of 100–101 that the cathedral would still be closed at Christmas. In response to *The Times*' story William Oddie, the former editor of the *Catholic Herald*, quipped in his old paper: 'will it matter?' (25 October 2011). For the *Telegraph* it was a 'squalid occupation' that had resulted in 'A Sullied Cathedral' (24 October). This description resonated with several comments by a number of lords and MPs in Parliament. Libby Purves in *The Times* memorably described the protest as a 'tented tantrum. A nylon-roofed, media-savvy, Twitterati, festival-inspired, Glasto-generation sulk', though she was 'very glad that St Paul's was gracious towards it at first'. The *Daily Express*, in a series of negative headlines articulating rage at the protest, claimed that: 'Mob threat to sabotage Poppy Day at St Paul's' (25 October).

The second significant series of twists in the story was the resignation of both Giles Fraser, the Canon Chancellor, on 27 October, and the Dean, Graeme Knowles, four days later. Another chaplain also resigned. After these resignations and the re-opening of the cathedral (on 28 October), the *Independent* used the headline: 'Carry on at the Cathedral'; while Riazat Butt's article in the *Guardian* was given the title: 'St Paul's brought to its knees by confusion and indecision' and the *Telegraph* reported that: 'St Paul's branded "laughing stock" as Dean Graeme resigns' (31 October). *Time* magazine offered an ironic score line: 'London Protestors 1 God 0: Anti-Capitalism camp scores PR Victory Against St Paul's'. On the same day the *London Evening Standard* ran a satirical comedy sketch by Nick Curtis, one of the creators of *Rev*, the BBC's comedy drama series. It was entitled: 'A loose Canon, his Bishop, the Dean and unholy war at St Paul's' (28 October). It is noticeable how some of these accounts employed irony and comedy while others resorted to framing this story in terms of conflict.

---

[8]   Tom Kelly et al. Available at: http://www.dailymail.co.uk/news/article-2051901/St-Pauls-Cathedral-shuts-doors-time-living-memory.html [accessed 1 December 2011].

Figure 3   Photographers and a cameraman document entrance doors opening
                at St Paul's Cathedral, London, following a week-long closure. The
                cathedral reopened at midday on Friday 28 October 2011, with a
                special Eucharist service, including prayers for the demonstrators.
                Courtesy of Press Association Images/Matt Dunham.

The third significant development came on 1 November after the resignation of
the Dean, when under the temporary leadership of the Bishop of London, Richard
Chartres, the cathedral chapter reversed their original decision and suspended their
legal action against the protestors. Melanie Phillips, in the *Daily Mail,* was less
than playful and wrote of 'the debacle at St Paul's' which 'threatens to inflict a
terrible blow on the authority of the Church of England itself' (2 November).
While on the same day Matthew d'Ancona wrote in the *London Evening Standard*
under the headline: 'The Church looks like a heritage society on the hop'. On
1 November *The Times* declared that 'the C of E' was in 'disaster recovery mode'.
Ruth Gledhill, *The Times'* religion correspondent, ascribed global significance
to the events: 'The resignations show the huge divisions at the leadership of the
cathedral. The cathedral in particular has been brought to its knees by it but I
think it's been extremely damaging for the Church as a whole in Britain if not
Christianity in the West' (1 November). The precise nature of the 'damage' or
'terrible blow' is not spelt out.

As can be seen from these brief descriptions the story evolved and attracted a
broad range of coverage. Read back over the last few paragraphs and it is noticeable
how this evolving story is invested with considerable dramatic significance. This

is achieved by heightened language, which on one level is 'entertaining' to read, while on another is in danger of sliding into hyperbole. The descriptive language employed varies in its tone, though amongst some commentators and headline writers it often slides into melodrama, exaggeration or even plain vitriolic attack. There is no single simple narrative but a range of stories and perspectives emerging out of a series of events. News stories need a new angle to remain fresh and attractive to editors and to audiences. The story about St Paul's evolved into many different forms, and was expressed and then circulated through a range of media. Used in different ways, it has been cited, adapted and twisted to make political, ideological and theological points.

The story continued to mutate and multiply. Initial controversial criticisms of the demonstrators based on images from a thermal imaging camera supposedly revealing that many of the tents were empty at night (e.g. *Daily Telegraph, Sun, Telegraph* and *Times*) were followed up with claims that cathedral staff had to clean up human waste (the *Mail*), sacrilegious graffiti and even cope with individuals urinating through the crypt restaurant windows (e.g. *Evening Standard*). Several papers quoted these claims uncritically, though some began to question their veracity, especially concerning how many tents were actually occupied at night.[9] For some papers the accuracy of such claims appeared less important than the fact that these stories appeared to support their editorial attitude towards the protest. The *Express* papers, for example, continued in the way they began: 'Protestors say that Poppy Sellers are Baby Killers' (*Sunday Express*, 6 November 2011). The *Daily Express*, illustrated their story with a photo of graffiti on one of St Paul's columns, declaring: 'Sick thugs daub 666 on St Paul's' (5 November), and two days later: 'Mob use St Paul's as a toilet' (7 November). The *Daily Express* may have maintained a 'consistent' line of coverage, but protestors and their supporters have hotly contested such stories and pictures, including an image of riot police in action against the Wall Street demonstrators, and the assertion by the *Express* that: 'New York shows how to deal with St Paul's mob' (16 November).

While this book was in press the story evolved further. The Occupy camp outside St Paul's was dismantled and the protestors evicted by the police and bailiffs, soon after midnight on 28 February 2012. Several journalists suggested that in spite of some scuffles and rough handling the eviction was 'largely peaceful', with only twenty arrests, very different from the extreme violence used against protestors in Syria. A 'staff reporter' for the *Ekklesia* (a British theological think-tank) news service led their description of the eviction with the claim that: 'Christians praying

---

⁹   See, for example, Sam Jones and Peter Walker's article on: 'Occupy London activists deny claims that few tents are occupied at night', the *Guardian*, 26 October 2011. They quote one of the demonstrators claiming: 'While it is quite possible that not every tent is occupied every night, we try to keep vacancy to a minimum and operate a sign-in/sign-out system to help ensure this happens. The camp attracts thousands of people every day. We do not expect all the people who are expressed through this movement to be able to stay overnight.' A figure of 70 per cent occupancy rather than 10 per cent as reported was cited.

on the Cathedral steps were violently pushed and kicked by police'. Later on the
same day Giles Fraser, temporarily working for the *Guardian*, wrote a detailed
article for their website suggesting that: 'The St Paul's demonstrators showed a
passion and caring attitude that contrasted with the cold indifference of the City'.[10]
A shorter version of his piece appeared on the front page of the *Guardian* the
following day (29 February 2012). The BBC news site offered swift analysis of
what the demonstrators had achieved, quoting David Allen Green, a City of London
lawyer, claiming that the protestors had 'been a useful if colourful corrective to
the arrogance and financial vandalism of many who work in the Square Mile'. By
contrast, the *Daily Mail* ran the story under the headline: 'Salvation of St Paul's:
Protest Camp that lasted 137 days is cleared in 137 minutes'. It showed several
pictures of cleaners carrying out 'a deep clean' on where the camp had been. On
the day of the police action Louise Sassoon in the *Daily Express* claimed that the
eviction 'marks a victory for the *Daily Express* which launched a crusade to Boot
Them Out'. The story has continued to evolve and to divide commentators and
journalists. Whether this is the end of the St Paul's Occupy Protest stories is an
open question. Reports may appear to drop off mainstream news agendas, but they
can re-emerge when they appear to have been completely forgotten.

News stories invariably take on a life of their own, reappearing in unexpected
places and forms. This story was no exception. The tales connected with St Paul's
are a mere drop in what Salman Rushdie describes as the never-ending 'sea of
stories'.[11] Some stories have the magnetic power to stand out from other tales.
Good images help. Photographs of bright, fragile tents with the solid pillars of St
Paul's in the background were commonly circulated over this Winter-long protest.
Digital images of banners proclaiming 'Capitalism is Crisis', 'We are the 99%' or
'Occupy London', and asking 'What would Jesus do?', were often used to provide
an interesting foreground or background.

In other photographs masked protestors wearing 'V is for Vendetta'[12] or
other dramatic masks, stood in the background while the Bishop of London and

---

[10]   Fraser was also widely quoted as saying: 'Riot police clearing the steps of St Paul's
Cathedral was a terrible sight. This is a sad day for the Church'.

[11]   Salman Rushdie, *Haroun and the Sea of Stories* (London: Granta, 1990).

[12]   These comic book Guy Fawkes' masks, including a pointed beard and moustache,
appeared in numerous press photographs of the St Paul's protests and other 'anti-capitalist'
demonstrations. Several journalists reminded readers that the mask had originally been created
by a British graphic novel artist David Lloyd for Alan Moore's comic book series *V for Vendetta*
(1982–1989), which has become even better known through a feature film of the same name
(2005, directed by James McTeigue). In both novel and film the protagonist is attempting
to overthrow a fictional ruling British Fascist party, by employing some of Guy Fawkes'
techniques. The mask's creator David Lloyd is often quoted as saying: 'The Guy Fawkes mask
has now become a common brand and a convenient placard to use in protest against tyranny
– and I'm happy with people using it, it seems quite unique, an icon of popular culture being
used this way.' (See, for example, Rosie Waites, *BBC News Magazine*, 20 October 2011.)
Waites also underlined how 'sales of the masks make money for Warner Bros'.

Figure 4   Occupy protest outside St Paul's Cathedral with the artist Banksy's
              donation, imitating the board game *Monopoly*, and a 'What would
              Jesus do?' banner in the background. 31 October 2011, in London.
              Courtesy of yampi / Shutterstock.com

the Dean spoke or listened to speeches outside the cathedral. There are, in the
words of Roland Barthes, 'numberless' narratives appearing in 'infinite forms'
throughout human history.[13] Why has this evolving story, about some protestors
camped outside a cathedral, attracted so much attention for a brief period of time?
Apart from the obvious answers, such as the symbolic significance of St Paul's and
the visually memorable scenes, a further set of explanations are to be found in the
various contexts in which this story emerged. These contexts have been described
in different ways by a wide range of interpreters.

Contested contexts

Second, those who use a *context centred-approach* tend to concentrate on the
historical, social and religious settings in which a story emerges. How does a
story relate to a wider context? How does this news interact with previous or
other current stories? Why has this news attracted so much attention? To

---

[13]   Roland Barthes, *The Semiotic Challenge*, trans. Richard Howard (Berkeley, CA:
University of California Press, 1989), p. 89.

understand some of the interactions that took place around St Paul's, and other recent significant religion stories,[14] it is vital to take into account the changing historical and communicative contexts.[15]

Earlier in the twentieth century, reports and interviews were commonly, though not exclusively, marked by respect towards religious leaders. This was part of a broader atmosphere of deference towards the establishment, characterised by interviewers sometimes even asking political leaders what they would like to speak about. News organisations and journalists were often highly deferential in public towards church leaders and institutions. The Pathé 1940 *Review of the Year*, for example, described how a bomb had destroyed the high altar of St Paul's, 'the Mother Church of the Empire'. Even after Lord Reith (1889–1971), himself a son of the manse, departed as Director General in 1938, the BBC collaborated closely with the churches and with selected religious representatives. The BBC may have been seen as a 'chaplain to the nation', but the relations between reporters and religious leaders, especially figures within the established church, were at times strained. Both journalists and producers covering religion were often critical of clerics, even though many programme-makers were themselves ordained.[16] Nevertheless, the co-operative approach continued even after the ebbing away of deference, the satire boom of the 1960s and the BBC's move from being a promoter of Christianity to a reflector of multi-faith Britain.[17] More and more news reports reflected challenges to the perceived Christian monopoly of the United Kingdom. Mainstream reporters, if they covered religion, increasingly reflected not only conventional, but also common religion as well as 'secular sacred' beliefs, alternative spiritualities, scientific materialism and expressive, even aggressive, forms of new atheism (see the following chapter).

As we have seen, news stories are constantly evolving, but this does not take place in a vacuum. Contexts matter, even if different settings are sometimes complicated to untangle. The interactions between the contexts in which a news story is produced (e.g. a newsroom), in which a story takes place (e.g. around St Paul's) and in which a story is received (e.g. in audiences' home, car or tent) are complicated. These interactions frequently lead to tension, disagreement and even conflict between individuals who primarily inhabit distinct settings. Consider the news production. As Roger Fowler, in *The Language of News*, suggests: 'News is

---

[14]   See, for example, the ongoing coverage of the child abuse scandals within the Catholic Church or the recurring discussion in this book of Rowan Williams' interview and lecture relating to Sharia Law.

[15]   For more detail on this see Kim Knott and Jolyon Mitchell, 'The Changing Faces of Media and Religion'. in Linda Woodhead and Rebecca Cato (eds), *Religion and Change in Modern Britain* (London and New York: Routledge, 2012), c. pp. 243–64.

[16]   Kenneth M. Wolfe, *The Churches and the British Broadcasting Corporation 1922–1956: The Politics of Broadcast Religion* (London: SCM, 1984).

[17]   Jolyon Mitchell, *Visually Speaking: Radio and the Renaissance of Preaching* (Edinburgh: T&T Clark, 1999), p. 107.

not a natural phenomenon emerging from 'reality', but a *product*. It is produced by an industry, shaped by the bureaucratic and economic structure of that industry, the relations between the media and other industries and, most importantly, by relations with government and with other political organisations. From a broader perspective, it reflects, and in return shapes, the prevailing values of a society in a particular historical context'.[18] Stories are produced in complex economic, political and social settings. The stories about religion considered throughout this book, and the St Paul's story considered in this chapter, are no exception.

The St Paul's story hit a raw nerve at a specific moment in history. Since the global financial crisis beginning in 2008, the subsequent recessions and the Eurozone crisis in 2011 and 2012, economic news has rarely been far from Western headlines. Combine this with stories about so-called 'fat cats' or bankers' extraordinary pay increases at firms where many workers are laid off and it is not entirely unexpected to find an international 'occupy' movement, which began on 17 September 2011 outside New York's stock exchange, attracts extensive coverage.[19] This was part of the news context in which the St Paul's protests took place. It ensured that a good number of commentators and journalists attempted to situate this story in a broader context.

The religious press also covered the story extensively. For example, the *Jewish Chronicle* observed that rabbis had signed a 'letter supporting activists' taking part in the occupy London protest outside St Paul's' (27 October 2011). Not surprisingly the *Church Times* devoted several pages of comments, letters, and articles to the story in late October and early November. The leader: 'Wealth and Safety: St Paul's dilemma', was both sympathetic and critical (28 October). The following week saw the British Museum's curator of manuscripts, Arnold Hunt, placed the St Paul's protest onto a broader historical canvas. He observed how in the sixteenth and early seventeenth centuries there were many protests, complaints and conflicts at Paul's cross, 'the open-air pulpit in St Paul's churchyard' (*Church Times*, 4 November). Hunt goes on to observe how: 'St Paul's was not only a centre for preaching, but also for publishing, bookselling, and information gathering. The churchyard was famous for its bookshops, and the nave of the old cathedral,

---

[18]   Roger Fowler, *Language in the News: Discourse and Ideology in the Press* (London: Routledge, 1991), p. 222.

[19]   According to a study by the *Global Language Monitor*, 'occupy' was the 'most commonly used word on the internet and in print' in 2011. 'Occupy' rose 'to pre-eminence through' the 'Occupy Movement, the occupation of Iraq, and the so-called 'Occupied Territories' in the Middle-East. See http://www.languagemonitor.com/global-english/ top-words-of-2011/ (accessed 17 December 2011). Some English-speaking journalists related this news about the global use of the word 'occupy' and the St Paul's story. For example, Murray Wardrop writing in the *Telegraph* cited this research stating that: 'Repeated references to the Occupy Movement, which inspired protests outside St Paul's Cathedral in London and in other major world cities, helped push the word into first place' (10 November 2011).

known as Paul's Walk, was a clearing-house for news'. Historical precedents can shed new light on existing stories.

Writers not only endeavour to put stories into their historical context, but also cite other papers as they attempt to place news into its broader communicative environment. Andrew Brown's observations on the press in the *Church Times* (e.g. 4 November) offered some critical distance, approvingly quoting the financier Ken Costa's article from the *Financial Times*, which interpreted the protest as a sign of something more significant: 'We are perhaps at a tipping point. While it is always risky to indulge in prophecy, I suspect that this deep-seated global concern about the way the free market operates will not go away' (28 October). This kind of incisive observation was lacking in many of the more hysterical commentaries. For several weeks Brown provided a brief and amusing summary of the media context in which the story was evolving. His approach demonstrates how juxtaposing stories can dissipate some of their critical power.

The common account (e.g. in several ITV television news reports) was that the leadership at St Paul's was deeply divided. The story was initially framed as an internal conflict. Even though some commentators professed delight at Giles Fraser's decision to resign, and while in the *Daily Mail* Richard Littlejohn described him as a 'daft vicar from central casting', Fraser was more commonly portrayed as man of principle who followed the way of Jesus by aligning himself with the poor. He 'refused to sanction use of violence' *(Today* programme), as this was a 'red line' that he would not cross (ITV News interview, 27 October). By contrast, the Dean, Graeme Knowles, and the rest of the chapter were caricatured as preservers of the status quo who were more interested in over £16,000 daily (which commonly became quoted as being over £20,000 per day) that the cathedral receives from visitors who are charged around £15 per head. The closure of the cathedral was deemed to be in order to protect this income. Here was a narrative with an apparent hero and villain.

As so often the reality was more complex. While still in post Giles Fraser, writing on the cathedral's website, vigorously rejected accounts that suggested finance was behind closing the doors of St Paul's. Robert Piggot, the BBC's religious affairs correspondent, also rejected these over-simplistic portrayals on BBC Radio 4's *Today Programme*, as early as 27 October, offering a different interpretation of the ecclesial context. He disagreed that 'relationships had collapsed' among the clergy, suggesting instead that the cathedral was being 'held to hostage' by actions of some of protestors. Creating heroes and villains may work for folk tales and Hollywood dramas, but they do little to help understand a situation fraught with emotion, complex responsibilities of care and passionate concern for economic justice and peaceful action.

In the previous section, I considered the language employed and the images used in relation to evolution of the story. But who was interviewed and how did they attempt to contextualise the story? Some commentators appear to have relied on secondary sources, while other journalists were more careful to visit the site and speak with actual protestors. Other interviewees included a wide range of clergy. James Naughtie, a presenter on BBC Radio 4's *Today*, visited the cathedral on 31 October and recorded an interview with two clergy from nearby London churches. One was Paul Turp, the rector of Shoreditch, who claims that in his church some of the richest and poorest people in the UK are able to 'sit side by side'. In the edited version of their interview, broadcast the following morning, they both expressed real frustration that the 'story has become the cathedral', rather than economic justice.

The claim here was that broader context had been overlooked because of the drama unfolding at St Paul's. Following the Dean's resignation, Rowan Williams' first public statement on the issue was ignored by some more critical commentators but it was still widely cited: 'The events of the last couple of weeks have shown very clearly how decisions made in good faith by good people under unusual pressure can have utterly unforeseen and unwelcome consequences, and the clergy of St Paul's deserve our understanding in these circumstances' (31 October 2011). The degree of empathy reflected here rarely translated to commentators' harsher judgements of individual clerics and religious leaders. Sometimes they were given the opportunity to respond. It was surprising to see and to hear so many clergy on mainstream news reports, at least touching upon theological issues. The Bishop of London, Richard Chartres, was interviewed at length on the *Today* programme (by Sarah Montague, 2 November). He memorably asserted that the 'cathedral is not a business' and just as St Paul's was rebuilt after burning down (in 1666), it would once again live up to its resurrection-like symbol of the phoenix.

In the days that followed, several papers claimed that the encampment had become a 'magnet' to the homeless, the mentally ill and some drug addicts (e.g. the *Telegraph)*. From the protestor's own newspaper, the *Occupy Times of London*, and online discussions it is apparent that some of the demonstrators invested considerable energy in looking after these marginalised individuals that the camp attracted, while others had concerns that this 'service' was deflecting them from their original purpose. Even though the cathedral chapter withdrew their legal claim to have them evicted, the Corporation of the City of London took out a court injunction for the eviction of the protestors and removal of the encampment. At one stage it was not clear whether the protest would end peaceably or violently.

Even though the protest ended relatively non-violently, many journalists still placed the eviction within a broader conflictual frame, with winners and losers. There is body of research that concludes that 'conflictual framing' has 'become *one* of journalism's dominant paradigms'.[20] To put it another way, within many news organisations conflict has become a 'crafted cultural norm' that is commonly used to interpret events.[21] By contrast, some researchers have discovered that audiences can be more concerned about human interest and morality frames than

---

[20]   See Jolyon Mitchell, *Media Violence and Christian Ethics* (Cambridge: Cambridge University Press, 2007), especially chapters 1–3.

[21]   Charles R. Bantz, 'News Organisations: Conflict as a Crafted Cultural Norm', *Communication*, 8 (1985), pp. 225–44.

conflict frames.[22] There is therefore an apparent discrepancy between what news providers and what audiences appear to be interested in. This is significant as it raises questions regarding journalistic attachment to conflict. This is partly explained by a professional context that may perpetuate a divisive construction of reality and allows some journalists to continue uncritically to believe that conflict increases interest in the story. Many religious leaders claim that they want to bring conflict resolution and build peace, so it is not surprising to find frustration with an industry, which frequently highlights conflict.

Creative journalists

Third, those drawing on a *journalist-centred approach* tend to investigate the role of the reporter, editor or broadcaster in creating a story. Who has covered it? Why have they covered it? What internal influences and external pressures made a difference to how they selected, framed and reported the story? Asking such questions as part of a journalist-centred approach, when analysing religion and the news, is valuable as it can help to reveal journalists' 'blind spots' or bias. Not many journalists write revealing autobiographies, nor are they themselves often the subjects of biographies, but even if they are outwardly committed to balance and impartiality, it is fair to assume that their own life story and beliefs inform their coverage of news about religion.[23] Taking these observations together leads to a further question: how does a journalist's background, news organisation or available technology shape her/his coverage of an individual story or evolving set of stories?

The perceived conflicts surrounding St Paul's attracted journalists, commentators and photographers like moths to a flame. Under the daily pressure of working within a 'stop-watch culture' many journalists still attempted to create something original,[24] offering their own perspective. The experienced reporter Joan Bakewell revisited the site during its fourth week for the *Telegraph*. While describing how the church had 'stumbled badly' in its early handling of the protests, she goes on to quote Rowan Williams approvingly when he suggested that: 'There is still a powerful sense around – fair or not – of a whole society paying for the errors and irresponsibility of bankers; of impatience with a return to "business as usual" – represented by still-soaring bonuses and little visible change

---

[22]   See, for example, W. Russell Neuman, Marion R. Just and Ann N. Crigler, *Common Knowledge: News and the Construction of Political Meaning* (Chicago: University of Chicago Press, 1992), pp. 60–77.

[23]   See Japp van Ginneken's discussion of a journalist's religious background in his *Understanding Global News: A Critical Introduction* (London, Thousand Oaks and New Delhi: Sage, 1998), p. 66.

[24]   See Philip Schlesinger's discussion of 'A Stop-Watch Culture' in his *Putting Reality Together* (London: Routledge, 1987), pp. 83–105.

in banking practices' (6 November 2011). In the final paragraph her own voice comes through as she declares that 'the Church has a fine new opportunity to speak out about what kind of new society we want'. Bakewell is doing what all journalists do; she selects, compresses and edits. She weaves together her own eyewitness account, a brief historical summary, an 'eminent' source, and her own conclusion. This is not framed around conflict but rather around a personal narrative that leads towards a challenge to religious groups.

Some journalists saw this entire episode in more symbolic terms. For Simon Jenkins, in the *Guardian*, 'these protests are not Tahrir Square ... whatever the claims of their occupants. Their protest is more a dull ache of frustration at power being dispensed in corridors rather than streets, at power that is ever further from their grasp' (31 October 2011). Other commentators saw the protest as more symbolically powerful. 'Occupy London is a nursery for the mind', according to the *Guardian*'s Madeleine Bunting, because with the help of the 'hapless Church of England' this 'obscure but interesting protest' has been propelled into the headlines ...'. For Bunting 'the Dean and chapter of St Paul's have superbly demonstrated in recent days the point Occupy London is making: that City interests have compromised and captured some of the most powerful institutions in the country'. The observation she fails to make, perhaps because she is closely related to one, is the way that the powerful media organisations within the United Kingdom are also largely beholden to their owners – many of whom derive much of their income from the city. Her concluding remark reads like a personal, critical, almost prophetic statement. 'One might have hoped that an institution such as St Paul's, conscious of its own history of civic purpose and national identity, not to mention the radical gospel of a Jewish itinerant carpenter, would have grasped the symbolism of the moment more astutely. That they failed demonstrates all the more starkly the ethical bankruptcy of our age' (31 October). Journalists are particularly sensitive to symbolic actions.

These reports by three highly experienced journalists, Bunting, Jenkins and Bakewell, illustrate the wisdom in seeing news as a creative act. In *Unreliable Sources: How the Twentieth Century was Reported*, John Simpson claims that: 'Reporting is an art form which has sometimes been mistaken for a science'. A veteran foreign affairs correspondent and former Christian Scientist,[25] Simpson also believes that 'Journalists are like portrait painters: their work will be accurate and fair, or inaccurate and distorted, according to their individual capability'.[26] This individualistic view of journalism is incomplete. It is more than just a journalist's individual capabilities that shape coverage of stories about religion. As we saw earlier, there are other factors, influences and pressures which colour a

---

[25] See John Simpson, *Strange Places, Questionable People* (London: Pan Books, 1998 [2008]), p. 48 and p. 89.

[26] John Simpson, *Unreliable Sources: How the twentieth century was reported* (London: Macmillan, 2010).

story.[27] There is a body of research that suggests that journalists in the USA tend to be more sceptical towards religious beliefs than the wider population.[28] There is less detailed empirical data on this topic in the UK and Europe, but nonetheless it is reasonable to assume that the background, training and beliefs of individual journalists had some influence on how they understood and covered the St Paul's story, as well as each of the stories discussed through this book.

Journalists are also influenced by their daily habits, repeated patterns and practices of what Philip Schlesinger describes as 'putting reality together'.[29] Other scholars speak of 'manufacturing the news', 'making' the news, and even a 'massive feat of social construction'.[30] This is shaped by a whole cast of characters: journalists, reporters, and editors, to name but a few. Each group, including more senior gatekeepers, is constrained by organisational structures, daily routines and corporate culture. There are also commercial considerations to take into account, both economic constraints and ownership. Journalists operate within a communicative environment significantly different from that in the days of Lord Northcliffe (1865–1922, former owner of papers such as *The Times* and the *Daily Mail*) and his brother Lord Rothermere (1868–1940, former owner of papers such as the *Daily Mirror*). Nevertheless, the owner of the paper or the broadcasting station or the internet site, and their control over news collection, production and distribution, contributes to the daily practice of creating news. An area ripe for further study is how the beliefs of owners impact upon coverage of religion and the news.

Alongside these internal influences there are significant external pressures from outside a news organisation.[31] This may include state or governmental attempts to censor or manage the news. Pressure groups, PR agencies, press officers and even the general public can all play a role, or at least try to play a role. As one of the founders of the Glasgow Media Group, John Eldridge, argues: 'Apart from the constraints of time, budget and resources there is, necessarily, selection, compression and simplification in the construction of news stories'.[32] Most journalists become skilled at selecting, compressing and simplifying. These

---

[27]   See, for example, Pamela J. Shoemaker and Stephen D. Reese, *Mediating the Message – Theories of Influence on Mass Media Content* (New York: Longman, 1991).

[28]   One of the earlier and best known of these studies is S.R. Lichter, S. Rothman and L. Lichter, *The Media Elite: America's New Power-brokers* (Bethesda, MD: Adler & Adler, 1986).

[29]   Schlesinger, *Putting Reality Together* (London: Routledge, 1987).

[30]   John Eldridge (ed.), *Getting the Message: News, Truth and Power* (London: Routledge, 1994), p.4.

[31]   John Eldridge (ed.), *News Content Language and Visuals: Glasgow University Media Reader, Vol. 1* (London: Routledge, 1995); Greg Philo (ed.), *Industry, Economy, War and Politics: Glasgow University Media Reader, Vol. 2* (London: Routledge, 1995).

[32]   John Eldridge (ed.), *Getting the Message – News, Truth and Power* (London: Routledge, 1994), p. 4.

skills are in evidence through much of the coverage of the St Paul's protests. The quality of the end result varies from crafted, thoughtful reportage to exaggerated, knee-jerk commentary.

Consider how in the *Daily Express* Leo McKinstry penned a scathing attack entitled: 'Anglican Church has been pathetic in tent city crisis'. Once again the Second World War was invoked. 'During the Blitz of 1940, St Paul's was a heroic symbol of defiance against Nazi Germany. Today, as the wretched rows of tents remain in place, the cathedral is a sorry emblem of the established church's institutionalised cowardice' (3 November). Nevertheless, some commentators were more sanguine. To the title of 'Murdering St Paul's cathedral', George Pitcher in the *Telegraph*, celebrated the hard work of the Bishop of London in the midst of a crisis, though still argued that the 'anti-capitalist' protest at St Paul's has done nothing so well as expose the divisions inside the Church of England' (1 November). George Pitcher is an ordained former public affairs director at Lambeth Palace while Leo McKinstry is well known for his sporting biographies and outspoken columns, which have opposed immigration, supported the execution of a drug smuggler and expressed fear that the Arab Spring would lead to the 'installation of hard-line Muslim theocracies in Cairo' (21 February 2011). McKinstry has even suggested in the *Express* that: 'Another £8 billion could be saved annually by abolishing the mammoth overseas aid budget, which is just a monument to Western guilt and does little for the developing world since most of the money is siphoned off by corruption and bureaucracy'(21 January 2010). Without detailing their personal histories and beliefs it is clear from their writing that McKinstry and Pitcher have very different approaches on how to order the world. Their backgrounds and views shed light on how and why they covered the St Paul's protests in the ways that they did.

With the proliferation of news and the increasing demands on many journalists to produce more material or copy, it is not surprising that reporters resort to well-worn pathways or firmly held personal beliefs. In *Unsecular Media: Making News of Religion* Mark Silk suggests that whilst the coverage of religious stories is rarely explicitly anti-religious in North America, journalists tend to rely upon commonplaces or 'topoi' to frame their stories. These include: 'Religious Leader Reveals Feet of Clay (or turns out to be a scoundrel)', 'Ancient Faith Struggles to Adjust to Modern Times', 'Scholars Challenge Long-Standing Beliefs', 'Interfaith Harmony Overcomes Inherited Community', 'New Translation of Sacred Scripture Sounds Funny', 'Devoted Members of a Zealous Religious Group Turn Out to be Warm, Ordinary Folks'.[33] This is by no means a conclusive list, with the steady decline of institutional commitment and religious belief being a recurring refrain in Western Europe. Intriguingly, the St Paul's story does not fit precisely into any of these themes, though some journalists did claim that several religious

---

[33]   See Peter Steinfels, 'Constraints of the Religion Reporter', *Nieman Reports* 47, Summer 1993:4, cited in Mark Silk, *Unsecular Media: Making News of Religion* (Urbana and Chicago: University of Illinois Press), p. 54.

leaders failed to exercise appropriate leadership and that the 'chaotic' protestors had challenged the 'order' of St Paul's and the city. Silk goes on to argue that the explanatory stereotypes that journalists all too often rely upon, need to be enlarged to ensure greater depth of insight. In the case of the St Paul's story, only after several weeks' coverage did some journalists begin to shed light on the power and economic relations between the church and city corporation. Few have explored how the religious leaders, such as the Bishop and Dean, can work in a city which is closely controlled by a corporation with little public accountability.

In this and the previous section of this chapter, we saw how the professional context of the journalist is commonly distinct from the contexts that religious leaders inhabit. Their primary discursive and interpretative communities are often very different. Theological language, from any religious tradition, can be seen as insider 'gobbledygook'. Distinct rituals, routines and 'liturgies' reinforce the divide. Put more simply, religious leaders and journalists commonly work in very different settings. This may partly explain why a range of authors, both scholars and journalists, argue in *Blind Spot: When Journalists Don't Get Religion* that 'key religious dimensions' within news stories are frequently 'ignored, overlooked or misrepresented' by non-specialist journalists.[34] In many cases journalists and religious leaders also hold contrasting sets of norms, values and expectations. This can lead to misunderstandings and even mistrust. These groups, of course, share many common experiences, collective memories and national histories. There are a few individuals who even work as journalists while also being religious leaders. In spite of this, both groups can find that what they particularly value, such as a 'good' story about division or a resolved conflict, is not necessarily entirely compatible.

Expressive audiences

The majority of scholarly studies and critical journalistic reflections have concentrated upon the content, the context and the creators of a news story about religion. More rare are approaches that consider the role of the audience. With the convergence of communication technologies, the growth of 'citizen' journalism and 'online' journalism, and the rise of interactive forms of news production this is changing. These less common *audience-centred approaches*, the fourth category, tend to investigate how readers, listeners and viewers respond and interact with what they learn? Those drawing on this approach increasingly recognise that there are multiple audiences, who bring different beliefs, theologies and traditions, as well as personal narratives and experiences, to any news story they encounter.

---

[34]   See: Paul Marshall, Lela Gilbert, Roberta Green Ahmanson (eds), *Blind Spot: When Journalists Don't Get Religion* (Oxford: Oxford University Press, 2009). This book focuses on examples from North America but the main insights emerging from this book are also pertinent to a European context.

The situation is complicated further as the communal context in which audiences watch, read or hear the news may also be different from the professional worlds of the paid journalist and religious leader. There are inevitably points of overlap, but audiences may belong to other religious communities or to none at all. The result is that individuals can bring a new set of narratives, experiences and beliefs to a news story that has emerged from outside their own religious tradition or world-view. This can provoke unexpected reactions. Audiences are now much more easily able to interact publically with news stories through online posts, blogs and comments. Audiences never were entirely passive, but now it is much simpler to express oneself to a wider public. For example, *Muhammad Al-Hussaini*, a Muslim writing on the *Guardian*'s public *Comment is Free* site, reflected on the experience of camping outside St Paul's: 'In reclaiming for the people this spiritual navel of London where the tectonic plates of Church and City, the sacred and profane, grate against each other in eruption and agony, the protesters have unwittingly stumbled upon the seat of England's tortured soul'.[35] Increasingly expressive audiences are adding to what Michel de Certeau describes in another context as the 'interminable recitation of stories'.[36] As stories are repeated they are edited, adapted and elaborated upon by audiences. As they circulate they can grow or dissipate in significance.

Nevertheless, the online engagement with the *Occupy* movement is an example of how expressive audiences may even be turning the process of 'agenda setting' on its head. It is commonly claimed that news media set the agenda for public debate. For instance, Bernard Cohen claimed that the press 'may not be successful much of the time in telling people what to think, but it is stunningly successful in telling its readers what to think about'.[37] This quotation appeals to journalists who claim that significant power resides with their craft.

In the light of active and dynamic audiences this is open to qualification, especially with the increase of citizen journalism through *Twitter*, *Facebook* and blogs. Even media magnate Rupert Murdoch (b.1931) is very aware that younger audiences (especially 19–34 years old) are increasingly turning to different parts of the web for news. He believes that this age-group 'don't want a God like figure from above to tell them what's important'.[38] Sometimes audiences want to tell journalists what stories are significant, though whether new media actually facilitate this process is open to debate. Some stories do circulate through

---

[35]   Muhammad Al-Hussaini, 'Occupy: the fault line between St Paul's and the Corporation of London'. This article was published on guardian.co.uk at 18.30 GMT on Monday 28 November 2011. Online: http://www.guardian.co.uk/commentisfree/belief/2011/nov/28/occupy-st-pauls-occupy-london (accessed 1 December 2011).

[36]   Michel de Certeau, *The Practice of Everyday Life*, trans. Steven Rendall (Berkeley, CA: University of California Press, 1984) p. 186.

[37]   Bernard Cohen, *The Press and Foreign Policy* (Princeton University Press, 1963), p. 13

[38]   Stuart Allen, *News Culture*, 3rd edn (Maidenhead: Open University Press, 2010) p. 143.

independent media and percolate into the public sphere in such a way as to put the issue onto the professional news journalist's agenda in unexpected fashions. In other words, the range of agenda-setting sources has radically increased for both audiences and journalists over the last two decades. This can be observed in the multiplicity of voices that were heard in the public sphere reflecting, debating and commenting on the St Paul's protests.

Audiences potentially have more channels for public expression and therefore have the capacity, even if it is underused, to influence what is included within mainstream news frames. In the light of this, the traditional news values,[39] which determine where and whether a story is covered, are open to further qualification. While the St Paul's story had consequences for many London commuters and tourists, it was prominent because of its location adjacent to a national symbol, it was proximate to many Londoners and immediate in relation to the international 'occupy' movement,[40] it was potentially rife with conflict and yet idiosyncratic in that the doors of St Paul's hadn't been closed since the Second World War. This provoked a wide range of strong audience reactions.[41] Here was an unusual, unexpected and initially surprising news story in an extremely well-known location, which touched on religion, economics and social divides. If a murder or sexual element was uncovered then it could have become an even more 'ideal news story'. The fact that, unlike in Syria or Iran, demonstrators have not been shot outside St Paul's may explain why if 'it bleeds it leads' does not apply here.

Some audiences increasingly realise that the 'fundamental problem' with such unstated or intuited 'criteria of news-worthiness is that they distort reality. They create some kind of surface to social reality, which has very little to do with the

---

[39]   J. Galtung and M. Ruge, 'Structuring and Selecting News', *The Manufacture of News*, S. Cohen & J. Young (eds), London: 1973.

[40]   Dick Skellington, editor of the Open University's *Society Matters*, underlined the international nature of these 'Occupy' demonstrations, claiming that: 'by mid-October there were occupations in 951 cities in 82 countries, worldwide', rising in November to '2,609 sites in towns and cities across the world'. See: http://www8.open.ac.uk/platform/blogs/society-matters/occupy-movement-now-worldwide-phenomenon (accessed 17 December 2011).

[41]   These reactions to the closing of the cathedral were expressed in a wide range of contexts, from letters in the *Church Times* (e.g. Richard Bauckham, a New Testament Professor, described it as a 'public relations catastrophe for the Church' because it had been 'a failure of prophetic witness') to personal reflections in public blogs (e.g. Alan Wilson, the Bishop of Buckingham, described it as a 'hysterical over-reaction' wondering aloud if the managers of St Paul's were 'overgrown public schoolboys playing indoor games in their own self-important Tourist Disneyland' (*Bishop Alan's Blog*, 28 October 2011). These were by no means the only audience voices, with others empathising with a Cathedral chapter who 'feel besieged' by 'protestors who encircle them like a revolutionary mob' (Simon Walsh, member of the London diocesan Synod, a letter beside Bauckham's letter in the *Church Times*, 4 November 2011). Several correspondents wrote to national papers ironically observing how: 'Sir, St Paul was a tent-maker'. (e.g. *The Telegraph*, 29 October 2011.)

world we live in'.[42] Even if the 'Occupy' camp has a permanent monument to its tent protest within the cathedral it will almost inevitably remain out of the headlines. New more spectacular stories swiftly replaced aerial shots of bedraggled tents. When a referendum date was set in Scotland and then a huge cruise liner ran aground off a small Italian island (January 2012) the St Paul's protest appeared to drop completely off mainstream news agendas. A half-submerged liner offers more spectacular images than familiar pictures of weathered tents in the city. It only briefly re-appeared with the late February eviction, where pictures of police surrounding demonstrators returned to news reports for no more than a few days.[43] The chronic, ongoing issues of economic injustice may lack sensational or spectacular images, but they will continue. The 'Occupy' protests in other parts of London and Britain (e.g. Adjacent to Bristol, Exeter, and Sheffield Cathedrals or Edinburgh's St Andrew's Square) received far less national or international news attention.[44]

What emerged from the online discussions around the actual coverage of this evolving story is that news is increasingly perceived as more than presidents, monarchs and film stars, or burning castles, embarrassed religious leaders or closed cathedrals. A recurring criticism, which goes beyond the St Paul's story, is towards 'news values that have been developed to meet the needs of individualistic societies'. In the light of the *News of the World* phone hacking scandal and the subsequent *Leveson* enquiry examining the 'culture, practice and ethics of the press',[45] some of the criticisms directed at the apparent lack of ethical behaviour in practices of the City might also be extended to attend to different parts of news media. It is increasingly understood that the 'sensational, the spectacular, the tragic, the sordid and the deviant, tend to get prominence over the orderly, the integrated, the normal and the constructive'.[46] The daily round of service, care and

---

[42] Michael Traber, 'Communication Ethics' (Ch. 18) in George Gerbner, Hamid Mowlana and Karle Nordenstreng, 'The Global Media Debate: Its rise, fall and renewal' (New Jersey: Ablex, 1993), p. 156.

[43] See, for example, the front page of the *Church Times*, which included a shot of about seven policemen surrounding a bearded young man with his hands together as in prayer. 2 March 2012.

[44] Local press and other local media did however cover these camps on a regular basis. See, for example, the *Evening News* coverage in Edinburgh during Autumn 2011 and early 2012. Some national papers, such as *The Scotsman*, also focussed on the Edinburgh protest. See, for example, 9 January 2012, http://www.scotsman.com/news/call_on_occupy_edinburgh_campers_to_quit_1_2044971 (accessed 14 June 2012).

[45] Formal evidence hearings started on 14 November 2011 at the Royal Courts of Justice in London, with the formal part of the enquiry scheduled to conclude by the end of July 2012. See http://www.levesoninquiry.org.uk/ (accessed 1 June 2012).

[46] Neville Jayaweera, cited by Crispin Maslog (ed.), *Communication, Values and Society* (Quezon City, Philippines: New Day Publishers, 1994), p. 121, see pp. 119–21 for section on 'News Values'.

worship through the cathedral was largely overlooked in most of the news stories, or simply used as a backdrop to the conflict outside the doors.

News relating to religion and conflict also provides cartoonists, satirists and comedians with rich material to play with. The St Paul's 'Occupy' story was no exception. The *Mac* cartoon, by Stan McMurty, in the *Daily Mail* depicted a clerical figure with one hand cupped to his mouth shouting into the cathedral: 'The last of the protestors have gone, bishop. But guess what?' The answer to his question is made clear visually: at the bottom of the Cathedral steps, all the tents have disappeared, only to be replaced by a forest of wind turbines (1 March 2012). An earlier *Mac* cartoon brings together religion and the St Paul's news story in humorous fashion. In the night sky a full moon floats above the encampment and placard 'Capitalism is Crisis'. Four aged clerics head out of the cathedral towards the tents gleefully carrying flame-throwers. Two of the elderly clergy smile as a flame emerges from their barrels. A bishop holds a lighted candlestick in one hand and a newspaper in the other, bearing the headline: 'Empty Tents at St Paul's'. The bishop's command is used as the caption: 'Go for it Lads. Any poor soul out there must be absolutely frozen' (26 October 2011).

'Go for it, lads. Any poor soul out there must be absolutely frozen.'

Figure 5   *Mac* Cartoon from *Daily Mail*, 26 October 2011. Courtesy of the *Daily Mail* and Mac (Stan McMurty).

Bishops in full regalia are easy prey. In Paul Thomas' cartoon in the *Daily Express* a bishop is portrayed outside the cathedral facing the tents and declaring: 'I've ordered a lightning bolt and a plague of locusts in case the water cannon doesn't turn up' (26 October). Steve Bell's cartoon in the *Guardian* parodies the black and white minstrel show and the song 'Mammy'. Archbishop Rowan Williams, surrounded by clergy, and backed up by a line of riot police, comes leaping and dancing down the cathedral steps singing: 'Maammon!! How I love Ya!' (28 October). It is noticeable how the vast majority of cartoons on the topic tend to place the clergy in opposition to the demonstrators. One variation, which vilifies the bankers instead, is Martin Rowson's cartoon in the *Guardian* on the 17 October 2011. Riot police hem in the demonstrators, to ensure safe passage for the obese suited bankers, with pigs' faces, who creep past in the foreground. The scene is entitled: 'Tale of Two cities'.

Conclusion

At first sight the approach taken in this chapter tends towards descriptive analysis rather than critical evaluation. This over-simplified dichotomy, however, is open to qualification. Journalists, themselves, are often very good at descriptions. How an evolving story is described is highly significant. What is left out of the news frame and what is left within it matters hugely to the tone, meaning, and implications of a story. Religious leaders are often involved in the practices of re-description and reframing of news events, in the light of their own traditions, practices and beliefs.[47] Sometimes this process can be reversed, so that journalists attempt to re-describe how a religious leader has originally described an event. Often a journalist's descriptions and a religious leader's re-descriptions clash, or even vice versa. Nonetheless, in both cases, they are plainly incompatible. This may be something to celebrate rather than to try to repair or reconcile. Journalists, as members of the so-called 'fourth estate', are often perceived as having 'power without responsibility'. For that reason the democratisation of communication and description is, whatever its drawbacks, to be welcomed, as it challenges not only religious hegemony, but also the mainstream media's monopoly on description.

This is more significant than at first meets the eye. Why? Because commonly embedded within the description is an evaluation of what has happened or how individuals have behaved. Sometimes this is obvious and explicit, but often it is hidden and implied. This should not be absorbed uncritically. In many ways, a form of description that combines all four approaches (considering the stories, contexts, journalists and audiences) is likely to produce a more complete and insightful analysis of reality than a descriptive approach, which only focuses on a single element within the ever-hungry news industries and audiences.

---

[47]   See Jolyon Mitchell, *Media Violence and Christian Ethics* (Cambridge: Cambridge University Press, 2007), especially chapters 1 and 2.

It is St Paul's itself that has remained a still point in the midst of evolving stories, contested contexts, creative journalists, and expressive audiences. In *The Phoenix: St Paul's Cathedral and the Men who Made Modern London*, Leo Hollis claims that following the Civil War, the execution of Charles, the plague and the 1666 Fire, medieval London, as well as many of its institutions and traditions were 'laid waste'.[48] The result was that 'the ancient fabric of the [medieval] cathedral mirrored the state of the city: devastated, pillaged, disrespected and finally broken almost beyond repair' following the Great Fire'.[49] St Paul's becomes a metaphor for rebuilding a shattered capital. Out of the ashes comes a phoenix. The 'gleaming Portland stone, defying political, religious and financial vicissitudes', may have been 'the first cathedral to be built in Britain for centuries' but 'with its astonishing scale and dome, Wren's radical design for St Paul's attempted to reinterpret the old to produce a symbol of reason, harmony and – above all – certainty'.[50] Following so much uncertainty, conflict and division, here was a confident assertion of order and rationality built in stone. Whatever one's personal feelings about the 'occupy' protest outside its doors in 2011 and 2012 it was hard not to be struck by the visual contrast between the solid, steady, structure of the cathedral and the fragile cluster of flimsy tents. Their future was far from certain.

Appearances, however, can be deceptive. For all its ephemeral qualities, the camp's presence perplexed, inspired and infuriated. Its place in history is far from clear, and now it has been removed it is possible that it will be largely forgotten as a minor news item. The same can be said for the many and varied news stories that have flapped and blown around this site of protest. News may be preserved online more effectively and accessibly than ever before, but significant, solid and lasting news is harder to find. As we have seen, news about religion is in a constant state of flux, evolving and adapting. It becomes a site of contest, where different voices with different perspectives encounter one another. There are interpretations, misinterpretations, and even plain insults. An eclectic approach, as outlined in this chapter, also includes listening carefully to the voice of the subject(s) of the story, in this case the demonstrators. This is not always comfortable, or straightforward, or peaceable for journalists, religious leaders or audiences. News stories, such as those that have clustered around St Paul's, have the potential to divide and to ensure that communities stop listening to each other. Nevertheless, both accurate description and thoughtful re-description can help to build bridges between divided communities. This can begin by journalists, religious leaders and audiences listening carefully to diverse voices, analysing complex situations, and imagining themselves into the worlds of others.

---

[48]   Leo Hollis, *The Phoenix: St Paul's Cathedral and the Men who Made Modern London* (London: Weidenfeld and Nicolson, 2008).

[49]   Kate Colquhoun, 'St Paul's Rises from the Ashes', book review on *The Phoenix* from the *Telegraph*, 24 June 2008. Also available online: http://www.telegraph.co.uk/culture/books/non_fictionreviews/3555296/St-Pauls-rises-from-the-ashes.html (accessed on 1 December 2011).

[50]   Ibid.

Chapter 2

Religion in the British Media Today

Teemu Taira, Elizabeth Poole and Kim Knott

Summary

How is religion represented in British media today? In this chapter, Taira, Poole and Knott provide a detailed answer, based on their research into television and newspaper reporting of religion in 2008–10. As well as surveying references to conventional religion, Taira, Poole and Knott also chart references to 'common religion' (things like fate, angels and luck) and references to the 'secular sacred' (things like human rights and freedom of choice). The resulting statistical picture contains some surprises. There are more references to religion on British television and in British newspapers today than there were twenty years ago. Other statistics are less surprising: our newspapers and television programmes reflect the increasing ethnic and religious diversity of the UK, and contain more references to Islam and the 'secular sacred' than twenty years ago, with much coverage of the former characterised by negative stereotyping.

Introduction: Research on religion in the media

Religion is often in the news, but media portrayals do not always match those of religious groups themselves. The way it is treated tells us a great deal about popular fears and prejudices, and the place of religion in Britain's cultural heritage. Research was conducted in 2008–10 to record the incidence of references to religion in the British media and examine how it was portrayed. The project repeated a research process used at the University of Leeds in 1982–3 (Knott, 1984), thus enabling comparisons to be made between the two periods.

In both projects data was collected and analysed from three newspapers (*The Times*, the *Sun* and the *Yorkshire Evening Post*) for a period of two months, and for three television channels (ITV1, BBC1 and BBC2) for one week. Despite the number of channels, newspapers and news websites available today, we were constrained in our choice by the selection used in the first project (when there were only three TV channels, for example). Repeating the process was essential to enable us to make comparisons. In addition, in both projects we conducted a reception study (in the first one, through a survey, and in the second, through focus groups). We also undertook an analysis of a media event. In 1982, this was the pastoral visit of Pope John Paul II to the UK; in 2009, it was the visit of the

Dutch MP and creator of the inflammatory film, *Fitna*, Geert Wilders. It was only as the second project began to draw to a close that we realised we could extend it to include the state visit of Pope Benedict, and a comparison with the previous UK papal tour. In examining these events we gathered data from a much wider range of media sources, but over a shorter time-frame.

Two further aspects of our research process need mention before we turn to some of the results. First, is the issue of how we defined religion in order to study its portrayal. Back in 1982 we were interested not only in media treatment of official, church-based beliefs and practices and world religions – what we called 'conventional religion' – but also in unofficial religiosity which acknowledged the supernatural but was not endorsed by formal institutions. We called this 'common religion' (Towler, 1974; Knott, 1984). Typically, the former type included references to the Pope and the Archbishop of Canterbury, Methodism, Judaism, new religious movements, prayer and miracles and the latter references to superstition, fate, luck, the paranormal, astrology and spiritualism. In the second project, observation of the changing social and cultural milieu as well as our own research interests led us to add a third type, the 'secular sacred': those beliefs, practices, places and symbols that are non-religious but are nevertheless held to be non-negotiable and often referred to as 'sacred', including such values as freedom of speech and human rights, and belief systems such as humanism and atheism.

We subdivided conventional and common religion and the secular sacred into categories and subcategories that we were then able to use in logging references in newspapers and on television. Our analysis of these was both quantitative and qualitative: we counted references and organised them by media source, genre, type and category; and we studied them in depth, looking at how they were used to portray religious and secular-sacred themes, at how discourse on such themes was constructed, and at how religion was represented through this process.

Secondly, we did not restrict our analysis to those articles and programmes that dealt explicitly with religious themes – journalism about religion and religious broadcasting. Instead, we examined all genres from news to entertainment and sports (with the exclusion of educational and children's TV); in fact, we considered all references and stories about religion and the secular sacred, no matter how small. We found that references in adverts and the racing tote were as important as those in *Songs of Praise* or church notices for building up a picture of religion in the media.

We turn now to our findings. The first section summarises the general results of the 2008–10 study. It is followed by two sections on media portrayals of Islam, the first on the general reporting of Islam in the papers and on television, and the second on terrorism and conflict. We turn then to Britain's media and how they differ in their stance on religious issues. We conclude with a final section on the coverage of the 2010 papal visit, showing how that coverage reflects the observations made earlier in the chapter.

Religion in the British media, 2008–2010

The results of these two research projects show that there is more religion in the media today than in the 1980s despite a decline over the same period in church attendance and in most areas of Christian belief and practice. There has been a small increase in the number of references to Christianity, but a large increase in coverage of other religions, particularly Islam, but also Judaism, Hinduism and Buddhism (Fig. 6). References to alternative spiritualities are few and far between.

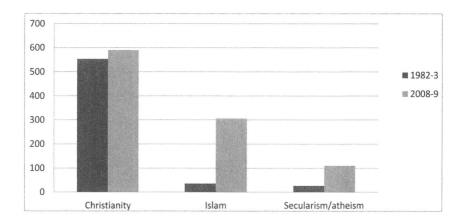

Figure 6   Media references to religion 1982–1983 and 2008–2009

As we will see later, most references to Islam in the newspapers and on TV portray Muslims as extremists, terrorists and radicals. Other coverage refers provocatively to the 'Islamification' of Britain, or shows Islam as problematic for social integration. This treatment is more pronounced in the conservative tabloid newspapers, but it can be found from time to time in all British news sources (see section 4 on media profiling). This view of Islam and Muslims is recognised by many as symptomatic of media 'Islamophobia'. As public knowledge and opinion about religion is informed in large part by what people read in the papers and watch on television, it is likely that negative portrayals perpetuate and reinforce negative perceptions.

Negative reporting is not confined to Islam, however. Christianity has been portrayed by the liberal press as anti-egalitarian and out of date on issues of gender and homosexuality. In response, a common conservative media story line, supported by evangelical Christians, has been the marginalisation of Christianity by public officials. This was a strong theme, for example, during the 2010 papal visit (see discussion below). Christian 'persecution', it has been claimed, arises from successive government's equality and diversity policy, and from its politically-correct favouritism of Muslims at the expense of Britain's Christians. This has been a matter of dispute, however, with some newspapers offering resounding critiques.

This kind of debate often receives media coverage, as does the criminal or immoral behaviour of clergy, recent cases of child abuse being an obvious example. This not only reflects the nature of contemporary ethical and political discussion in the churches, but the media's own culture and rhetoric – their recurring love of drama and controversy. The popular news media commonly attracts audiences by focusing on conflict, deviance and, of course, celebrity.

But there is more to media religion than Islam and Christianity. Findings show that there has been a rise in the number of references to common religion as well as conventional religion. A quarter of all references in the early 1980s were to supernatural beliefs, practices and issues not endorsed formally by churches and other official religious organisations. That figure has risen to 40 per cent today (Fig. 7) and includes references to magic, ghosts, fate, luck and fortune-telling.

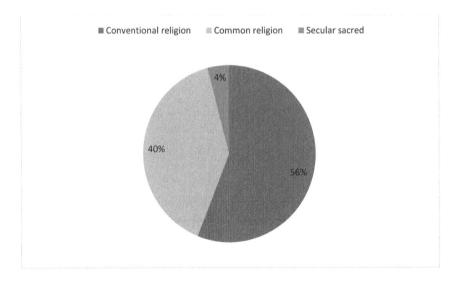

Figure 7   Media references to religion and the secular sacred, 2008–2009

Along with metaphorical and often humorous references to miracles, angels and prayer, they appear not in news coverage or programmes about religion, but in newspaper sports reporting, entertainment (soaps, sitcoms and murder mysteries) and in TV adverts. Prayers for victory on the football pitch, suspense and tension in thrillers and horror movies, the superhuman feats of consumers of popular brands of footwear or alcohol and the miraculous results delivered by household products are all expressed with reference to religious images and language.

As TV viewers, these references generally pass us by unnoticed, but our research shows that,

- nearly 40 per cent of all references to religion on television do not focus overtly or in depth on current religious affairs, Islam or the churches, but refer in passing to religious practices, such as weddings and funerals, to cosmology, including heaven and hell, and to the place of religion in the landscape and heritage;
- 30 per cent of all references to religion on television appear in adverts;
- on ITV there are nearly twice as many references to things like luck, magic and the unexplained as there are to conventional religious themes, whilst on BBC1 and BBC2 the trend is reversed.

Irrespective of how many people actually participate in religion, it continues to provide many key terms in the English language for expressing wonder, hope and fear, honouring and praising celebrities and high achievers, contemplating the unexplained, and for coping with unaccountable horror and global crisis.

Another major change in coverage since the 1980s has been the rise in references to non-religious beliefs, particularly to secularism and the new atheism: the 'secular sacred'. Freedom of speech, human rights, personal choice, and belief that religion should be a private not public matter are just some of the secular sacred views discussed in the media and often held by media professionals themselves – who, according to a *YouGov* poll in 2005, were less likely to hold religious beliefs than the public at large (Holmes, 2010).

In the sections that follow, we will examine some of these findings in more depth, focusing on the media portrayal of Islam, the nature and range of newspaper stances on reporting religion, and coverage of the 2010 papal visit.

The reporting of Islam

There are several political explanations for the increasing visibility of Islam in the news media. These relate to global and local politics. For example, globalisation has seen the increasing movement of peoples across the world and military intervention in the Muslim world by Western governments. Islam is salient in the current historical political moment.

Previous research has shown how, in the British news media prior to 9/11, Islam and Muslims were associated with fanaticism, violence and terrorism (Richardson, 2004). However, on a local level the representation of British Muslims was more complex. The need to maintain harmonious social relations in a multi-faith society and lack of terrorist activity by British Muslims at that time resulted in a focus on cultural issues, integration and the 'Islamification' of the UK (Poole, 2002). 9/11 and 7/7 changed all this. There was a shift from a focus on Muslims abroad to Muslims at home, and terrorism became the dominant topic of coverage in relation to Islam home and away (Poole, 2006). More recent research has demonstrated (since the decline in visible terrorist activity in the UK post 7/7) a shift back to cultural difference at the centre of coverage in the case of British Muslims (Moore, Mason and Lewis, 2008).

Our current study demonstrates a continuation of these themes. The quantitative analysis shows a huge – though not unexpected – rise in coverage of Islam since 1982 (Fig. 6) in both newspapers (two months) and on television (one week), from a total of 38 references to 306, making it the largest single category of coverage in the reporting of religion in newspapers and the fourth largest topic in coverage of religion on TV. Coverage of other religions has also increased. Although this rise appears insignificant compared to that of Islam, it is important to note that, taking newspaper coverage alone, if we remove all references to Islam that deal with extremism and terrorism, as a faith its coverage is not dissimilar to others (Table 1). The number of remaining references for Islam is less than the number for Judaism (73 as compared with 81). However, this also illustrates an important point: whilst there are media acknowledgments to Britain as a multi-faith society, interest in these faiths is marginal unless they have acute political significance, as in the case of Islam. The fact that references to Islam on TV mainly occurred in news and current affairs programmes reinforces this.

Table 1   References to different religions on television and in the newspapers

Religion	Number of references on television	% of total TV references to religion	Number of references in newspapers	% of total newspaper references to religion
Islam	51	3.1	255	9.5
Hinduism	6	0.4	29	1.1
Buddhism	15	0.9	28	1.0
Sikhism	3	0.2	10	0.4
Judaism	10	0.6	81	3.0
Other religious traditions	14	0.8	6	0.2

References to Islam on TV were located mainly in domestic productions but were concerned with Muslims living outside the UK (Turkey, Afghanistan, Iran). In our period of coverage, references to all religious traditions occurred mainly on BBC2, partly due to the airing of the series *Around the World in 80 Faiths*. In the papers, whilst *The Times* reportage of Islam was the highest, this was partly a reflection of the greater quantity of copy in *The Times* more generally. However, extremism was more likely to be covered by the *Sun* (stories on 'Preachers of

Hate' for example); the *Yorkshire Evening Post* was just as likely to cover other religions such as Buddhism and Sikhism.

So what were the predominant themes in the media coverage of Islam? Unsurprisingly, terrorism, extremism and conflict prevailed, with a significant emphasis on the cultural differences that result in problems of integration in the UK. In order to examine the type of meanings being constructed around Muslims at this particular historical moment, a qualitative analysis of three-quarters of the newspaper articles from October 2008 was undertaken. Out of the 87 articles analysed, 55 could be said to cover topics relating to terrorism, conflict and extremism. Seven articles could be described as broadly positive in their approach: articles about anti-racism and community relations. The remaining articles showed Muslims in a predominantly negative light as a cultural threat.

Terrorism and conflict

Articles on terrorism were mainly about British Muslims (all but two). Stories included: British Muslims on trial for planning terrorist activities, a Muslim convert's failed toilet bomb attempt, coverage of the trial of the perpetrators of the Glasgow airport attack and accusations that terrorist groups were transmitting coded messages in child porn. There were four common elements to these stories. The first was that agency is clear. The central protagonists were the 'terrorists' whose actions were always negative when seen against the less frequently featured heroic action of the police and public. Secondly, rather than providing any historical or political context, the acts of terrorism were clearly linked to Islamic belief (though this was not contextualised). The perpetrators were categorised interchangeably as terrorists, extremists, fundamentalists and militants. This slippage allowed for articles about extremists to be infused with ideas of terrorism, and justified calls for tougher action to be taken against them. Finally, a process of Othering took place, which linked the British suspect to their 'indoctrinators' abroad, thus locating the origin of violence at a distance. This treatment of terrorism demonstrated the consensus around it where further discussion or debate was not seen to be needed. Articles featured, in general, non-Muslim, official sources.

Articles on conflict included extremism, fanaticism, radicalisation or conflict in world conflict zones such as Iraq and Afghanistan in which reference to Islam or the Taliban was made. The predominant story was about the murder of an aid worker in Afghanistan by the Taliban (October 2008). As well as emphasising the violent acts and extremist speech of 'Muslims', these articles highlighted the 'persecution' of Christians, problematised Muslims (by suggesting that problems such as radicalisation come from within the faith or community), and focused on the increasing 'Islamification' of the UK made permissible by weak government. This was a dominant theme in the treatment of cultural difference. It was also a factor in coverage of Geert Wilders, which we gathered for our analysis of a significant media event. Wilders, a Dutch MP for the Party for Freedom (PVV), was refused entry to Britain on public order grounds (on 13 February 2009). Lord Pearson of the UKIP party had invited him to a screening of *Fitna*, his anti-Islamic film, in the House of Lords. The Home Secretary deemed *Fitna*, in tandem with Wilders' presence, as 'threatening community harmony and therefore public security' and denied him entry. Aware that he would be turned back at the airport, Wilders flew to London, thus achieving a huge publicity coup. Rather than choosing to protect a minority group from attack, media coverage centred on the juxtaposition of freedom of speech (constructed as a liberal Western value) versus censorship (portrayed here as a product of Islam's prohibitionist nature). This led to a homogenisation of both 'us' and 'them' presented as an exclusive dichotomous relationship resulting in a 'clash of cultures'. The government was represented as undermining 'British values' by tolerating 'preachers of hate' whilst banning Wilders. Appeasement and double standards then were key themes.

It is important to note, of course, that this type of coverage was not homogenous. There were spaces where counter voices could be heard. In the liberal press, the local press, and in letters and features a greater diversity of opinion was apparent. However, these tended to be present at the margins of coverage and were dwarfed by the negative reporting illustrated here.

The frameworks within which Muslims are represented and understood continue to problematise and homogenise a diversity of people. Difference is highlighted. Categorising and classifying people in this way divides them along the constructed categories, concealing commonalities and obstructing understanding. Despite increasing public awareness of the discrimination experienced by Muslims in Britain and the dissemination of a growing body of research on this, there seems if anything to have been a reduction, post 7/7, in the variety of discourses circulating in Britain about Islam.

Having examined the media coverage in our period of analysis of a key category, Islam, we turn now to a consideration of the differential treatment of religion by particular newspapers and TV channels.

Profiling the British media

An important aspect in our research has been the profiling of selected media sources. Although our sample was limited to three newspapers and three terrestrial television channels, the profiling – which, in the case of newspapers, was based on a quality 'broadsheet' (though now in smaller format), a popular tabloid and a local paper – generates hypotheses for future studies.

In our two-month period, there were more references to both religion and the secular sacred in *The Times* (1,409) than in the *Sun* (783) and the *Yorkshire Evening Post* (506) taken together (Fig. 8). This was partly due to the larger number of pages in *The Times*. Likewise, the *Sun* had more references than the *Post*, which again had fewer pages. Nevertheless, it is obvious from a regular reading of both that religion is higher on the agenda of *The Times* than of the *Post*.

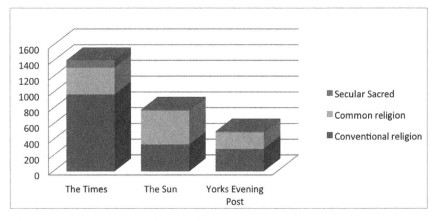

Figure 8   Newspaper references by type, 2008–2009

Conventional religion and the secular sacred were emphasised in *The Times*, whereas the *Sun* was filled with references to common religion. The *Yorkshire Evening Post* was evenly balanced in portraying the two, but neither the *Sun* nor the *Post* gave much attention to the secular sacred. *The Times* made far more reference than average to conventional categories such as Roman Catholicism, Islam, Judaism and church history. Of common religion categories, folk religion stood out as being strongly covered; and of the secular sacred it can be said that all the issues were dealt with more often than in other papers. The *Yorkshire Evening Post* had relatively more references to Quakers, Buddhism and Sikhism than other papers, but fewer references to Islam and Judaism. This suggests something about the local dimension of the paper's coverage. It does not offer as much foreign news or elite history as *The Times*; instead, it focuses on what is nowadays a more multicultural and religiously-diverse local community and the events that take place within it.

Turning now to television, the great majority of references – a total of 1,013 – were on ITV1, compared with 313 on BBC1 and 346 on BBC2 (Fig. 9). There were two contributory explanations for this, the first of which is methodological. There was a longer viewing duration for ITV1, because both BBC1 and BBC2 had educational and children's programmes, which were excluded from our analysis. But this gave ITV1 only ten more hours of air-time than BBC1, so viewing duration is not a wholly convincing explanation in itself. Furthermore, with exclusions, BBC2 had 22 hours less broadcasting time than BBC1, but still had more references to religion. The second explanation concerns the high number of references in advertisements. This accounts in part for the amount of coverage on ITV1, but even if advertisements are excluded the total number of references still exceeds those on other TV channels. We are left to conclude that ITV1 is more likely than BBC1 or BBC2 to have religion references in its schedule, even though it has very little specifically religious broadcasting.

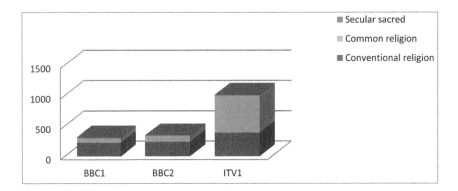

Figure 9   Television references by type, 2008–2009

The comparison between the type of references on different TV channels shows that the profile of the BBC is more on the conventional side, whereas common religion dominates on ITV1, especially its day-time profile. In that sense ITV1 is more akin to the *Sun*, and the BBC more like *The Times*. Despite this, there were still more references to conventional religion on ITV1 (390) than on either BBC1 (224) or BBC2 (238).

BBC1 had references to Protestant churches, church history, religious texts and even new religious movements. It covered all established non-Christian religious traditions except Hinduism more than average. In terms of common religion, its emphasis was on folk religion and folk practices, whilst spiritualism, spirit possession, gambling and the unexplained were covered more on ITV1. In relation to the secular sacred, the channel focused on atheism and the relation between religion and science. BBC2 was more like BBC1 than ITV1.

On the basis of this profiling, we suggest that references to religion in the current British media are usually conventional, with references to common religion more likely to be in the tabloids or on ITV1 than in broadsheets, local papers or the BBC. Most references to the 'secular sacred' are in the broadsheets. Religion features more often in broadsheets than tabloids, and more often in tabloids than local papers. The broadsheets are both more traditional and more diverse in their coverage of religion, whereas tabloids pick up mainly Christianity, Islam and common religion and ignore the non-established religious traditions and minor Christian denominations. Local papers cover any of these as long as the topics have some local relevance. References to religion in newspapers and on television are not limited to specifically religious reporting or religious broadcasting. They are found in news, current affairs, editorials, comments, supplements, sports, letters, light entertainment, plays and films and advertisements.

It is important to emphasise that these findings on profiling should be taken more as hypotheses based on a limited sample rather than generalised results telling us about the British media as a whole. The current project has, however, something to say about other television channels and newspapers.

As Channel 4 was not part of our sample (see Introduction), its profiling is not based on statistical data. Nevertheless, it is clear from a cursory analysis that the channel offers a considerable amount of religious broadcasting, especially documentaries. It is also known for giving airtime to more critical and sometimes even anti-religious viewpoints, for example in *The Root of All Evil?* (2006) and *The Enemies of Reason* (2007), hosted by Richard Dawkins. If Dawkins is an important secular figurehead and authority on religious issues on Channel 4, for the BBC it is Robert Winston, who is not anti-religious as such but a credible scientist with a Jewish background.

Our profiling of newspapers other than *The Times*, the *Sun*, and the *Yorkshire Evening Post* was based on our analysis of two events – the aforementioned case of Geert Wilders and the recent papal visit (see below). It was further supported by interviews with newspaper editors and religious correspondents conducted by journalist Annikka Mutanen (2009). Evidence from these sources shows that it is the conservative tabloids and the *Daily Telegraph* that take a particularly pro-Christian stance. But none of the editors and journalists actually thought themselves or their papers to be anti-religious, and even the editor of the *Independent* maintained that the paper opposed 'aggressive secularism'.

The content of the national newspapers illuminates more clearly the variety between them (we restrict ourselves here to comments on English dailies). Even though they may choose a more positive or negative approach case by case, a broad pattern may still be discerned. The papers can be placed on a pro/anti religious continuum, which at one end includes overtly pro-Christian papers such as the *Daily Telegraph* and *Daily Express*. The *Daily Mail* and the *Sun* are aligned next to them. The opposite end consists of the more secularist, sometimes openly critical papers, the *Independent* and the *Guardian*. The *Daily Star*, *Daily Mirror* and *The Times* are in the middle, with the *Star* closest to the pro-Christian end of the continuum. *The Times*'s overall approach, despite its embrace of moderate secularism, is still much closer to the pro-religious than anti-religious end of the spectrum. Across the board, attitudes towards Islam and militant atheism vary, but generally the tabloids are more negative than the broadsheets, even though the *Telegraph* and *The Times* are also highly critical of representatives of atheism.

If these attitudes are then related to distribution and sales – the *Telegraph* being the most popular broadsheet, the *Sun* and the *Mail* being most popular of all dailies – we may conclude that, in general, there is a conservative and pro-Christian emphasis in British newspapers. This conclusion is perhaps rather surprising, given that media professionals are less religious than British people in general (Holmes 2010). It also runs counter to common complaints by religious commentators about the 'secularist media'.

The Papal visit

Turning our attention now to a recent media event, we can show that most of our earlier observations are in fact exemplified in the media coverage of the papal visit to Britain in September 2010.

The coverage confirmed our profiling of the British media. On television, most of the religious programming relating to the visit took place on the BBC. In addition, there were mainly critical documentaries on Channel 4, with much less broadcasting on ITV1. Different commentators complained that the BBC was either too critical or not critical at all, but with many hours of live coverage and some slightly critical – and also positive – pre-visit documentaries, the overall balance of the BBC coverage was moderately positive, as is the case more generally on the basis of our sample. Newspapers were divided: the tabloids complained about 'left-wingers' and secularists for criticising the Pope and classified him as a 'force for good'. While the *Guardian* and the *Independent* provided some positive coverage of the visit and criticised Richard Dawkins and Stephen Fry who were leading the 'secularist' protest, they placed much emphasis on victims of Catholic child abuse and criticised the way the Pope had dealt with the abuse controversy. Despite there being no Yorkshire event on the papal itinerary, the *Yorkshire Evening Post* was able to find a local aspect when it included a story on local choir children who were going to sing for the Pope. All the papers saw the occasion more or less as a success: their narrative of the Pope's visit went from the pre-visit doubts and the image of 'God's rottweiler' to 'a resounding success' (*Daily Telegraph*, 20 September), 'beyond all expectations' (*The Times*, 20 September) and a 'warmer, more human and less rigid' image of the Pope (the *Independent*, 20 September).

Three of the themes discussed earlier were all found in the media coverage of the papal visit: increased religious diversity (especially Islam), supposed marginalisation of Christianity and the rise of atheism and secularism. The Christian ecumenical tone during the previous visit in 1982 – when the Pope actually talked about the 'restoration of unity among Christians' (in an address on 30 May 1982) and signed a declaration for improving Christian dialogue – had changed to a more inter-faith approach in the media. In an interview on BBC1 a Sikh confirmed that the Pope speaks beyond Catholics, and that to be religious today is to be inter-religious (16 September); BBC's *Look North* ran a story about Muslim children who attended the choir to sing for the Pope (15 September); *The Times* published an article on Muslims who welcomed the Pope to Britain (15 September); Prime Minister David Cameron was quoted as saying that the visit was a 'unique opportunity to celebrate the good works of religious groups' (*Daily Telegraph* 15 September); the *Daily Mirror* ran a headline 'A Man for All Religions' (18 September).

The distinction between good and bad religions was evident in stories about the 'Muslim plot to kill Pope', which turned out to be false alarm but which served as an opportunity to reinforce the connection between Islam and terrorism. Some papers were in retrospect embarrassed to have exaggerated the story while others hurried to defend themselves by claiming that there had been a serious threat.

The inter-faith aspect, despite its presence, was not there at the expense of Christianity. The marginalisation of Christianity was perhaps the Pope's main message to Britain. Some newspapers took it as an evidence of diversity gone too far, but mostly it was turned against the 'political correctness' of 'atheist left-wingers'. It was seen to be compatible with the Pope's battle against 'aggressive secularism'. This message was adopted with surprising agreement in the more pro-Christian papers, especially in editorials, compared to the more cautious stance that had been taken some months earlier on the public letter, signed by many British Christians, asserting the marginalisation of Christianity.However, dissenting voices were raised to varying degrees in comments throughout the newspapers. The more secularist papers thought that the warnings against aggressive secularism were far-fetched in relation to British everyday reality. This shows how the British media, whilst continuing to demonise Islam, operates increasingly with a distinction in which secularists and atheists are put on one side and religious people on the other.

Conclusion

Increasingly, religious diversity in Britain since the 1980s has led to a rise in references to all types of religion and non-religious belief. Islam, in particular, is widely covered, though when references to terrorism and conflict are excluded, its numerical treatment is proportionate. Religion is still widely reflected in the language and images of popular culture, and, despite claims that it is marginalised, Christianity continues to be discussed and represented as part of national heritage and the British landscape. Religion is undeniably a subject of great global significance, and, in a nation, which is increasingly religiously illiterate because of declining participation, the media are more important than ever for informing the public about religion.

Chapter 3

Religion, News and Social Context: Evidence from Newspapers

Robin Gill

Summary

What can be learnt from newspapers about perceptions of the social and religious context in the UK? In this chapter Robin Gill answers this question by providing a detailed analysis of the religious content of several leading British newspapers, from over the last forty years. On the basis of his original research, which focuses on three specific periods of coverage (during 1969, 1990 and 2011), Gill claims that it is possible to observe divergent perceptions of the social and religious context in the UK. This includes the 'persistence' of religious belief, 'secularization', 'hostility to Islam', indifference and hostility to Christianity, 'interest in New Age religion and occasional interest in peak (commonly worldwide) religious events'. Gill considers how these perceptions have changed over the last four decades, and whether they are in tension. His chapter provides some contrasting conclusions from the previous chapter and further evidence of the evolving relationship between religion and the news in the UK.

In 1969 I undertook a survey of the religious content of eight English national newspapers.[1] For four weeks in August I recorded daily the proportion of total page space (including advertisements) given to religious issues in the following newspapers: *The Times, The Daily Telegraph, The Guardian, The Daily Express, The Daily Mail, The Mirror, The Sun* and *The Sketch*. On the first two days of that month Pope Paul VI made his historic Peace Mission to Uganda which received quite an amount of attention in all of the newspaper except *The Telegraph*. In proportional terms *The Mail* had the highest level of coverage (2.5 per cent of overall space) with an overall mean for all the newspapers of 1.5 per cent, but only 0.7 per cent for *The Telegraph*. For the most part the newspapers appeared to welcome the Peace Mission.

I struggled at the time to find a satisfactory way of defining the term 'religious content', aware that Thomas Luckmann's study *The Invisible Religion*[2] had made

---

[1]   An earlier version of this chapter appears in Robin Gill, *Theology in a Social Context: Sociological Theology Volume 1* (Ashgate: Farnham, 2012) pp. 187–205.

[2]   Thomas Luckmann, *The Invisible Religion* (London: Macmillan, 1967).

this task immensely more complex. How wide a definition of 'religion' might be adopted in a survey of this nature? In the end I decided that the sort of wide definition adopted by Luckmann raised the issue of the doubtful sociological practice of imposing labels upon others which they personally reject. So I concluded that a narrow, conventional definition would be more appropriate in this context – namely 'items referring explicitly to religious institutions, their functionaries, or their central transcendent beliefs.' More difficult still was the attempt to distinguish between hostile and non-hostile religious content. Finally I adopted a perceptual definition of the notion of 'deemed hostile': namely, 'items which mainstream religious institutions might themselves deem to be hostile – for example, reports about clergy or their families involved in sex scandals or crime.'

From the work of the sociologist J.D. Halloran at Leicester University I was aware at the time that it was exceedingly difficult to measure the social significance of different forms of mass communication.[3] Instead what I sought to produce was a snapshot of the different ways that national newspapers perceived religious institutions, their functionaries and their central transcendent beliefs. My survey was clearly not going to establish whether these perceptions were accurate mirrors of these institutions, functionaries or beliefs in contemporary British society, let alone whether they significantly shaped popular perceptions and attitudes towards them. It was argued by some at the time (perhaps somewhat disingenuously) that even advertising in the media probably reflected public tastes rather than shaped them. Instead what I hoped to achieve was a fresh and largely unexplored way of recording this particular form of public perception.

The exercise, however, did generate a number of insights about social context as perceived by different newspapers. The overall mean of deemed hostile material was 18 per cent of all religious content of the newspapers, but was considerably higher within the populist newspapers *The Sun* (28 per cent) and *The Sketch* (35 per cent). In contrast *The Guardian* had the highest overall proportion of religious content (1.1 per cent) of which only 13 per cent was deemed hostile. Another important insight was that, with the exception of *The Express*, readers appeared in their letters to be much more interested in religious issues than were the news and feature editors. If the overall mean of the religious content of the newspapers was 0.8 per cent, among all the letters they carried, 4.5 per cent were concerned with religious issues. Finally within the popular newspapers (that is, not *The Times*, *The Telegraph* or *The Guardian*) horoscopes were given as much space proportionately as the total religious content (given my definition *above* horoscopes were not deemed to be 'religious').

All of this suggested that the different newspapers' perceptions of religion in British society in the late 1960s varied very considerably. They expressed different levels of hostility, scope and interest, just as sociologists of religion were doing at

---

[3]   J.D. Halloran, *The Effects of Mass Communications* (Leicester: Leicester University Press, 1964). For recent studies on the social effects of the media, see Knut Lundby (ed.), *Mediatization, Concept, Changes, Consequences* (New York and Oxford: Peter Lang, 2009).

the time. The radically differing perspectives of Bryan Wilson, David Martin at the time[4] found echoes within the different newspapers.

None of this gave any clear indication of change. This survey was a static snapshot and did not provide the sort of longitudinal evidence needed to test rival theories of secularization or persistence. So when I was doing the longitudinal research needed for *The Myth of the Empty Church* I decided to repeat the survey for four weeks in July 1990.[5] Since I was looking for longitudinal evidence I realized that, whatever the limitations of my original definitions of 'religious content' and material 'deemed hostile', it was methodologically imperative that these definitions were not altered (longitudinal research depends upon like being compared with like over different points of time). However, inevitably the peak religious event was different. This time around it occurred on 26 July 1990 when it was announced that the relatively unknown Bishop George Carey was to become the next Archbishop of Canterbury.

Comparing the evidence from these two surveys it soon became clear that the relative proportion of space given to religious items in national newspapers had declined overall (from 0.8 per cent of total space to 0.6 per cent) between 1969 and 1990 and in all the newspapers except *The Telegraph*. Most dramatically, it had more than halved in *The Guardian*. Now it was a new newspaper, *The Independent*, which had the highest proportion of religious items and percentage of letters with religious content. However, material perceived as 'hostile' had also declined over all (from 18 per cent to 16 per cent of all space given to religious items in the newspapers). Only *The Mail* (in which 'deemed hostile' material had risen from 18 per cent in 1969 to 30 per cent now), *The Sun* (in which it had risen from 28 per cent to 47 per cent) and the new popular newspaper, *The Star* (25 per cent: *The Sketch* was now defunct) were by then noticeably hostile. In those papers that still published general letters from readers, there was always a far higher religious content than in the paper as a whole.

In so far as newspapers might give some indication of contemporary popular sentiments, a shift away from mainstream religious institutions, but with little outright hostility, was apparent. Both of these pieces of evidence, if interpreted as indicating decline and popular indifference, were consonant with a secularization theory. In addition, there also appeared to be a decline in the percentage of readers' letters concerned with religious topics (from 4.5 per cent to 3.2 per cent of overall letters).

Less consonant with Bryan Wilson's understanding of secularization – which explicitly linked secularization with a general increase in 'rational ... cause-and-

---

4   Bryan Wilson, *Religion in Secular Society* (London: C.A. Watts, 1966) and David Martin, *The Religious and the Secular* (London: Routledge & Kegan Paul, 1969). For Martin's most recent perspective, see his *The Future of Christianity* (Farnham: Ashgate, 2011).

5   See Table 17 in Robin Gill, *The Myth of the Empty Church* (London: SPCK, 1993), p. 322.

effect thinking'[6] – was the evidence that horoscopes seemed to be more popular than ever. In the tabloids (including *The Daily Express* and *The Daily Mail*) the space given to horoscopes in 1969 was, as just mentioned, approximately equal to that given to religious items, but in 1990 it was half as much again. In addition, letter writers were still decidedly more interested in religious issues than the newspapers themselves. Finally the peak religious event in 1990 attracted far more attention (with an overall mean of 2.5 per cent) than it did in 1969 (1.5 per cent). Of course this peak event in 1990 was home-grown, but even *The Star* (3.0 per cent) and *The Sun* (2.4 per cent) gave it considerable attention. *The Telegraph*, perhaps not surprisingly given that a relatively conservative evangelical was appointed as Archbishop, had the highest proportion of coverage of any the newspapers (3.6 per cent).

What patterns can be observed in 2011? Eight out of nine of the newspapers included in 1990 (only *The Mirror* was absent) were surveyed for four weeks during January and February 2011: *The Times*, *The Daily Telegraph*, *The Guardian*, *The Independent*, *The Daily Express*, *The Daily Mail*, *The Sun* and *The Star*. In order to provide longitudinal evidence, once again the 1969 definitions were used, but percentages were adjusted for overall means for 1990 (that is, by removing data for *The Mirror*) when comparisons were made with 2011.

Overall changes

A word of caution is necessary at the outset. In the last 21 years newspapers have changed immensely. Ironically they have become both physically larger and less widely read. Many newspapers have supplements in 2011 both at the weekend and during the week. In order to maintain a valid comparison with newspapers published in 1969 and 1990 the religious content of these supplements was noted but not included in the 2011 statistics. However, these supplements still create some ambiguity, since sport or television, for example, are sometimes placed in them and sometimes not. In addition, there are now online versions of many newspapers (some subscription only and others not). For *The Guardian*, for example, the online version in 2011 appears to be used much more widely by the general public than the printed version. So any assessment of the social significance of *The Guardian* today would need to take full account of both the online as well as the printed versions.

My purpose again is emphatically *not* to assess social significance here but only social context. That makes an important sociological difference. By focusing on the continuing printed versions of the main body of each newspaper, the question is whether it is possible to detect *within them* different perceptions of religion in England over the last 42 years? The issue here is whether the approach of *newspapers* (whatever their role in an online age) to religion changes over time

---

6   Wilson, *Religion in Secular Society*, p. 17.

and then whether this offers an independent and relatively unexplored clue about different perceptions of social context.

Two striking differences are apparent immediately. This time around the overall religious content has increased slightly (to 0.7 per cent of total space from 0.6 per cent in 1990) rather than declined (as happened between 1969 and 1990) and the material deemed hostile has almost doubled (to 29 per cent of all space given to religious items). Evidently the perception of journalists is that religion is somewhat more newsworthy than it was 21 years ago (although not quite as newsworthy as it was 42 years ago), but that, in some of its manifestations at least, religion is to be regarded with considerable suspicion. In particular, Muslim extremists are given considerable attention in all of the tabloids and in some of the broadsheets.

In earlier research I puzzled about why,[7] with the important exception of Bernard Lewis,[8] religious fundamentalism was given so little serious attention before the 1979 Iranian Revolution. Even after this crucial event it was possible for academics to argue that it would be a short-term phenomenon and for newspapers to assume an ongoing process of declining interest in religious issues in the modern world. Once religious extremism linked to violence became a reality *within* the West – most dramatically with the shocking events of 9/11 and 7/7 – then it seems that religious coverage in newspapers has both increased and become distinctly more hostile. Academics such as Bernard Lewis,[9] Olivier Roy,[10] and Mark Juergensmeyer[11] also found a new and more attentive audience.

Of course these two striking differences are in part related. Precisely because Muslim extremism is being given more attention so the religious content of the newspaper rises. Yet, as will be seen in a moment, the rise in overall religious content is not accounted for wholly by the rise of material deemed hostile (nor is the latter always about Muslims). Much of the peak religious content in 2011 (at least in the broadsheets) was concerned with the announcement by the Dalai Lama that he is to retire from active politics, an announcement that caused little hostile comment. If the overall (adjusted) peak was 2.7 per cent in 1990, it is still 2.6 per cent in 2011. Furthermore, the overall (adjusted) percentage of letters concerned with religious issues has also remained static (3.6 per cent in both surveys). Seemingly readers are still more interested in religious issues than are

---

[7]   See Robin Gill, *Competing Convictions* (London: SCM Press, 1989), chap.2 and updated in Robin Gill, *Theology in a Social Context: Sociological Theology Volume 1* (Farnham: Ashgate, 2012).

[8]   Bernard Lewis 'The Return of Islam', *Commentary*, 61 (January 1976), pp. 39–49.

[9]   Bernard Lewis, *The Crisis of Islam: Holy War and Unholy Terror* (New York, NY: Random House, 2004).

[10]   Olivier Roy, *Globalised Islam: The Search for a New Ummah* (London: Hurst, 2004).

[11]   Mark Juergensmeyer, *Terror in the Mind of God: The Global Rise of Religious Violence* (Berkelely, CA: University of California Press, 2000) and *The Oxford Handbook of Global Religions* (Oxford: Oxford University Press, 2006).

news or feature editors. The latter, on this reading, are simply catching up slightly with the former.

None of this suggests a straightforward process of secularization (especially if secularization is understood as indifference to religion) in the way that the differences between 1969 and 1990 might have done. A more complicated pattern is present. Four distinct sets of perceptions emerge when the newspapers are grouped together in pairs: general persistence (*The Times* and *Independent*); considerably increased interest and hostility (*The Telegraph* and *Guardian*); marginally increased interest with New Age tendencies and greatly increased hostility (*The Express* and *Mail*); and static low level interest of any kind and very considerable hostility (*The Sun* and *Star*). If these papers accurately represent different sections of English society, then persistence, secularization, hostility to Islam, indifference to Christianity, interest in New Age religion and occasional interest in peak (frequently worldwide) religious events all can have some claim to be depicted now as the social context of theology. A thoroughly confusing set of trends emerges. Perhaps *that* is why British sociologists of religion remain so at odds with each on the issue of secularization.

Pattern 1: General Persistence

The Times shows remarkable continuity over the 42-year period. Overall space given to items with an explicit religious content was 0.8 per cent in 1969 and 0.7 per cent in both 1990 and 2011. Letters with an explicitly religious content amounted to 5 per cent in 1969 and 1990 and to 6 per cent in 2011. The peak religious content changed little between 1990 and 2011 (1.9 and 2.1 per cent respectively). The only striking change was the reduction of religious items deemed hostile. In 1969 this amounted to 17 per cent, but in 1990 it reduced to 6 per cent and in 2011 to just 4 per cent. *The Independent*, as already mentioned, did not exist in 1969, but in 2011 it is the only other newspaper surveyed that has a similarly low level of hostile material (amounting to just 3 per cent in 2011 and 2 per cent in 1990).

Compared with the other six newspapers it is evident that both *The Times* and *The Independent* go to considerable lengths to avoid identifying extremists as being 'Muslim' in their headlines and photo captions. Attention was given in many newspapers to the trial of extremists who had publicly burned poppies on Remembrance Day. *The Times* reported the trial but avoided headlining the fact that they were 'Muslims'. *The Independent* did identify them as Muslims on one occasion but gave the item little space, as did *The Times* when reporting that some Muslim schools were teaching hate and violence. *The Times* also had occasional, but very fleeting, mentions of Christian priests who had been suspended or jailed for sexual acts.

In its 2011 religious coverage *The Times* gave considerable space to the murder of the Catholic politician, Shabaz Bhatti, in Pakistan, including a full-page article by the Archbishop of Canterbury on this issue. Again it was careful to avoid religiously hostile comments. *The Times* was also the only newspaper to cover at length Anglicans becoming Roman Catholics under the new papal dispensation. It had a full-page interview with Dame Julia Neuberger who had recently been appointed Senior Rabbi of the West London Synagogue. Every Saturday it also has a *Credo* piece. Letters in *The Times* in 2011 included items debating gay marriages being conducted in churches, Jewish women being able to say the Kaddish, St George's Day, and George Fox. None were about Muslim extremism. Nor were they in *The Independent*. Here 2011 letters included, instead, discussions of the merits and demerits of hospital chaplains, Catholic schools, the religious question in the Population Census, the cost of the Pope's recent visit, women bishops, and bishops in the House of Lords.

The main difference between *The Times* and *The Independent* was that overall religious content and letters declined in the latter between 1990 and 2011. However, as already noted, the levels in both were exceptionally high in 1990 compared with other newspapers. Overall religious content in *The Independent* declined to 0.9 per cent in 2011(from 1.4 per cent in 1990) and letters with religious content declined to 3 per cent in 2011 (from 8 per cent in 1990). But the unusually high levels in 1990 may possibly reflect the fact the first editor of *The Independent* (1986–1993), Andreas Whittam Smith, is the son of an Anglican priest and himself a committed Anglican who was appointed First Church Estates Commissioner in 2002. Whether or not this had an influence, this paper retains remarkably low levels of religious material deemed hostile and overall religious content well above the mean (0.7 per cent) for all eight newspapers in 2011. Like *The Times* it suggests general persistence.

Pattern 2: Considerably Increased Interest and Hostility

Space given to religious items continued to rise proportionately in *The Daily Telegraph*. In 1969 it represented 0.5 per cent of total space in the main body of the newspaper, rising in 1990 to 0.7 per cent. With the elapse of another 21 years it has now just over 1 per cent. So within 42 years it has doubled proportionately. Since the actual size of the newspaper has expanded very considerably during this period, the volume of religious news within it has also increased significantly.

However, there still remains a very considerable gap between the interests of readers as reflected in the proportion of letters with a religious theme that are published and the overall contents of the newspaper. In 1969 letters with a religious theme represented some 6 per cent of all letters and in 1990 they represented 4 per cent. By 2011 they once more represented 6 per cent.

All of this suggests remarkable resurgence in overall interest in religious issues in *The Daily Telegraph* readers and editors. But there is a sharper point to note as well. In both 1969 and 1990 some 11 per cent of the overall religious content was deemed hostile, whereas in 2011 this had risen significantly to 23 per cent. Even if this hostile material is removed altogether from the overall religious content, there has still been a slight rise in 2011. So the increase in interest is not entirely hostile. Indeed, among 2011 letter writers it is for the most part not. They express differences of view on, say, whether gays should be allowed to be married in church or whether Christians objecting to homosexuality should be allowed to foster children, but they are also just as inclined to debate the merits of having pipe rather than electronic organs in church.

Within the body of the newspaper just over a third of the material deemed hostile was concerned with Muslim extremists. For example, considerable space was given to the trial of the poppy burners. Headlines and photographs in *The Telegraph* explicitly identified them as 'Muslims'. Prominence was also given to one of the 7/7 bombers who had apparently attempted to convert boys to Islam and to an 'abusive' Muslim who had murdered his 'converted' wife and children.

Yet it was not just Islamic fundamentalists who were highlighted by *The Telegraph*. A Northern Irish former policeman, who had murdered his wife and the husband of his lover, was explicitly identified as 'Baptist' in the headline. Similarly a mother who murdered her children was again explicitly identified in the headline as 'a churchgoer' at an evangelical congregation. Evangelical fundamentalism appears to be regarded by *The Telegraph* as a threat to social order alongside that posed by Islamic fundamentalism.

The attention given to both of these 'threats' in 2011 represents a significant change from 1969 and 1990. In the earlier years of *The Telegraph* material deemed hostile was much more likely to consist of stories about adulterous clergy. A Queen's Chaplain who had left his wife was still reported in 2011, as well as a Roman lay chaplain who had apparently made a false accusation of rape, but neither story was given as much space as that on stories about fundamentalists. Even a short item on Scientology was more satirical than critical and only a brief mention was made of evidence that the Pope's visit to Britain in 2010 was going to cost 'taxpayers' 7 million pounds.

The Guardian also showed a pattern both of increased overall interest in religion and of increased hostility. Yet there were differences on both of these points as well. The overall religious content of *The Guardian* had more than halved from 1.1 per cent in 1969 to 0.5 per cent in 1990, before returning to 1.1 per cent in 2011. And the proportion of material deemed hostile had dropped from 13 per cent in 1969 to just 1 per cent in 1990, but now had jumped to 21 per cent.

A clear difference between *The Telegraph* and *The Guardian* in 2011 is that material deemed hostile in the latter is concerned almost entirely with radical Islam. As might be expected in a left-wing newspaper, adulterous clergy went largely unnoticed. In addition, the 'Baptist' or 'churchgoing' identity of particular family killers was not remarked upon. Apart from an item about 'the leader of seaside sex cult', all of the other items deemed hostile were about the actions of individuals identified in headlines as being radical 'Islamists', Muslim 'hate preachers' or a 7/7 bomber who had attempted to 'convert' pupils. If anything more attention was paid in the general/political news of *The Guardian* than of *The Telegraph* to the effects and implications of Arab/Asian terrorists. The main difference between the two newspapers was that *The Guardian* did not always identify them explicitly as Islamists or Muslims whereas *The Telegraph* habitually did so.

As in *The Telegraph*, the letter writers to *The Guardian* appeared to express more interest in religious issues than the journalists/editors. The 1.1 per cent proportion of overall religious content did not match the 3 per cent of letters published that were concerned with religious issues. Nonetheless, this 3 per cent in *The Guardian* in 2011 actually represented a continuing slight decline from 6 per cent in 1969 and then 4 per cent in 1990.

Another contrast between the two newspapers was in their peak religious content. In 1969 *The Guardian* gave more space to the Pope's Peace Mission (1.8 per cent) than *The Telegraph* (0.7 per cent). In 1990 on George Carey's appoinment they were more equal, with *The Telegraph* giving this 3.6 per cent of space and *The Guardian* 3.1 per cent. In 2011 *The Telegraph* gave 2 per cent of space to the announcement by the Dalai Lama and *The Guardian* 2.4 per cent. However, the latter also had on the same day a lengthy obituary of Shabaz Bhatti, bringing the overall religious content that day to a remarkably high 4.5 per cent.

If it appeared by 1990 that *The Guardian* was becoming a purely secular newspaper with neither much interest in religious issues (compared with other broadsheets) nor even active antipathy to certain forms of religion, in 2011 it seems very different. *The Guardian Online* might campaign against *Thought for the Day* on Radio 4, but its printed paper on a Saturday still has a regular column *Face to Faith*. It ran a three-page feature in its *Review* (not counted of course in the overall religious content here) on the anniversary of the first publication of *the King James Bible* and it had several (perhaps over-optimistic) articles on the possibility of the Church of England authorities agreeing to allow gay partnerships to be conducted in churches. Like *The Telegraph* it also had an extended and sympathetic obituary of the Anglican Canon Donald Allchin, even though, less surprisingly, it ignored the death of the Conservative Life Peer Canon Peter Pilkington. *The Guardian*, it seems, can no longer be accurately depicted as being simply disinterested in religious issues.

Coming from radically different political positions both *The Telegraph* and *The Guardian* now show a fascinating combination of increased interest in and hostility towards (at least some aspects of) religion.

Pattern 3: Marginally Increased Interest with New Age Tendencies and Greatly Increased Hostility

The Express and *The Mail* display another pattern again. They both have an overall religious content (0.6 per cent) in 2011 that is slightly below the mean for all eight papers, yet both have increased slightly since 1990 (from 0.4 per cent for *The Express* and 0.5 per cent for *The Mail*). Neither of them displays anything like the resurgent interest of *The Telegraph* or *The Guardian*.

However, like *The Telegraph*, both *The Express* and *The Mail* now have considerable amounts of material deemed hostile concerned with Muslim extremists, Christian fundamentalists and the sexual misbehaviour of Catholic clergy. In *The Express* this hostile material has risen sharply in the last 21 years (it represented 11 per cent of overall religious materials in 1969, 12 per cent in 1990 and 31 per cent in 2011). 2011 headlines explicitly identify the poppy burners as 'Muslim extremists', schools of hatred are 'Muslim', it is a 'religious teacher' who commits a mortgage fraud and a 'royal chaplain' who leaves his wife, and the dentist who murders his wife has 'church guilt'. All of the 2011 letters with religious content in *The Express* were concerned with Muslims.

Levels of hostile material in *The Mail* have always been higher in every survey (18 per cent in 1969, 30 per cent in 1990 and 35 per cent in 2011). The 2011 headlines here are 'Muslim mob burned poppies', a female, lay Catholic 'chaplain cried rape after the priest finished their affair', 'Life for killer Sunday School teacher', and ' 'Rot in hell' fanatics told the UK's Muslim Miss Universe girl'. Unlike the letters in *The Express*, only one letter here was about Islam. With a higher proportion of letters with a religious content (here 5 per cent of all letters but only 2 per cent in *The Express*) their topics were more varied, including the date of Easter, life after death, funerals, whether or not Lincoln was a Christian, and about a Christian bed-and-breakfast husband and wife who refused to accommodate a gay couple.

Unlike the broadsheets, there is also a New Age element in both *The Mail* and *Express*. *The Mail* gave considerable (hostile) space in 2011 both to 'Satanists of Ash Tree Close' and to the rituals of a Wiccan warlock. It also had a full-page (non-hostile) feature on 'Wild child found God (and lost 10 stone)' and another on evidence that belief in God makes people happier and healthier. *The Express* had a two-page feature with the headline 'We've been visited by the spirits of our dear dead pets', as well as a half-page feature on 'The Zen way to sleep soundly' and a third on 'Angels and Ghosts'. Both *The Mail* and *Express* in 2011 also continue to have a daily (non-hostile) astrology column almost rivalling in space their overall religious content (0.4 per cent for *The Express* and 0.5 per cent for *The Mail*).

Evidently interest in Christianity in 2011 was much lower in both of these newspapers than in the broadsheets. In 1969 it was quite low in *The Express*. However, in *The Mail* then it was almost double the present rate of interest and less concerned with either Islam or New Age religion. The marginal increase in interest in religion since 1990 does not reflect any raised interest specifically in Christianity within either of these family tabloids.

Pattern 4: Static Low Level Interest of any kind and Very Considerable Hostility

Trends evident in the family tabloids are enhanced strongly in the popular tabloids, *The Sun* and *The Star*. Their low level of overall interest in religion remains from

1990. *The Star* stays at 0.4 per cent overall religious content (the lowest for any of the newspapers surveyed) and *The Sun* has moved only from 0.5 to 0.6 per cent.

The Star was first published in 1978. It is possible to see the former *Sketch* as occupying a similar niche in 1969 (even though it was taken over by *The Mail*, whereas *The Star* was launched as a popular tabloid by the owners of *The Express*). On this assumption *The Sketch* had an overall religious content of 1 per cent in 1969, together with the highest proportion at the time of material deemed hostile (35 per cent). In *The Star* this overall level was less than half in 1990, while the material deemed hostile was a comparatively high 25 per cent. By 2011 the latter has raised very sharply indeed to 65 per cent (once more the highest level of any of the newspapers surveyed). Hostile material in *The Sun* changed more sharply in the earlier period (from 28 per cent in 1969 to 47 per cent in 1990) maintaining this high level today (49 per cent).

Both *The Sun* and *The Star* direct a considerable amount of hostility explicitly at Muslims. *The Star* headlines depict poppy burners as 'Muslim fanatics', 'shameless' and even 'vile Muslims'. In *The Sun* poppy burners are 'Muslim fanatics' and 'Muslim extremists', and it is a 'Muslim' who kills US airmen. Every letter published with religious content in either newspaper (1 per cent in *The Sun* and 3 per cent in *The Star*) is also about Muslims.

However, in common with *The Express* and *The Mail*, *The Sun* in 2011 also extends hostility to the Catholic, lay chaplain ('Jail "Rev" romp rap') and identifies the 'night stalker' as a Jehovah's Witness. In each of these popular tabloid newspapers it is not the largely ignored announcement of the Dalai Lama that causes its peak religious content, but rather long articles and editorials on the poppy burners, accompanied on the same day in *The Sun* by an article by Archbishop John Sentanu defending St George (a religious peak amounting to 3.2 per cent for *The Sun* and 2.2 per cent for *The Star*). This defence of St George, together with a comparison of Cardinal Keith O'Brien with Baroness Warsi and a mention of Cliff Richard's Christian faith is most of what a reader of *The Sun* would discover about Christianity during this period. Readers of *The Star* would similarly learn that David Beckham has angel tattoos and that there is a book claiming that 'Jesus can cure gays'.

Even New Age material is largely confined to the daily astrology columns in both newspapers. In terms of overall space these astrology columns represent 0.5 per cent in *The Sun* and a remarkable 0.9 per cent in *The Star*. So the newspaper with the lowest overall religious content, the highest percentage of material deemed hostile to religion, and a tendency to ignore most items of news relating to Christianity (hostile or non-hostile), now gives more than twice as much space to astrology as it does to religious issues in any form.

Tensions between these Four Patterns

It is worth emphasizing again that this is not an attempt to assess the social significance of newspapers – for example, trying to assess whether they facilitate or deflect some process of secularization. Nor it is it an attempt to measure secularization or persistence. It is an attempt instead to offer under-explored clues about differing perceptions of social context. Journalists act as professional filters of particular perceptions aimed at different markets. Manifestly the perceptions emerging from these four patterns in the way that different printed newspapers represent religion in the world today have radical and unresolved internal tensions. Is religion a threat or a comfort in the modern world? Is Christianity worth reporting? If it is not, is this because it is fast disappearing in England or because it is simply part of the wallpaper? Is Islam to be demonized or integrated? Is New Age religion to be treated with any credence?

It is probably impossible to get widespread agreement on any of these questions. As a cultural paradigm predicts, with the long-term demise of religious socialization and belonging in Britain over the past century, it is only to be expected that religious believing is becoming increasingly fragmented. In this context the four patterns emerging from this newspaper survey may represent four distinctive paths in tension with each other. The newspapers themselves are consciously targeted at differing socio-economic, gender and even age groups. This of course is related to the density and level of language, the depth of analysis that they offer, the political bias they adopt and the pictures they use. Yet behind all of this, the different assumptions about religion in the modern world that they make may have much wider resonance.

As we have seen, four distinct religious types seem to be present: general persistence; considerably increased interest and hostility; marginally increased interest with New Age tendencies and greatly increased hostility; static low level interest of any kind and very considerable hostility. Hostility is present in three out of four of these types. This appears to be consonant with the rhetoric of the so-called 'new atheism' expressed particularly in Richard Dawkins' *The God Delusion*,[12] Christopher Hitchens' *God is Not Great: How Religion Poisons Everything*,[13] Sam Harris' *The End of Faith: Religion, Terror and the Future of Reason*[14] and (in more scholarly terms) Daniel Dennett's *The Breaking of the Spell: Religion as a Natural Phenomenon*.[15] The use of words such as 'delusion', 'poisons', 'spell' and

---

[12]   Richard Dawkins, *The God Delusion* (London: Bantam Press, 2006 and Boston: Houghton Mifflin, 2008).

[13]   Christopher Hitchens, *God is Not Great: How Religion Poisons Everything* (London: Atlantic and New York: Warner, 2007).

[14]   Sam Harris, *The End of Faith: Religion, Terror and the Future of Reason* (New York: Norton, 2004).

[15]   Daniel Dennett, *The Breaking of the Spell: Religion as a Natural Phenomenon* (New York: Viking and London: Pelican, 2006).

'terror' in the titles of these books clearly signals hostility. In sociological terms it represents an important shift from secularization theory more typical of the 1960s and 1970s. The latter was more akin to the assumptions about secularization that characterized Weber and Durkheim – a regretful acceptance that religion (with its beneficial features of social cohesion and moral values) is simply disappearing from the modern world. In contrast, the new atheists more typically argue that religion, far from disappearing quietly, is still far too dominant and pernicious in the modern world. This latter perspective might more accurately be depicted as polemical secularism rather than secularization. Rather than regretting or simply noting the disappearance of religion, it strongly resents its persistence.

So is polemical secularism now the dominant culture in modern Britain? Is this what is reflected in the sort of hostility found in six out of eight of the 2011 newspapers surveyed? If a positive answer is given to both of these questions, then that would have very profound implications for the social context of theology in Britain today. It might well mean that those theologians today, such as Stanley Hauerwas and John Milbank, who construe their central task in terms of so-called 'culture wars' are justified.

Before reaching this conclusion too readily, however, it is worth noting an important difference between the hostility found in the six newspapers and the hostility that is more typical of the new atheism. In stylised form the new atheism may be depicted in terms of a series of propositions:

1. We should govern our lives by reason (exemplified by science) not by faith.
2. Belief in God depends upon (blind) faith not reason.
3. Belief in God is a delusion.
4. All religion is a delusion.
5. Religion can be explained away by science.
6. Religion, since it is a demonstrable delusion, results in irrational behaviour.
7. Religion is especially dangerous because it causes war.
8. Religion poisons everything.
9. Humanity would be better off without religion.
10. Religion should be eliminated.

Of course this stylised form is much too crude to capture the arguments of all of the new atheists. Few might actually reach proposition 10. And Daniel Dennett, unlike Christopher Hitchens, would be unlikely to subscribe to proposition 8, since he concedes that 'there is growing evidence that many religions have succeeded remarkably well … improving both the health and the morale of their members, quite independently of the good works that they have accomplished to benefit others'.[16] He does still wish to balance these benefits against harms caused by religions and to explore purely secular means of achieving the same benefits, but generally he avoids the more dogmatic negative claims made by other new atheists.

---

[16]   Dennett, *The Breaking of the Spell*, p. 272.

That point conceded, it is characteristic of all the new atheists (including Dennett) that they draw conclusions about religion or religions as a whole, whereas the six newspapers are predominantly hostile towards radical Islam (and, more occasionally, towards fundamentalist forms of Christianity). The 2011 survey of newspapers detected little or no hostility towards mainstream Christianity or to the Church of England in particular. If anything hostility in this form was more characteristic of the 1969 and 1990 surveys (although the coverage in 1990 of George Carey's appointment was largely benign). Nor were the 2011 newspapers hostile to the Dalai Lama and his form of Mahayana Buddhism. In terms of the 10 stylised propositions only a modified version of proposition 7 might resonate strongly in the six newspapers that expressed hostility – that is, hostility specifically directed at those forms of religion that promote acts of terrorism and violence.

Mark Juergensmeyer, with an early background in religious activism and journalism, approaches religiously inspired terrorism and violence in a manner more in line with the broadsheet newspapers than the new atheists. It has been seen that *The Times* and *The Independent*, especially, were both careful in 2011 not to express even this more specific form of hostility. Terrorists were typically depicted as 'terrorists' not as 'Muslim terrorists'. It was the broadsheets on the political left and right – *The Guardian* and *The Telegraph* – which characteristically and with apparent hostility identified this as a specifically Muslim issue. Juergensmeyer does discuss 'the global rise of religious violence' at length, interviewing in the process many of its perpetrators. However, he finally distances himself from confrontational and bellicose policies towards these perpetrators:

> The ... scenario for peace is one in which the absolutism of the struggle is defused, and the religious aspects are taken out of politics and retired to the moral and metaphysical planes. As long as images of spiritual warfare remain strong in the minds of the religious activists and are linked with struggles in the social world around them, the scenarios we have just discussed – achieving an easy victory over religious activists, intimidating them into submission, or forging a compromise with them – are problematic at best. A more moderate view of the image of religious warfare has been conceived, one that is deflected away from political and social confrontation.[17]

He argues that this 'more moderate' view involves a recognition both that religion can contribute positively to public life (as the broadsheets generally acknowledge) and that religion should be tempered by the 'rationality and fair play' of the Enlightenment: 'religious violence cannot end until some accommodation can be forged between the two – some assertion of moderation in religion's passion, and

---

[17]   Mark Juergensmeyer, *Terror in the Mind of God: The Global Rise of Religious Violence* (Berkeley, CA: University of California Press, 2000), pp. 240–41.

some acknowledgement of religion in elevating the spiritual and moral values of public life'.[18]

Another tension between the newspapers was between those that showed a renewed or ongoing interest in (non-Muslim) religious issues and those instead that were or remained largely indifferent to them. This was mainly a tension between the broadsheets and the tabloids. *The Times*, *The Independent*, *The Telegraph* and (unexpectedly) *The Guardian* all showed strong patterns of persisting or renewed interest. Only in *The Independent* did the proportional coverage drop between 1990 and 2011, but even after this drop the level was still comparatively high. In contrast, readers of *The Express*, *The Mail*, *The Sun* and *The Star* would have been hard pressed to have learned anything much about mainstream Christianity during the period surveyed in 2011. All were characterized by indifference. But again, this was not exactly the sort of *religious* indifference premised by secularization theory, since New Age issues were still in evidence alongside regular horoscopes. In 1990 and 2011 *The Star* showed itself to have the lowest level of interest in religious issues, allied to the highest level of hostility expressed on the few issues it actually reported, compared with any of the other newspapers surveyed. Yet, as has been seen, it also almost doubled the proportionate size of its astrology column in that same period of time. Here too this hardly fits the assumptions of the new atheists. With the slow demise of Sunday schools in Britain following the first decade of the twentieth century (when they had involved a majority of children even in impoverished urban areas) and their widespread collapse in the 1960s, it may be guessed that many readers of *The Star* are several generations away from any formal religious socialization.

---

[18] Juergensmeyer, *Terror*, p. 249. See also Andrew R. Murphy (ed.), *The Blackwell Companion to Religion and Violence* (Malden, MA and Oxford: Wiley-Blackwell, 2011), Part 5.

Chapter 4

A Relationship Worth Getting Right

Paul Woolley

Summary

The relationship between religion and news media is often difficult and fraught with mutual misunderstanding. Nevertheless, as Paul Woolley argues, it is a relationship worth getting right. In this chapter, Woolley suggests how the relationship between religions and the media (and the news media in particular) could be improved. He argues that much coverage of religion currently demonstrates a lack of religious literacy, and that religion editors need to be as well informed and experienced as their counterparts in economics or business reporting. He also argues that religions need to play their part in getting the relationship right, by engaging more readily and more clearly with different media, especially the news and journalists.

Introduction

In a lecture to the public theology think-tank *Theos* in October 2008, the BBC's Director-General (2004–2012), Mark Thompson, addressed the relationship between religion and the media. 'The relationship matters', he argued, 'because quite simply religion is back. It's not just in the news, but often leads the news'.[1] The Director-General went on to note that 'The media can't avoid religion ... if they want to reflect the world'.

Unsurprisingly, Mark Thompson's speech attracted considerable media interest and comment. It was not his claim that religion was 'back' which proved contentious but, rather, his assertion in the Q&A following the lecture that Islam should be treated more sensitively than Christianity. 'BBC Put Muslims Before You' screamed the *Daily Star* on its front page later that week. 'BBC supremo Mark Thompson has banned jokes about Muslims – because they are "more sensitive" than Christians' the Star's report continued – ironically alongside a full length photo of a semi-naked 'Lucy' advertising a poster of her 'available inside' the paper. The *Daily Telegraph*'s coverage was more subtle. 'Mark Thompson claimed that because Muslims are a religious minority in Britain and also often from ethnic minorities, their faith should be given different coverage to that of more

---

[1] M. Thompson, 'Faith, Morality and the Media', *Theos* Annual Lecture, 14 October 2008.

established groups' the paper's Martin Beckford (who, unlike the *Star's* reporter, was present at the lecture) reported. 'The BBC will tackle Islam differently to Christianity, admits its Director-General', ran the headline in the *Daily Mail*.

Mark Thompson's comments were, of course, rather more subtle than some of the news headlines implied. 'What Christian identity feels like to the broad population is a little bit different to people for whom their religion is also associated with an ethnic identity which has not been fully integrated', he said. 'There's no reason why any religion should be immune from discussion, but I do not want to say that all religions are the same. To be a minority I think puts a slightly different outlook on it.'

The reporting of the Director-General's comments powerfully illustrated the point he was making – the relationship between the media and religion can indeed be a tricky one. 'It's a relationship', Thompson said prophetically, 'where accusations and grievances often fly back and forth – though one cannot help thinking that it may be more a matter of mutual misunderstanding than of malice. But it's also a relationship that matters to both the parties: a relationship it's worth getting right.'

In an interesting footnote to this episode, the morning after the speech I received a number of telephone calls from the BBC press office. Despite the fact that the lecture was a public one and that journalists were present, I was put under pressure not to release the recording of the Q&A to the media. It was clear that the BBC's press office was trying to bury what it considered to be bad news. On that occasion, out of respect for our guest lecturer, I held the recording of the Q&A back, only releasing the podcast of the lecture at a later date. Of course, it made no difference; the majority of reporters had already filed their stories.

In this chapter, we examine the relationship not only between religion and the media but religion and journalism. In order to consider the relationship, it is necessary to explore, first, the state of religion nationally and globally. Secondly, we assess the extent and nature of the media's coverage of religion. Does the relationship matter to both parties? If so, what steps might be necessary to improve it? We conclude with a couple of case studies by way of 'worked examples'. The chapter will focus primarily, although not exclusively, on Christianity.

Desecularisation

Despite predictions of religion's decline throughout the twentieth century, rumours of God's death – to misquote Mark Twain – have been greatly exaggerated. In 1968, sociologist Peter Berger confidently predicted that by 'the twenty-first century, religious believers are likely to be found only in small sects, huddled together to resist a worldwide secular culture'.[2] In *The Desecularization of the World* in 1999, however, Berger admitted that he had been mistaken, arguing that 'the assumption

---

[2]   P. Berger, 'A Bleak Outlook Seen for Religion', *The New York Times*, 25 February 1968, 3.

that we live in a secularised world is false: The world today, with some exceptions ... is as furiously religious as it ever was, and in some places more so than ever'.[3]

Despite the vocal objections of some well-known public atheists, religion is a resurgent force across the world. In *God is Back*, John Micklethwait and Adrian Wooldridge argue that the proportion of people attached to the world's four biggest religions – Christianity, Islam, Buddhism and Hinduism – rose from 67 per cent in 1900 to 73 per cent in 2005 and is expected to increase to 80 per cent by 2050. The failure of communism and the rise of globalisation helped to spark the global religious revival in the twenty-first century, and it is now being fuelled, they argue, by market competition and a customer-driven approach to salvation. In regard to Christianity, Philip Jenkins in *The Next Christendom* predicts that by 2050, six countries (Brazil, Mexico, the Philippines, Nigeria, Congo and the United States) will each have at least 100 million Christians. Europe will have long been displaced by Sub-Saharan Africa as the principal centre of Christianity, while Brazil itself will have at least 150 million Catholics and 40 million Protestants. More than one billion Pentecostals, among the poorest in their various populations, will be spreading their own beliefs to the rest of the world.

After a slow retreat over the past decades, religion explosively re-entered the media space on 11 September 2001. The re-emergence of religion into the public and political consciousness was not, however, simply due to radical Islam. What are the reasons for the renewed interest?

First, religion is contributing significantly to the renewal of civil society. One of the findings of the *Citizenship in Britain* study in 2004 was that those individuals who regarded themselves as belonging to a particular religion often exhibited atypical characteristics.[4] They recorded comparatively high levels of interpersonal trust, of trust in the police, of respect for the law and of a commitment to the citizen's duty to vote. They also recorded higher than average levels of group membership, of engagement in informal activities, of political participation and of time 'donation'. Clearly, the 'Big Society' agenda presents a potentially significant opportunity for faith groups. In recent history, the public and politicians alike have tended to look to either the state or the market to solve the problems of society. The left have seen the market as the problem and government as the solution. On the right, the opposite view has been taken. In reality, both left and right have failed to recognise the centrality of everything that exists in between the market and the state. People find meaning and belonging in families, clubs, faith communities, fellowships, neighbourhoods, voluntary organisations – all of which are bigger than the individual, but smaller than the state. In the words of the Chief Rabbi, Lord Sacks, 'They operate on a different logic. Families and communities are held together not by the coercive use of power, not by the contractual mechanisms

---

3   P. Berger, in J. Coffey, 'Secularisation: is it inevitable?,' *Cambridge Papers* Vol. 10, No. 1, March 2001.

4   C. Pattie, P. Seyd, and P. Whiteley, *Citizenship*, 57–107.

of exchange, but by love, loyalty, faithfulness and mutuality: being there for one another when we need one another'.[5]

Secondly, there is the emergence of evidence regarding the correlation between religious belief and human well-being. Study after study demonstrates the importance of religion as a contributory factor to happiness. In 2008, for example, research presented to the Royal Economic Society indicated that the more religious a person is the happier. The research, conducted by Professor Andrew Clark, drew on data across Europe including the UK. It found that religious people report better 'life satisfaction' than their non-religious counterparts.[6] Richard Layard of the London School of Economics boldly claims that: 'One of the most robust findings of happiness research is that people who believe in God are happier'.[7]

Thirdly, religion is increasingly significant in the emerging identity politics. It is clear that well-formed and deeply-rooted religious identities form an inescapable part of the growing identity politics in the UK political arguments that focus upon the interests and perspectives of social minorities, or self-identified social interest groups. Today, people are as likely, perhaps more so, to define themselves according to their religious faith as they are to their ethnicity or nationality.

Fourthly, and related to the above, unprecedented levels of migration are reviving religiosity in the UK, not least in (though not limited to) the Catholic Church in England and Wales. For example, in 2007 a report by the Von Hügel Institute, entitled *The Ground of Justice*,[8] examined how Catholic migration into the UK has caused the Catholic community to undergo a shift in its ethnic makeup: according to one agency director interviewed by the authors, over 2,000 people, often with strong religious convictions, arrive at Victoria coach station from Central and Eastern Europe every week.

Statistical analysis

Statistics concerning the nature and extent of religious belief are inevitably contested. Still, the 2001 census showed that a significant majority of people, voluntarily and in the privacy of their own homes, chose to designate themselves in religious terms. In the census of England and Wales, Christianity was the major religion (71.6 per cent of the population), followed by Islam (2.7 per

---

[5]   J. Sacks, 'Faith communities and the renewal of civil society', June 2000: http://www.ccfwebsite.com/archives/Dr_Jonathan_Sacks_the_Chief_Rabbi_calls_for_faith_communities_to_renew_civil_society.pdf (accessed 1 September 2011).

[6]   A. Clark, and O. Lelkes, 'Deliver Us From Evil: Religion as Insurance', the Royal Economic Society's annual conference, 17–19 March 2008.

[7]   R. Layard, *Happiness: Lessons from the new Science* (London: Allen Lane, 2005).

[8]   Davis, F., Stankeviciute, J., Ebbutt, D., Kaggwa, R., *The Ground of Justice, The Report of a Pastoral Research Enquiry into the Needs of Migrants in London's Catholic Community*, Von Hügel Institute, St Edmund's College, Cambridge, 2007.

cent), Hinduism (1 per cent), Sikhism (0.6 per cent), Judaism (0.5 per cent) and Buddhism (0.3 per cent).[9]

In 2008, *Theos* undertook an extensive research project in conjunction with the polling company ComRes on the extent and nature of religious belief in the UK.[10] The research revealed that 58.9 per cent of the population self-identify as Christians, although only 9 per cent are 'practising Christians'. Significantly, the denominational spread of those in the 'practising Christians' group has some notable, though perhaps not entirely surprising, differences from Christians as a whole. While 58 per cent of Christians give their denomination as 'Church of England', only 39 per cent of practising Christians do. 20 per cent of practising Christians are Catholics, compared with 17 per cent of all Christians, and 41 per cent attend other churches, including Baptist, Methodist, Pentecostal and independent churches, compared with 23 per cent of Christians as a whole. As we will see below, well over 39 per cent of news stories relating to Christianity are concerned with the Church of England. Though this can be partly explained by the Anglican Church's historical role within the nation, it is far from representative of the experience of most Christians today.

There is a popular misapprehension that there has been a continual decline of religious observance over the past two hundred years. In their comprehensive study *Churches and Churchgoers*, Currie et al. estimate that there were 577,000 Easter Communicants in the Church of England in 1800, equating to 3.54 per cent of the population (the 1801 census gives a figure of 16.3m for total population).[11] In 2006 the Church of England Easter communicants figure was 1.85m out of a population of 50.8m equating to 3.64 per cent of the population. It could be argued, therefore, that the proportion of Church of England communicants has increased in comparison with 1800, and, as we have seen, the Church of England by no means accounts for all UK churchgoers. If communicants in other denominations and networks were taken into account, the figure for 2006 would be considerably higher. The data referenced indicate that the state of religion in the UK is quite different from the narrative of decline often presented in the news media.

Religion and the broadcast media

This book is about religion and the news, but some brief comments about religion and the media more generally seem apposite. On 6 February 2010, the *Sunday Telegraph* reported that the BBC's Head of Religion and Ethics had accused the

---

[9]   See Census figures for England and Wales in 2001: http://www.statistics.gov.uk/cci/nugget.asp?id=984 (accessed 1 September 2011).

[10]   To see the full data tables, go to http://campaigndirector.moodia.com/Client/Theos/Files/DarwinTables1.pdf (accessed 1 September 2011).

[11]   R. Currie, A. Gilbert, and L. Horsley, *Churches and Church-Goers: Patterns of Church Growth in the British Isles since 1700* (Oxford: Clarendon Press, 1977).

Church of England of 'living in the past'. Aaqil Ahmed was responding to the news that the Synod of the Church of England was going to debate a motion criticising the BBC for its treatment of Christianity. Mr Ahmed added: 'I think all the faiths should be treated in the same way. I do not believe in treating any faith differently'. Mr Ahmed evidently disagrees with his Director-General.

It is clear that religious programming is in decline as a proportion of broadcast output. In June 2010, it was reported that ITV would broadcast only one hour of religious programming in 2010. Channel Five would not show any.[12] In contrast, Aaqil Ahmed said that 'The [BBC's] Charter says that we should be doing 110 hours. We're doing 164 this year'. In real terms, however, the Corporation's religious output has also fallen. To be exact, it has fallen from 177 hours of religious programming on BBC television in 1987/88 to 155 hours in 2007/08 – a period during which the overall volume of programming has doubled.[13] Sticking with the BBC, the Corporation spends significantly less on programmes dealing with religious and ethical issues than on entertainment shows that attract the same size of audience. *Friday Night* with Jonathan Ross regularly attracted a similar audience to *Songs of Praise* (4 million viewers). The difference is that the contribution of Mr Ross was valued at £18 million. Strikingly, in 2005, the funeral of Pope John Paul II was the largest televised event ever.[14]

What are we to make of all of this? The first point is that there is no position of neutrality when it comes to programming. The BBC's output reflects certain notions of what 'good' programming should look like, as set out in its Charter. Of course, its understanding of the 'good' might simply be based on securing as high an audience share as possible. However, the BBC as a publicly funded broadcaster has a wider role, which goes beyond the commercial; it, like charities, is required to demonstrate its 'public benefit', which has moral meaning. It is notable that the BBC had a Central Religious Advisory Committee (CRAC) up until the end of 2007 which met regularly to discuss religious broadcasting issues and advised the BBC and Ofcom (the Office of Communications) on religion-related policies and coverage. Since 2009 it has been replaced by the *Standing Conference on Religion and Belief*, which performs a similar role, though it now includes a humanist among its members. Secondly, it is important that the BBC produces programmes that reflect the diverse interests and belief commitments of its audience. The BBC's coverage of religion should broadly reflect the religious composition of the

---

[12] 'ChurchofEnglandis"livinginthepast",saysBBC'sheadofreligion',the*DailyTelegraph*: http://www.telegraph.co.uk/news/newstopics/religion/7174716/Church-of-England-is-living-in-the-past-says-BBCs-head-of-religion.html (accessed 1 September 2011).

[13] 'ChurchofEnglandis"livinginthepast",saysBBC'sheadofreligion',the*DailyTelegraph*: http://www.telegraph.co.uk/news/newstopics/religion/7174716/Church-of-England-is-living-in-the-past-says-BBCs-head-of-religion.html (accessed 1 September 2011).

[14] J. Ford, 'Most-watched Television Events through History', http://technology. ezine1.com/most-watched-television-events-through-history-77369aee7e8.html (accessed 1 September 2011).

society it serves. In that sense, the methodology used to determine the extent of religious broadcasting should be no different to that used to determine the extent and nature of coverage of other topics. Contrary to Aaqil Ahmed's comments about 'equality' in the coverage of religious faiths, referred to earlier, it seems entirely reasonable that a religious faith ascribed to by 70 per cent of the population should receive more coverage than one with 3 per cent.[15] Isn't that democracy? Thirdly, it is not perhaps the role of the BBC to 'promote' Christianity any more than to 'promote' politics or the Arts or anything else for that matter. However, it does have a responsibility to ensure that its coverage of religion and programmes with 'religious' content promote religious literacy.

Religion and the news in print media

The fact of de-secularisation is implicitly evident in the extent of the coverage devoted to the subject of religion by the newspapers and their websites. Ruth Gledhill, *The Times*' religion correspondent (see chapter 6), observes that when she began reporting on religion 'everyone assumed it was heading towards extinction, like God'.[16] However, she concludes that today 'the profile of religion as a whole has never been higher'. In a comment piece on the *Guardian*'s website in 2005, 'Readers' Editor' Ian Mayes responded to the following letter from one of his readers: 'I was brought up in a secular society and one of the reasons I read the *Guardian* was because it was a secular, progressive paper. Now it has more religion than any other paper'.

Is that true? [Mayes wondered]. Well, viewed in the round, it probably is … [I] put the following to journalists; 'A reader writes to complain that there is too much religion in the *Guardian*. Is there?' Very few respondents thought that there was. A large majority thought that, considering the role of religion in world affairs, not only in conflicts, the paper had a clear responsibility to report, investigate, and seek to understand and explain.

This sense of responsibility is reflected in the extremely active and popular 'belief' section of the *Guardian*'s 'Comment is Free' (CiF) blog. Interestingly, despite its evident reputation as a 'secular' paper, the *Guardian*'s engagement with religious issues (as distinct from its reporting of religion) is exemplary. CiF invites writers from a wide variety of perspectives and religious traditions to contribute to its popular blog, and, to the irritation of some of its respondents, treats an impressive breadth of viewpoints with respect. Its editor, Andrew Brown (see chapter 9), writes sensitively, intelligently and with great nuance on topics that can so often be reduced to hyperbole and sectarian abuse.

---

[15] See Census figures for England and Wales in 2001: http://www.statistics.gov.uk/cci/nugget.asp?id=984 (accessed 1 September 2011).

[16] R. Gledhill, 'Religion's death has been widely exaggerated', *The Times*, 22 October 2007.

Despite examples like CiF, the problem remains that a significant amount of religious reportage is conducted through a lens of secularisation, the belief that as societies 'progress', particularly through modernisation, religion declines and loses its authority in all aspects of social life and governance. The 'default' settings of a majority of journalists appear to be aligned to those of Peter Berger in the 1960s. Similarly, many journalists continue to view religion and religious believers as a problem and cause of concern, rather than a source of hope. Undoubtedly, religion can be inflexible, inhuman, sectarian and inaccessible, but that is more the exception than the norm. The point is that a majority of news media coverage regarding religion reveals a serious lack of religious literacy.

The coverage of religion commonly focuses disproportionately on a narrow set of issues, including declining attendance, women bishops and human sexuality. The point is illustrated by reference to the 'religious' headlines, which appeared in the national press during a single week in April 2010. They can be divided into three categories – persecution and religious liberty, Catholic sex abuse and religious sectarianism.

Persecution and religious liberty

- 'Persecuted Christians' Join Forces
- It Can Only Harm Christians To Bleat About Persecution
- After Nurse Shirley Chaplin Is Banned From Wearing A Cross, Remind Me, What Country Am I Living In?
- 'Anti-Christian' Judges Should Be Banned From Religious Cases, Says Lord Carey
- Lord Carey: Christians Are Being Crucified By Top Judges
- Church Leaders Head For Showdown With Top Judges Over Bias Against Christians
- Thank God For The One Man Who Has The Courage To Stand Up To Our Ruling Elite's Assault On Christianity
- Muslim Nurses CAN Cover Up … But Christian Colleagues Can't Wear Crucifixes
- NHS Rules Relaxed For Muslims As Crucifix Is Banned
- Religious Tolerance Has Put A Fatwa On Our Moral Nerve
- Lord Carey's Bloated Conscience
- Lord Carey Warns Of 'Unrest' If Judges Continue With 'Dangerous' Rulings
- Civil Unrest Over 'Unchristian' Rulings
- Lawyers Reject Calls For Christian-Sensitive Judges
- Britain 'Risks Civil Unrest If Gay Rights Win Over Religious Beliefs'
- Insult Doesn't Need To Come With Injuries

Catholic sex abuse

- Catholic Church In England Criticises Vatican
- Vatican Climbdown Over Sex Abuse Remarks By Senior Cardinal
- Senior Catholic At Odds With Vatican Chief Over Abuse Row
- Catholic Church Dismisses Vatican Chief's Abuse Claim
- The Mob Should Lay Off. The Pope Is Completely Innocent
- Seizing The Pope? What An Arresting Idea. Will It Work?
- Catholic Church And Child Welfare
- Vatican Tells Bishops To Report Abuse Cases To Police
- Paedophile Priest 'Needed Protection From Unfounded Claims'
- The Pope On Trial Would Show What Equality Before The Law Means
- Pope Decided To Let It Be After 40 Years
- Top Cardinal, Tarcisio Bertone, Blames Paedophile Crisis On Homosexuals
- Pope Benedict XVI 'Can't Claim Abuse Immunity'
- Catholics May Just Have To Sit Out This Anti-Papal Media Frenzy
- Arrest The Pope? I Rather Think We Should
- Pope Calls For Catholic Church Repentance Over 'Sins'
- Pope Says Catholic Church Needs To Do 'Penance'
- Pope Calls On Catholic Church To Do 'Penance For Its Sins' In First Public Acknowledgement Of Child Sex Abuse Scandal
- Pope Benedict Turns His Back On A Church In Crisis

Religious sectarianism

- Not All Religious Explanations Of Tragic Events Are Harmless
- Amy Jenkins: School Lottery System Is The Way Forward

In view of the above, it is unsurprising that Tony Blair criticised the media in July 2010 for 'an ignorance which is dangerous' when it comes to covering religion. Speaking at an international short-film event run by the Tony Blair Faith Foundation in London, he said 'What most of the media focus on is religious conflict and division. And the idea we are trying to get across is that faith is inspiring people to great acts of progress'.[17] The Faith Shorts competition produced winners and runners-up from Europe, the Middle East, Asia, and North and South America. Blair said the films 'challenged some of the lazy stereotypes about religion'. Why does the news focus on religious conflict and division beyond the fact that 'conflict' is part of the media's definition of news generally? I want to suggest two factors.

In the first place, it is striking how few religion 'specialists' in the news media are specialists in any real sense of that word. It is unthinkable that the BBC's

---

[17] 'Blair: British Media have a dangerous ignorance of faith', *Church Times*, 30 July 2010: http://www.churchtimes.co.uk/content.asp?id=98376 (accessed 1 September 2011).

political, economics or science editors would not have studied the subject at University, have worked in the industry or developed specialist knowledge over a long journalistic career. Imagine the BBC appointing an individual to the post of Business Editor without a background or proven experience in business or economics. Consider, for example, the indefatigable Robert Peston: a Philosophy, Politics and Economics graduate of Balliol College, Oxford, Peston worked briefly at stockbroker Williams de Broë before he became a journalist in 1983 for the *Investors Chronicle*, joining the *Independent* newspaper for its launch in 1986. In 1990 he was appointed City Editor of the *Independent on Sunday*. Peston was at the *Financial Times* between 1991 and 2000, after which he was appointed editorial director of the online financial analysis service Quest, and became a contributing editor of *The Spectator* and a weekly columnist for the *Daily Telegraph*. In 2001 he moved to the *Sunday Times*, where he wrote a weekly business profile, 'Peston's People', and left *The Spectator* for the *New Statesman*, where he wrote a weekly column. In 2002 he joined the *Sunday Telegraph* as City editor and assistant editor. He became associate editor in 2005. Later that year it was announced that Peston would succeed Jeff Randall as BBC Business Editor, a post he has held ever since, becoming a household name during the financial crash of 2008. In contrast, it is very difficult to find a religion correspondent who read Theology or Religious Studies at University. Degrees aside, no religion correspondent has anything approaching a CV equivalent to Robert Peston's. Of course, it is not necessary to subscribe to a particular religious faith personally to report effectively on the subject. Jerome Taylor at the *Independent* is an example of someone in this category who reports religious news accurately and exhibits a high level of understanding of the complex issues involved.

Secondly, the media itself is rather unrepresentative of society. It is notoriously difficult to secure reliable statistics on the extent or nature of religious belief in media organisations, but the evidence that is available indicates that the media space is a disproportionately secular environment. In an (admittedly unscientific) snapshot survey conducted amongst media professionals at the Edinburgh Festival Fringe, the proportion of people claiming a religious belief was a fraction of the national average. Similarly, the political, religious and social attitudes of media correspondents tend to be more libertarian than those of society as a whole. Despite the claims of journalism to be objective or impartial, the reality is that individual journalists and their papers narrate news through a particular worldview with certain theological and philosophical presuppositions.[18]

It is easy to generalise, so let us consider two case studies, which offer an insight into the nature of the relationship between religion and the news. In both examples, we consider how the news media covered comments of the Archbishop of Canterbury in 2008 and 2010 respectively.

---

[18]   See also Chapter 1 for a more detailed discussion of this topic.

The Archbishop and Sharia law

On the evening of 7 February 2008, the Archbishop of Canterbury delivered the Temple lecture on 'Civil and religious law in England: a religious perspective'. In the afternoon, before the lecture, he gave an interview to Christopher Landau (an exceptional religion journalist who has two degrees in Theology and Religious Studies from Cambridge University and is now training for ordination in Oxford, see chapter 5) on BBC Radio Four's *World at One* programme. In the interview, the following exchange took place:

> CL: ... the application of Sharia in certain circumstances ... seems unavoidable?
> ABC: It seems unavoidable and indeed as a matter of fact certain provisions of Sharia are already recognised in our society and under our law. So it is not as if we're bringing in an alien and rival system. We already have in this country a number of situations in which the law, the internal law of religious communities, is recognised by the law of the land as justifying conscientious objections in certain circumstances. So, I think we need to look at this with a clear eye and not imagine either that we know exactly what we mean by Sharia and just associate it with what we read about Saudi Arabia or whatever.

Christopher Landau made a point of pressing the Archbishop to explain his position, asking about issues such as the stoning of women, especially rape victims. In response, the Archbishop said:

> Nobody in their right mind I think would want to see in this country a kind of inhumanity that sometimes has been associated with the practice of the law in some Islamic states, the extreme punishments, the attitudes to women as well.

The last part of the interview proceeded as follows:

> CL: In the end, do you think that some people might be surprised to hear that a Christian Archbishop is calling for greater consideration of the role of Islamic law?
> ABC: People may be surprised but I hope that that surprise will be modified when they think about the general question of how the law and religious community, religious principle, are best, most fruitfully accommodated.

In the lecture later that evening, the Archbishop basically argued the same point:

> There is a position – not at all unfamiliar in contemporary discussion – which says that to be a citizen is essentially and simply to be under the rule of the uniform law of a sovereign state, in such a way that any other relations, commitments or protocols of behaviour belong exclusively to the realm of the private and of individual choice. As I have maintained in several other contexts,

this is a very unsatisfactory account of political reality in modern societies; but it is also a problematic basis for thinking of the legal category of citizenship and the nature of human interdependence.[19]

The reaction of the media to the Archbishop's comments was extraordinary. The headlines, which conflated the interview and the lecture, included 'Archbishop backs sharia law for British Muslims' (the *Guardian*) and 'Archbishop of Canterbury argues for Islamic law in Britain' (*The Times*). Despite stating in the lecture that 'if any kind of plural jurisdiction is recognised, it would presumably have to be under the rubric that no "supplementary" jurisdiction could have the power to deny access to the rights granted to other citizens or to punish its members for claiming those rights', the interview and speech were widely understood to be arguing the exact opposite. The Home Office Minister Tony McNulty commented, 'To ask us to fundamentally change the rule of law and to adopt sharia law, I think, is fundamentally wrong'.

The episode certainly illustrates the challenging nature of the relationship between religion and the news. It is unlikely that the lecture without the interview would have generated any significant media coverage or that either would have been reported before 9/11. Shami Chakrabarti expressed the problem well: 'Archbishops are better at sermons than sound-bites and sometimes this can become confused in the translation. Dr Williams has clarified his position with dignity and humility. There must be equality under one single law of the land, but if the law continues in the best democratic tradition, there can be reasonable room for individual conscience and expression'.[20]

It is clear that some news reporters and media commentators both misunderstood and misreported the argument the Archbishop was seeking to develop. However, the episode also highlights the importance of media awareness and literacy on the part of religious leaders and spokespeople. Perhaps the biggest mistake on the part of the Archbishop's media team was not to anticipate the subsequent reaction to the interview and provide 'rapid rebuttal' to some of the accusations levied at the Archbishop. In the words of James Carville, the lead strategist of the successful presidential campaign of then-Arkansas governor Bill Clinton, 'speed kills'. It is striking also that, even now, the transcript of the interview on the Archbishop's website contains a number of typographical errors. In all the hullaballoo, the most important point of the Archbishop's lecture was lost, namely that the law is important,

---

[19]   Rowan Williams. 'Civil and Religious Law in England: a Religious Perspective', 7 February 2008, the foundation lecture at the Royal Courts of Justice: http://www. archbishopofcanterbury.org/1575 (accessed 1 September 2011).

[20]   'Williams tries to defuse row over sharia law but refuses to apologise', the *Independent*, 12 February 2008, http://www.independent.co.uk/news/uk/home-news/ williams-tries-to-defuse-row-over-sharia-law-but-refuses-to-apologise-781009.html (accessed 1 September 2011).

but it is not all-important. It is critical that we create a society in which civil issues can be dealt with in communities without automatic recourse to the courts.

Catholics and credibility

On Saturday 3 April 2010, the BBC's Religious Correspondent, Robert Piggot, reported comments of the Archbishop of Canterbury that the Catholic Church in Ireland had lost 'all credibility' over the way it had dealt with paedophile priests. In the *Start the Week* interview, which was only broadcast in full two days later, Mr Piggot reported Rowan Williams as saying that the problems, which had been a 'colossal trauma' for the Church, also affected the wider public.

Stating that Dr Williams' words represented unusually damning criticism from the leader of another Church, Piggot went on:

> 'Rowan Williams' assessment of the Roman Catholic Church in Ireland as having lost all credibility is unusually blunt and damning.
>
> It should be remembered that relations between the two Churches have been strained since Pope Benedict offered disgruntled Anglicans easy conversion to Catholicism last October.
>
> But Dr Williams' remarks do reflect a growing sense of alarm at what is perceived to be the Catholic Church's disastrous loss of moral authority. His comments will strike a chord with increasing numbers of people who feel the Vatican has yet to realise, let alone accept, the seriousness of the plight it shares with the Church in Ireland.
>
> While it is very unusual for one Church leader to make such comments about another, Dr Williams will feel the Roman Catholic Church in Ireland and the UK's Anglican Churches are fighting the same battle against secularism and the erosion of Christian influence and status.
>
> On the most important weekend in the Christian calendar, when the Church is supposed to be talking about renewal, it faces a real crisis which Dr Williams believes needs to be sorted out.'[21]

The story not only featured prominently in the BBC's own news reports but was also subsequently picked up by the national and international media. The *Guardian* reported 'Williams criticises Irish Catholic Church "credibility"'. *The Times* went with 'Ireland Archbishop stunned by Dr Rowan Williams' criticism of Catholic Church'.

The pressure generated by the headlines was such that, even before the actual interview was broadcast on the Bank Holiday Monday, the Archbishop of Canterbury had telephoned the Archbishop of Dublin, Diarmuid Martin, to

---

[21]   'Rowan Williams expresses 'regret' over Church remarks', 3 April 2010, http://news.bbc.co.uk/1/hi/8601381.stm (accessed 1 September 2011).

apologise for difficulties that may have been created by his remarks. How was the apology reported? *The Times* stated that 'Rowan Williams expressed "deep sorrow and regret" after a furious reaction from Irish Catholic leaders to his earlier claim that some priests in Ireland found it "quite difficult" to walk down a street wearing a clerical collar'.

The first time I heard Dr Williams' comments in context was on BBC Radio 4's *Start the Week* programme. What did Rowan Williams actually say? The precise words of the Archbishop were as follows:

'I was speaking to an Irish friend recently who was saying that it is quite difficult in some parts of Ireland to go down the street wearing a clerical collar now. And an institution so deeply bound into the life of a society, suddenly becoming, suddenly losing all credibility – that's not just a problem for the Church, it is a problem for everybody in Ireland.'[22]

This case is possibly one of the worst examples of religion news (mis)reporting that I have come across in recent years. Although the words were correct, the context was not. Theologians know that a text without a context is a pretext. It was difficult not to conclude that the media coverage was prompted either by the desire to advertise a flag-ship Radio 4 programme, deal with the challenge of a slow news day or support a default narrative about ecumenical tensions and decline. Or perhaps it was a combination of all three. Either way, the BBC made an error in its reporting.

Of course, there are probably lessons for the Lambeth media team too. The interview was pre-recorded at the Archbishop's Palace. In political circles, a member of the interviewee's media team would normally sit in on the interview and record it, enabling a transcript to be produced for their own records. Did the same happen with the Archbishop? If so, the media team could have immediately released the full transcript of the interview with a request that the BBC correct any errors in its news report and set the record straight.

Faith in the future

In view of these two case studies, what of the future relationship between religion and the news? How can the relationship be improved? In this chapter, I have intimated that there are two key needs and they are linked: to improve the quality of journalists' coverage of stories with a religious dimension and to improve contributions to the media by religious leaders, their spokespeople and religious experts. We are living through a media revolution, with a huge growth in news reporting precipitated by the internet. The explosion of blogs and the rapid development of social networking mean that there is likely to be an even greater volume of religious coverage across different media channels and platforms in the

---

[22]   *Start the Week*, Monday 5 April 2010, BBC Radio 4, http://www.bbc.co.uk/programmes/b00rrhyd

future, which makes the relationship even more important. So, how can we get the relationship right?

In the first place, religious people and organisations need to engage with the media more effectively and understand the demands of news journalists, especially in a 24-hour rolling news culture. I am constantly surprised by the number of press releases I receive from faith-based organisations that appear designed not to be read. Individuals working in religious organisations should, more than most, recognise the importance of communication and undertake media training. It is critical that religious organisations engage more positively and less defensively with the media.

Secondly, media organisations have a responsibility to ensure that the news producers and reporters who cover religion are religiously literate. It should be a basic requirement for religion correspondents to have undertaken a course in religion. Positions should be filled by experts in the field. The effect of this would be to end or radically reduce the sloppiness and inaccuracies evident in certain reports.

Thirdly, media organisations should attempt to reflect the broad diversity of the populations they exist to serve not only politically, socially and ethnically, but also religiously. It is difficult to understand why media organisations are disproportionately secular. Commitments to equality and diversity should extend to religion.

Finally, there is space for organisations engaging with faith and society to increase the public understanding of religion by working to promote more balanced, accurate and rational coverage of the controversial religion stories that hit the headlines.

Conclusion

It is clear, as Mark Thompson noted in his *Theos* lecture, that religion is not only in the news, but often leads the news. On the basis of the upward trend in religious belief, religion is set to increasingly lead it. So, the relationship between religion and the news must be improved if we want to be better informed about the complex world in which we live. The relationship between religion and the news matters to both parties. In order to get the relationship right, significant steps will need to be taken by journalists, headline writers, religious spokespeople and the groups and organisations they represent. The media need to be better educated about religion and religious groups need to be better educated, and more realistic, about the media. The relationship is worth getting right, especially if we value the journalistic values of accuracy, fairness and impartiality, and the potential of religion to contribute positively to the creation of open and generous societies where people are able to truly flourish.

SECTION 2
Covering Religion

Figure 10   An unusual view of a group of photographers focusing down towards the viewer. Courtesy of Losevsky Pavel / Shutterstock.com

Introduction to Section 2: Covering Religion

*In this section, journalists and media experts provide a range of perspectives on
the relationship between religion and the news media in the UK. Many of the
contributors in this section raise the question of the purpose of news in general,
and religion reporting in particular. To what extent is the task of the news media
to pursue 'stories', even if this focus on the extremes means providing a distorted
picture of a given religious group, and reinforcing public prejudice against it?
How far does the news media have the task of holding religious groups to account
by drawing attention to their extremist fringes or hypocritical practices? How
far does the news media have the responsibility to treat religious groups in a
balanced way, including the duty to treat some religious groups more sensitively
than others? All these questions also raise the issue of the difference between
media discourse and religious discourse – characterised by one contributor as the
difference between utilitarianism and virtue.*

*Another theme that emerges from the contributions of this section is the
changing nature of various media in the UK. On one hand, print newspapers face
an uncertain future as advertising revenues fall and readers increasingly find
news and information from online sources. On the other, the rapid expansion of
new online media and the rise of what one contributor calls 'citizen journalism'
provide journalists and religious leaders with both new opportunities and new
challenges.*

Chapter 5

What the Media thinks about Religion: A Broadcast Perspective

Christopher Landau

Summary

Landau begins his chapter by offering a distinct definition of news: news is information that people would rather was not in the public domain. The task of broadcasting media is to bring such information to light – the pursuit of a 'story' is their raison d'etre. This means, Landau argues, that journalists do not always have to represent religions in proportion to their size: while a tiny minority of Muslims may be terrorists, the story is nevertheless an important one. While Landau acknowledges that there will always be tension between the religious news that journalists want to report and the 'good news' that religions would rather was heard, he makes some recommendations for improving the relationship between religion and the news. Journalists, he argues, need to become more religiously literate, so that they are better able to present informative discussions on religious issues. Religious groups need to engage more proactively with broadcasting media as they are, rather than hoping that they will change.

It was only relatively recently that I discovered a pre-twentieth century definition of the verb 'broadcast': to scatter seed by hand. For the contemporary television or radio journalist who reports on religious affairs, it is a definition worth careful consideration, not least in the context of the Biblical parable of the sower.[1] That parable explores whether scattered seed has fallen on fertile or infertile ground, having assumed that the seed itself is of good quality. But in today's journalistic climate, the question is not merely about where the 'seed' falls after it's broadcast, but also the nature of the seed itself.

In these reflections, as I consider the way in which matters of faith and religion are dealt with by news broadcasters – drawing particularly on my own recent experience as a religious affairs correspondent at the BBC – I hope to offer some insights into the factors affecting how broadcast journalists report on religious affairs. This will involve considering whether the 'seed' that news broadcasters choose to 'scatter' will ever be regarded by religious people themselves as containing within it fruitful potential for future growth, and exploring whether

---

[1]   Matthew 13:1–23, Mark 4:1–20, Luke 8:4–15

'religious news' will ever bear much resemblance to the 'good news' religious organisations strive to proclaim.

Such a discussion necessarily needs to begin with a frank assessment of what constitutes 'religious news' in the eyes of journalists working in the newsrooms of national broadcasters. One working definition of 'news' is 'something that somebody somewhere would rather was not made public knowledge'. For journalists, uncovering and then conveying such information is the very essence of their trade: the more exclusive or unusual a particular story is, the greater its value to the news organisation.

If religious organisations are to better understand why they get the coverage they do, a realistic appreciation of what makes 'a good story' – the journalistic holy grail – is an essential prerequisite. It is only by fully appreciating the context within which journalists are working, and the criteria by which their work is judged by editors, that religious groups themselves might learn to be more confident in their media engagement.

What makes religion hit the headlines?

The recently-retired Bishop of Southwark, Tom Butler, often spoke of the danger presented by the domination within British media of people who represented what he referred to as a metropolitan, liberal, secular elite.[2] The point is simple: if journalists are disproportionately unlike the people about whom they report, the process of journalism begins from a potentially unhelpful starting point. There is certainly a danger that journalists with little or no personal appreciation for the relevance of religion might risk assuming that their audience shares similarly secular convictions, even when the statistical evidence points otherwise.

A helpful set text for this discussion is the book *God is Back*,[3] briefly cited in the previous chapter, written by two journalists with impeccably 'mainstream' credentials: the editor of the Economist magazine, and its Washington bureau chief. Their contention is that the mass media risks overlooking the significance of religion in twenty-first century world affairs. The popular postwar notion that religion was irrelevant, and would gradually fade away, has been shown to be spectacularly untrue. The events of 11 September 2001 offer a stark demonstration of why religion needs to be understood as a force in world affairs. For those journalists whose view of the world creates little space for religion, a notion of 'God is back' may indeed seem compelling – though I suspect that most religious

---

[2]   One example is his appearance as a witness before the House of Lords select committee considering the BBC Charter Review, 2 November 2005, see http://www. publications.parliament.uk/pa/ld200506/ldselect/ldbbc/128/5110204.htm (accessed 3 March 2011).

[3]   John Micklethwait and Adrian Wooldridge, *God is Back: How the Global Rise of Faith is Changing the World* (London: Allen Lane, 2009).

affairs specialists would simply remark that it is not so much the case that God is back, rather that God never went away.

But even if news about religion is seen as relevant, and worthy of broadcast coverage – and this is by no means a given, particularly among commercial broadcasters – the sorts of stories that will receive substantial attention are unlikely to be those which church or other religious leaders would hope to see reaching the widest audience. It is often the least edifying aspects of religious life that gain the largest amount of airtime – just as with any other aspect of human existence when under the media spotlight. So debates or conflicts within religious groups inevitably grab headlines, particularly when they involve the consideration of topics that highlight disparities between religious views and the emerging norms of contemporary society. Questions about gender roles and sexuality within Western churches offer the most obvious example: the arguments are not merely of interest to followers of the faith itself, but also for anyone interested in how social attitudes are changing, and how religious groups react.

Also of substantial interest are stories that highlight oddity or curiosity, which in part might be seen to emphasise an unspoken insinuation that all religions constitute a form of eccentricity, inflicting varying degrees of harm on their adherents. The growth of Paganism in Britain is sometimes presented in such terms, as were the activities of the Catholic group Opus Dei following its prominence in Dan Brown's novel *The Da Vinci Code*.[4] It is something I have experienced in the course of my own reporting. On a visit to what could have been described as a 'worthy but dull' interfaith dialogue event in South Korea, it was a supplementary interview I conducted with the son of the founder of the Unification Church (better known as the 'Moonies') which attracted substantial hits on the BBC News website.[5] It is not just editors, but audience members themselves, who have an eye for the unusual.

The potential danger is that stories about religion end up spending rather too much time consigned to what you might call the 'oddity slot'. The clear appetite for such stories raises an important question about how media outlets determine the sort of coverage different faiths receive, and why. The simple truth is that no journalist would ever wish to respond to a quota that demanded any particular group in society was afforded an amount of airtime in direct proportion to the size of the community. The problem comes when the gap between media profile and actual presence in society is perceived by some to have become too wide. Some Christian groups are becoming increasingly vocal about what they see as the sidelining of Christianity in Britain. One (perhaps apocryphal) letter of complaint to Radio 4's weekly religious affairs programme, *Sunday*, suggested that given the level of consideration given to Islam within a particular edition of the programme, it should be renamed *Friday*. The clear implication was that Islam had been given disproportionate attention given the size of Britain's Muslim population. But in

    4   Dan Brown, *The Da Vinci Code* (London: Bantam Press, 2003).
    5   *'Moonies' mull future without founder*, BBC News website, 8 October 2009, http://news.bbc.co.uk/1/hi/world/asia-pacific/8293607.stm (accessed 3 March 2011).

journalistic terms, of course, such a consideration is irrelevant when the 'story' – terrorism carried out in Islam's name – is an important one, regardless of the fact that such acts of violence are carried out by a tiny minority.

Maintaining an appropriate sense of balance and perspective in coverage of issues affecting different religious groups is a necessarily inexact science, but questions about whether some groups are too often overlooked cannot be ignored. Sometimes terminology gives an unhelpful slant to controversial stories. The debate about 'faith schools' has often ended up being focused on the rights and wrongs of Islamic schools, and questions about the integration of Muslims into wider society. The simple fact that the overwhelming majority of so-called 'faith' schools are in fact church schools, with a much longer history and continuing support from parents, has all too easily been overlooked. So a debate about the education of Muslims in Britain has become conflated with a general debate about faith schools, with the implication that concerns about segregation are as relevant to a Church of England primary in a rural English village as they are to a Muslim secondary in Leicester. Both journalists and religious leaders bear a responsibility for attempting to ensure that mistaken impressions are not simply regurgitated by numerous outlets, gradually becoming regarded as fact in the public consciousness.

The ever-present danger is of what one might call 'template journalism' – where hard-pressed hacks pick a tired cliché off the shelf and repackage it as a 'new' story.[6] This is the sort of journalism that reveals little, but confirms plenty of prejudices – so stories about Catholicism will tend to involve paedophile priests; interior shots of Church of England buildings will feature empty pews; and Islam will only be considered in a story also featuring the word terrorism. This is not, of course, to suggest that stories about paedophile priests, declining Anglican congregations or Muslim terrorists should be overlooked. The real question is why such stories 'run and run', potentially overshadowing other developments or issues that might otherwise be worthy of journalistic attention.

Added to this danger that religious news will only ever tell you what you already know, is the rapidly evolving context within which all journalism is produced. Twenty years ago, I suspect that the dangers of 'template journalism' were every bit as great, but the time pressures on journalists were substantially fewer. The advent of online journalism, including the blogs and tweets of social media, means that it is now not only television or radio journalists who are counting the minutes rather than hours – let alone days – to the next deadline. What in fact constitutes 'broadcast journalism' is itself now an open question, as the traditional boundaries between content that is seen, or heard, or read, break down in the online environment.

It is, of course, a moment of great opportunity. But the proliferation of outlets, and the relentlessness of the twenty-four hour news cycle, risks not only reducing the capacity for genuinely original journalism to happen at all, but also creates a constant buzz of noise, above which it can become increasingly difficult to discern

---

    6   See Nick Davies, *Flat Earth News* (London: Chatto & Windus, 2008).

what constitutes news of real value. In this new, emerging environment, the rise of blogging has placed a particular value on comment as a journalistic medium in its own right. While old-world journalists might have struggled to provide verifiable facts to substantiate a challenging piece, no such concerns need restrain an enthusiastic contributor to the blogosphere. And while blogs can and do in themselves offer journalists an invaluable insight into the internal wranglings of particular groups, they also raise fundamental questions about the role of journalists themselves: the privileged access to information that journalists once took for granted has now in large part been removed by the internet, and both journalists and consumers are still coming to terms with what this means for the transfer of information in the digital age.

Reporting on religious affairs

In this rapidly changing, potentially bleak, and certainly challenging environment, it may be little wonder that religious leaders often despair of the media coverage they receive. Religious stories will often be handled by journalists with little or no specialist knowledge of the subject matter, and precious little time to undertake background research on the key issues of the day. The basic level of 'religious literacy' among such journalists is a potential cause for concern. Sometimes I hear radio discussions about a religious matter and despair at the lack of nuance. A typical exchange might involve a religious participant from an extreme, fringe group up against a spokesperson from the National Secular Society. In the 'car-crash' school of radio discussions, the level of angry debate might signal success in programming terms, but can be almost guaranteed to have failed to shine any real light on the issue in question.

This is not to suggest naively that radio broadcasters will surrender their desire for fiery discussions that make for captivating radio. But there is a real question about the religious literacy of those producers responsible for casting such discussions. I have sometimes compared the situation as regards religion with the general ability that would be expected of such a journalist to cast a discussion after the publication of a Labour government budget. To have Lord Tebbit in conversation with a representative of the Socialist Workers Party might make for a lively exchange, but would be patently absurd if you were presenting it as a serious examination of the issues. When the subject-matter is the latest row in the Church of England, the danger is that a similarly polarised debate happens all too often. Fringe groups claiming wide support may well end up on air – at times because the programme-makers themselves have lacked the ability to make an independent assessment of the credibility, or strength of support, that a particular group claims for itself.

The point is that a lack of literacy that would be unacceptable in relation to politics or business is somehow tolerated when it comes to religion – which might make sense if religious news never made it onto mainstream outlets, but while it does, crass mistakes are potentially embarrassing. It remains inevitable that from time to time unfortunate howlers make it as far as the television screen. My favourite example is the occasion when BBC *Breakfast* interviewed a cleric, and the on-screen caption described him as a 'Cannon' rather than 'Canon'. That particular occasion was not, perhaps, entirely in vain: it was one of the examples I cited when warmly backing a proposal for a training course on religion for BBC journalists. The result is now publicly available online, and the hope is that even the most hard-pressed producer facing an impossible deadline can usefully spend a few moments consulting one of the online guides.[7]

The production of such training material is a response to the recognition that religious literacy in newsrooms is not everything it might be. But it would be crass to suggest that there is a total lack of specialist understanding of religion within the British media. While dedicated religious affairs specialists are conspicuous by their absence in the newsrooms of other national broadcasters, the BBC continues to invest in such journalism at both local and national level. For seven years from 2003, I was one of the small band of specialists reporting about religion. I would often find myself being consulted by programme teams from various parts of the BBC about religious matters. When it came to my own reporting of the specialism, my experience was that the challenge was not so much about overcoming an inherent hostility towards religion itself, but rather to find ways of telling the stories that justified airtime in news programmes with no shortage of subjects to consider and no particular remit to cover religion. The point is that compelling material will always be attractive to editors, and in that sense, the religious affairs specialist simply has the same challenge as any other reporter – to 'sell' their story in such a way that programmes are keen to broadcast it.

Seldom did I encounter the sort of knee-jerk opposition to a religious affairs story appearing on air that some religious leaders infer must be routinely par for the course. But what I did find, from time to time, was that a comment might be made about a particular report on a religious matter that I am confident would not have been deemed appropriate in another context. I was once challenged as to why I was doing a piece on a new plan to promote unity in the Anglican Communion, given the proportion of listeners to Radio 4 who were not Christians, let alone Anglicans. I suspect a similar comment would not have been made about a report on mortgage lending being of little interest to listeners living in rented accommodation. The danger is that an editor for whom religion is an entirely irrelevant aspect of their own human existence fails to recognise its significance in the lives of their listeners. It is a mistake that the BBC used to make in relation to coverage of business-related matters. The former presenter of Radio 4's *Sunday*, Roger Bolton, has argued that just as the BBC appointed a Business Editor to address such concerns, so too it should appoint a Religion Editor – to ensure this defining aspect of human life receives the coverage it deserves.

---

[7]   http://www.bbc.co.uk/journalism/briefing/religion/ (accessed 3 March 2011).

It is not just the media that needs to change

The implication in discussions such as this can often seem to be that if only the media approached religion in a more literate, less sensationalist way, all would be well. But of course, religious leaders and organisations themselves also have a real contribution to make. In a speech to the religious think-tank *Theos* in 2008 (also cited in chapter 4), the BBC Director General Mark Thompson defended the corporation's record, saying: 'I believe that the BBC has maintained the daily and weekly presence of religion on its services with more consistency and commitment over decades than any other British media organisation, and also more than most of the rest of what you could call public Britain'.[8] His clear defence of the BBC's continuing commitment to religion – in terms of its journalism, factual programming and broadcast acts of worship – offered a clear rebuff to some of the criticism of the corporation from religious quarters. It is worth reminding the BBC's critics that if they think religion is sidelined in BBC schedules, they should consider its lack of prominence on other networks.

For religious organisations seeking to engage more fruitfully with the broadcast media, it is essential that they themselves have a greater level of literacy about those with whom they are seeking to build relationships. Within the BBC, there is a vast difference in terms of the prominence given to matters of faith and religion on different radio networks or television channels. Religious groups hoping to see their stories or issues covered well need to be realistic about what constitutes news of interest to a particular network's audience.

There is also the challenge of whether religious groups are willing to engage in a pro-active way with journalists. There are plenty of fringe groups, holding relatively extreme viewpoints within their particular faith, which nonetheless have won substantial numbers of media appearances, and boosted their public profile, having achieved such prominence simply as a result of their dogged pursuit of journalists and their clear self-belief in the importance of their own viewpoint reaching a wider audience. The time-poor producer seeking to cast a radio discussion, who knows little about religion, might be forgiven for thinking that a group called 'Christian Voice' was a mainstream organisation. Its campaign against *Jerry Springer the Opera* being televised by the BBC certainly attracted blanket media coverage, but that was in part fuelled by too many journalists mistakenly assuming that the group represented the Christian view – as if such a unified response existed. The truth was rather different, and while religious organisations might wish that journalists had the ability to sort pressure group wheat from chaff, the reality is that more balanced media coverage would also be helped by the larger denominations seeking to engage more effectively, especially with those media platforms and organisations lacking in-house religious expertise.

---

[8]   *DG defends Beeb's record on religion in Theos lecture*, 15 October 2008, http://www.theosthinktank.co.uk/DG_defends_Beeb's_record_on_religion_in_Theos_lecture.aspx?ArticleID=2590&PageID=14&RefPageID=13 (accessed 3 March 2011)

The row that followed the Archbishop of Canterbury's lecture on Sharia law in Britain in February 2008, also discussed in the previous chapter, can be viewed as a case study in the dangers of failing to engage with the media when a story has grabbed the headlines. I was personally involved: my interview with the Archbishop for Radio 4's *World at One*, previewing the lecture, ensured his suggestion that Sharia Law should have a place within the British legal system was heard by a very wide audience. By 5pm the same day, Downing Street and the Opposition had both issued statements distancing themselves from the Archbishop's comments – but it was only the following week, during an address to the General Synod, that the Archbishop was heard clarifying his previous remarks. In the intervening days, no other story came along to knock 'Shariagate' out of the headlines, and the silence from Lambeth Palace meant that extreme voices, wilfully distorting the Archbishop's original more nuanced comments, received wide coverage – while a robust defence of the Archbishop's views was lacking in the public arena.

It was a hard lesson for the church in realising that once a story has become headline news – however complex and unsatisfactory the reasons for that may be – a silent retreat behind the gatepost of Lambeth Palace will not help that story fade away. Indeed, in the twenty-four hour news cycle, a lack of response from key protagonists simply adds fuel to a story's fire: television journalists can stand in front of closed doors reminding their viewers of an interview request that has been refused. The question for religious leaders in such circumstances is whether they are prepared to admit that the media is a complex and difficult arena in which to try to convey ideas about religion, but also an essential one within which to engage if there remains a desire to promote such religious ideas beyond the internal communications channels of a particular institution or group.

The Archbishop had attempted to do just that by previewing his lecture with a mainstream broadcast interview: it was the subsequent failure to respond to the several criticisms of his views that were being made during the ensuing media storm that caused – to use public relations jargon – lasting reputational damage. A written statement on the Lambeth Palace website was of limited use to broadcast media; there was a conspicuous lack of either Christian or Muslim voices who might have been briefed on the lecture's content and thus able to speak out in support of the Archbishop. And while many within religious organisations might hope that the media climate would be one in which such tactical responses would not be necessary – because the media response itself would not have been so hysterical or ill-informed – it seems to me that the question going forward is whether religious groups are prepared to find ways of engaging confidently with the media, accepting its faults and limitations but without using those as a justification for a nervous withdrawal from public discourse.

It may be worth drawing a comparison with the British Monarchy, which in the 1990s had numerous occasions on which to lament the caustic attitude towards it of many British media outlets. One response to such coverage would have been to retreat from media engagement – but the Royal Family has clearly recognised that such a strategy, however attractive it might seem, is simply inconceivable given the influence that the media has in contemporary Britain. That influence may well be undesirable in several ways, but it is a reality within which any public figure has to operate. Religious groups, unless they simply want to exist within their own private worlds, also need to find ways to engage with the media as it is, rather than approaching it in the vain hope it will always deal with subjects fairly and without sensationalism.

In the current media climate, both journalists and religious leaders are struggling to come to terms with the digital age, and its profound impact on how information is conveyed and received. The picture is a complex and constantly changing one, and within it the individuals at work represent the full range of religious conviction or otherwise. In fact, in my experience, the worlds of religion and news broadcasting both contain 'saints and sinners' – a blanket condemnation of one by the other is not going to help either cause. If mutual suspicion and mistrust is going to be alleviated, the long, hard work of building constructive relationships will remain essential – particularly in those places where the relevance of religion is too often overlooked, or even wilfully ignored.

At root, there needs to be a candid recognition that journalists and religious leaders are not attempting to do anything like the same sort of work. In a Christian context, the 'good news' of the gospel is about positive transformation and hope – qualities that are generally lacking in the often 'bad news' which is the necessary content of news bulletins. The challenge in a complex and imperfect media environment is for religious leaders to make the most of the opportunities that do exist: to do so with confidence and realism, not expecting miracles, but confident that when their religion hits the headlines they will feel empowered to play the media at its own game – however much they continue to hope that the rules of that game might one day change for the better.

Chapter 6
Mirrors to the World

Ruth Gledhill

Summary

Gledhill uses autobiographical reflections to explore the changes in religious journalism since 1987, with the fundamental change being the rise of religion to ever-greater prominence in global news. 2001 marked the turning-point: the fact that seven in ten British citizens who counted themselves as Christian in the national census surprised 'even the Bishops' and gave the lie to the supposedly declining interest in faith, and 9/11 intensified the focus on religion in the news. The ongoing scandal of clerical child abuse and the rumbling divisions over homosexuality and gender ensure that there is often something to report. If these issues seem unfairly biased towards negative portrayals of religions, Gledhill offers a robust response: People say they want us to report harmony. But not only would they need to supply it, they would need to buy the newspapers in which it was reported.

The structure of journalism has also changed in the past decades: blogs, Twitter, Facebook and the increased interaction with readers has radically altered the nature of religious reporting. It has altered, too, the way in which journalism can be monetised. Gledhill, and others in the book, refer to The Times' *paywall, but no contributor quite knows whether this will be the model that will ensure the profitability of journalism in the future. A Novel, Poetry and Drama are used to go behind the 'wall' of several recurring stories to a 'world there for the mending'.*

In this chapter I hope to explore how, fundamentally, we journalists, in my case religion journalists, are mirrors to the world, which means that while we reflect it we might also obscure it. You might see through us darkly, or even not at all, to what lies beyond.

From when I joined *The Times* in 1987 and beginning to write about religion soon thereafter, my work has existed in a journalistic paradox that I believe is unique to this specialism. The subject, religion, is one which subsists upon 'eternal truths'. I started out facing the challenge of how a news journalist, dealing in the immediate, finds something new to say about a 2,000-year-old story, or a 5,000-year-old one. And then, having found a way to make the old seem new, came the new challenge when these stories from ancient times exploded into the modern world in stories of death and martyrdom in the name of faith in such a way that none had ever expected.

Truly, when I started out in journalism most news editors, perhaps in common with many if not most people, expected religion to be dead or dying by the new millennium. In the 1980s and early 1990s bishops would talk quietly but freely to me of how they were 'managing a church in decline'. One senior cleric confided over coffee at General Synod in York in about 1992 that the advances in biblical scholarship were such that by 2000 no cleric would be preaching a gospel any more. He said they should focus on simply finding a way to tell this to their flock, in as pastoral a way as possible. I will never forget telephoning leaders of the faithful for comment after the 2001 census showed a British population where more than seven in ten counted themselves Christian. Of all I spoke to, the bishops were the most astonished. Used to a world where the consensus was that few believed the sacred texts any more, some voiced doubt at the empirical credibility of government statistics. They had confused faith with churchgoing.

I thought of this confusion when Richard Chartres, Bishop of London, came to *The Times* to talk to the News International Christian Fellowship. Chartres reminded us that he used to work as the religious affairs correspondent for the *Daily Telegraph* until he was sacked by Max Hastings. Until that point, most religious affairs correspondents had been clergy. At *The Times* we had Clifford Longley, not quite a clergyman but the next best thing. Without any disrespect to the clergy, this is surely to be welcomed warmly. The fact that the correspondents were clergy (until recently, even the religion editor of the *Telegraph* still was) but no longer are, is testament to the fact that, however the media does view religious news, it is different now to how it once did.

The subject which was once regarded by news editors as soft has now risen to such prominence that religious affairs are not just stories in their own right, but they also sit at the heart of news areas traditionally viewed as hard. The most obvious example would be foreign affairs, in particular the rise of Islam to prominence in the news. This was already in evidence before the turn of the millennium, but with 9/11 these developments were accelerated in the most dramatic way.

Even though religion correspondents have not been personally implicated in the hacking scandal – (the Archbishop of Canterbury does not even possess a mobile telephone!) – all journalists have been affected by the poor reputation of our trade as a result of what has been exposed about these practices. Further, on my patch there is what I described in a recent article in *The Times* as the 'Anglican Autumn', the Church's struggle to find a response to the crisis of capitalism and also to fulfil its mission to the poor, a conflict that appears in the Bible in the 'render unto God' and 'render unto Caesar' saying of Jesus, and was brought into new focus by the issues arising from the Occupy LSX protest at St Paul's (discussed in detail in the first chapter of this book). These elements are linked by the rise of the web. What has happened is that the 'word' is more widely available to the individual than it has ever been, and likewise access to information, from both private and official channels, which might previously have been unavailable either through active censorship or simply the difficulty of getting hold of it.

The event which sparked the Arab Spring was the online appearance of the ex US-ambassador-to-Tunisia's criticisms of that country's government. His remarks were witty and mocking but also well informed and insider, and it was these which confirmed the public's worst fears about their country's leadership. So, just as the Reformation led to a more personal and less institutional relationship between the citizen/worshipper and his/her God, so the e-revolution (e-volution?) did something similar for the individuals' relationship with their rulers – rulers who may have worn their faith as a public garment but who were effectively no better than secular tyrants. Just as their abuses of power came to light through the web, so too, eventually, did those of their partial exposers, the 'messengers' of the press, at least in the UK. So what has continued to happen here since the dawn of the Arab spring is the continuous training of a bright light into dark and publicly unfamiliar corners of the professions. Of course, it had already started, with the embarrassing expenses revelations from our own Parliament. For journalists, politicians, bankers and even some church people, events of the last months and years have provided plenty of challenging opportunities for apology and confession, famously good for the soul.

Although at 52 I may still be relatively young in comparison with many of the constituents I cover, I am old enough to remember a time when most religion correspondents were men of the church themselves. If they were not actually preaching to the converted, they were nonetheless covering the subject in a way which presumed a degree of specialist knowledge among their readership. As a vicar's daughter, I saw myself as part of this select little club. This impression, which I now know to have been seriously in error, was nevertheless reinforced upon my first meeting with Robert Runcie, then Archbishop of Canterbury, at the 1988 Lambeth Conference. His opening gambit after we were introduced was to establish who my father was. We quickly established that Rev. Peter Gledhill had been educated at Rugby, Balliol and then Cuddesdon, where Runcie had later been principal. The Archbishop looked benignly down at me in his inimitable fashion, eyes twinkling happily. 'Ah. One of us', he said. But I never was. Soon after that encounter, Clifford Longley was promoted to leader writer and I formally applied for the job. Friends at *The Times* said I was going into a backwater. Indeed, I rather hoped I was.

The ivory towers of an Oxbridge-style enclave at *The Times*, writing about obscure encyclicals and Lambeth Conference resolutions, appealed strongly. I couldn't wait to climb up there and hide away in the back pages of *The Times*, between the court and social pages. This was not to be.

In Samuel Butler's novel, *The Way of All Flesh*, his heroine Alathea talks about her marital prospects and what her spouse would do with his inheritance after she died. 'Of course', she says, 'he will go and paint Academy pictures, or write for *The Times*, or do something just as horrid the moment the breath is out of my body'. When my own father was studying classics, he thought of writing for *The Times*. His tutors advised it was not a profession for a gentleman. Next, his father suggested the civil service. Too suspect, he was told. So he followed his own true calling, to the church.

Now it is all so different. So many people are encouraged to dream of writing for *The Times*. If I think about it too closely I feel a bit faint. All these brilliant undergraduates wanting to become journalists. Yet I still find reassurance in the lowness of our reputation. Maybe I can make do after all in a profession that is still so universally despised. Some of our reputation is deserved, and some not. I do believe we have an important role as messengers of fact and comment. Whether or not I have wanted it, I have found myself writing stories which are regularly printed on the most prominent pages of the newspaper, the front.

'A thousands ages in Thy sight are like an evening gone', from Isaac Watts' famous hymn *O God Our Help* – one I often find myself humming when on my way to another press conference or meeting with angry Church press officers – is a good image about the impact of time passing. The 'evening gone' is this relatively short time I have been covering this specialism. And yet it seems to have contained the changes of a thousand ages.

I have been shocked by the impact of much of the religious extremism, which it has been my responsibility to report. Often, I have been almost as shocked by the immoderation of the responses to what I have written. Good journalists always try to achieve balance and objectivity in news reporting and I am no different. Some believe the ability to achieve this ideal has been compromised by the new media, with its proliferation of comment and blogging. I am open about my own views and affiliations, which are both mainstream and eclectic at the same time. I believe it helps the reader if they know where a writer is coming from. Nevertheless, objectivity in news reporting still remains, in my view, an achievable aim. As a result of a childhood as a devout Prayer Book Anglo-Catholic, the rhythms of the church are deeply embedded in my consciousness.

Although it falls to me to ask searching questions of men and women of faith, there is one question in which they are oddly united in wanting to ask of me, namely 'Am I a believer?' It still surprises me how often I am expected to declare and account for my own religious beliefs in the public domain in a way that would never be expected of a political correspondent or any other specialist on a newspaper such as *The Times*. But I do not object to this and I accept also the right of the reading public to 'shoot the messenger' if upset by something, legitimately or not. I do not always enjoy, but see as necessary, the rough and tumble of debate, both in the letters pages of *The Times* and in the more hurly-burly world of new online media. I see it as my responsibility to answer for and be accountable for what I write. I take comfort from knowing that 'angel' in Biblical Hebrew is mal'ak. Its main meaning is 'messenger'. I do not actively seek evangelical status, but nor do I wish to be a martyr to news. A bearer of so much bad news actively runs this risk, as with any job that is inevitably so focused on reporting dissent and decline. My own quest for the grail of impartiality is immensely worthwhile to pursue, but it is also Arthurian in elusiveness in this spiritual landscape so crowded by the shapes of passionate involvement.

For what it is worth, I regard myself as the following: a liberal catholic member of the Church of England who believes unequivocally in the one God but has the usual range of Anglican-style doubts about aspects of Christianity as presented by some today. Like many others, for example, I believe God welcomes love, whether by gay people or heterosexual people, for each other. I suspect this gives me more in common with believers of all faiths than some might care to admit.

This is an epoch of religious ferment and, as stories come and go, I find that the best gauge of the balance which I am striking or failing to strike in my coverage is the correspondence of detractors. In other words, if both sides are jeering at me in similar numbers and at the same volume, I reckon I am getting it just about right. Politics, defence and industry can no longer be regarded as any 'harder' than religion in terms of being newsy enough for the front of the book. And while it did not take 9/11 to bring about this change of status, it certainly helped. Already in the years before the end of the millennium, religion not only found itself as newsworthy as any other subject on national papers' daily agendas; it also embraced and contained elements of many of those other specialisms, such as politics, crime, terrorism and social affairs. Religion itself is the interior politics of faith communities. In all the faiths, whether Islam, Judaism, Christianity, Hinduism or Sikhism, both religious and political debate are passionate and complex beyond belief and sometimes, it has to said, beyond understanding. Although my work benefits from the fact that I am writing about good men and women who often make the best copy when they 'fall' because they are falling from a greater height, how disappointed I sometimes am to see such palpably good people showing themselves in the ugliest light as they engage in bitter infighting.

So, what constitutes religious news today? Some of the criteria are more or less unaltered. Although there are already signs that news priorities are changing in response to the phone-hacking scandal, tabloid news desks remain interested in the sex lives of vicars, of course, and probably always will be. But the last decades have seen a growing interest in the internal politics of both Christian and non-Christian communities, from a religious as well as a civil perspective.

But what makes religion stories work is similar to all specialisms. A sense of a row or confrontation is always a welcome ingredient, up to and including the prospect of schism. Doctrinal disputes and disagreements of procedure or sacrament are welcome news to the media which enjoys them almost as dress rehearsals for schism. Schism, in terms of news criteria, hangs over the specialism not so much like a cloud as a prospect. Andrew Brown, of the *Church Times*, often jokes that whenever I get a good story, I write it as the greatest 'schism' since the Reformation. There is some truth in that, at least with the Church of England, although now that true schism does seem to loom, I find myself unable to use the phrase. Is this 'schismatic' approach right or wrong? I would defend it with the defence that can be applied to other areas of news coverage. The plane that arrives at its destination is not news: the crash is. Discord arrives from the heavens in 'manmade' crises. I do not want to be an ambulance chaser, but I do sometimes feel that we have the role of the assessor thrust upon us, reporting the damage on the ground.

People say they want us to report harmony. But not only would they need to supply it first, they would need to buy the newspapers in which it was reported. Neither prospect seems likely. I must, of course, address the changes in the working environment as well as the religious one. This is a time of a major revolution which can be compared to the Reformation in magnitude. Certainly what has been set in motion is as far reaching in its own way as Caxton and Gutenberg. The availability of the printed word was crucial to the rise of Protestantism, the acquisition of a personal relationship with God not mediated by the authorities. Now we see the same thing happening over again, but we are right in the middle of it and so it is not possible to predict with certainty what the outcome will be, beyond that it will be far-reaching and possibly cataclysmic in our understanding of the world, of each other and even of God. Here is the nexus of where my paralysis with writing this chapter lay.

To make an observation on the arena in which I work, the speed of evolution of technology sometimes strikes me as running ahead of our ability to cope with its implications. Its dynamic is so fast that sometimes it seems to leave everyone, those who service it and those who use it, slightly struggling in its wake – almost as if it were a comet streaming a trail across the sky, sharp and clear at the front but tailing away into a more amorphous and disputed shape. The blaze of new technology is like a modern augury that we, for all our powers of interpretation and analysis, simply do not know yet how to interpret properly. I love the connectivity, and am a compulsive user of Twitter, Facebook and the wider web. Another contributor to this book covers this aspect of my work so I will only briefly acknowledge that the world of faith has traditionally been at the fore of exploiting the power of the word in every sense. This was behind the rise of Protestantism. Now religious groups use the internet, often with positive results, but at the same time the violence in the Middle East is a direct result of the web. These are populist rather than religious movements, supported by millions of aggrieved and dispossessed people who are finding the power to oppose and dethrone tyrannies. Many in my world believe religion will be central to the outcomes.

To move from the global to the parochial, the web's effect on my own working life in Thomas More Square, just east of the City of London, has been equally revolutionary. Things are produced very quickly and then stay out there forever. Or not. Sometimes they disappear for ever as well. If not saved onto a hard-drive or printed out, hours of work can just vanish with the erasure of a link. It might seem the opposite of papyrus, which took months of painstaking work to produce and then was so perishable, and yet the online word can vanish quicker than the eye can blink.

One big change that's taken place at *The Times* is the paywall. Just like you can find something in the Bible or the Koran to guide you through almost any event in the modern world, the same is the case with Shakespeare. In *Midsummer Night's Dream*, some the characters are putting on a play within a play. And within this scene, there is a play wall – Shakespeare was perhaps even further ahead of his time than he could have guessed:

QUINCE
Ay; or else one must come in with a bush of thorns
and a lanthorn, and say he comes to disfigure, or to
present, the person of Moonshine. Then, there is
another thing: we must have a wall in the great
chamber; for Pyramus and Thisby says the story, did
talk through the chink of a wall.
SNOUT
You can never bring in a wall. What say you, Bottom?
BOTTOM
Some man or other must present Wall: and let him
have some plaster, or some loam, or some rough-cast
about him, to signify wall; and let him hold his
fingers thus, and through that cranny shall Pyramus
and Thisby whisper.
So the wall is played by a character.
This man, with lime and rough-cast, doth present
Wall, that vile Wall which did these lovers sunder;
And through Wall's chink, poor souls, they are content
To whisper.
The wall stands between the lovers but Pyramus finds he likes it.
He says: 'Thou wall, O wall, O sweet and lovely wall,
Show me thy chink, to blink through with mine eyne!'

He is trying to woo and flatter the wall so it will yield him a prospect of Thisbe. Pyramus commits suicide when he mistakenly believes his lover is dead. The world has been full of walls, religious and secular: Israel, Berlin, Jericho, Pink Floyd. Walls are emblematic. They are often dwarfed by their own symbolic potency. Hostility has been levelled at *The Times*' paywall but behind the wall, I can assure you, there is life. We are well on now from its implementation, it is becoming more and more accepted. I feel certain we will see other newspapers follow suit before too long. From the inside, I must confess it is regarded as a success and I share that view, even though at the start it felt a little scary.

The labourer is worthy of his hire, whether building bridges or walls, or working with them or behind them. Even clergy with their ethic of service are not expected to give their work away for nothing. Render unto Caesar, Jesus tells us. People like my boss are trying to monetise the internet, not because they are greedy, but because they want to keep the world going round. If giving away a product for free becomes the norm, one day there will be no product to give away. Many of us recall the shock when cathedrals began charging for entry. It seemed 'wrong'. Now many do so. The ethics are still being debated. The argument about how those ex-cathedra funds might be redistributed is a different one, not for this chapter.

The economic debates around new and old media are also still in their infancy and the form has yet to evolve. That is just one area in which the new environment has had a particular effect on us at *The Times*. Areas of the church are equally affected, but in different ways.

The case of the present Archbishop of Canterbury is particularly interesting to reflect upon. As soon as light shines on politicians, it shows them to be as fallible as the next party. Wikileaks and the expenses scandals of certain British members of parliament have had dramatic and unexpected effects on the world, still being played out as I write. The church leadership has also found itself struggling to keep everything under control in a world where the most vociferous debates are played out on the internet. Dr Williams has more integrity than many politicians and from where I sit, he looms high as a spiritual icon, a hero for our age. He is witness to how to hold fast to the old traditions while doing business with a world wedded to the new. He will not be compromised. Yet as anyone reading this will know, the stories I write rarely reflect this truth. This is because of the nature of news, of what I am called upon to report, of what makes news and why.

We report division and ferment. And even with all his vast intellectual, spiritual and pastoral resources, the Archbishop has found the business of holding things together harder than he can have ever imagined they would be and must have wondered whether it is worth the candle. Rather like the LibDems in the coalition government, he is a man of liberal impulses who finds himself 'in bed' with a dominant right wing. And, of course, it all makes fantastic newspaper copy. In terms of communication, his style has improved a lot and has become much less cryptic. Poetic ambiguity can be useful, even beautiful, but is not much use if it leaves people completely bamboozled. We in the media, or perhaps it is just me, grappling with these texts, can run into the danger of forgetting that the Archbishop has many different politickings to deal with. There are the internal church battles, more than enough for an army of archbishops never mind one, but there is also the equally if not more important interchange between the Church (the established church as representing all churches) and all faiths with the other secular organs of society.

Can liberal religion as epitomised by Dr Williams, true catholic or universal liberalism, survive? Liberalism means tolerance; liberal religion, therefore, is one that best embodies the tradition of human tolerance. Yet liberal tolerance does not lend itself well to the style demanded by modern debate and dispute. It gets trampled over and its advocates too easily lose respect. Somehow the Archbishop remains in the argument. And it has to be stated that the 'greatest schism since the Reformation', if that is what it is shaping to be, has not actually happened yet. The warring Anglican factions might not be talking to each other but they are still talking to the Archbishop of Canterbury. Maybe, just maybe, he is going to make it work and realise his ultimate goal of unity.

Like the people I write about, my specialism reaches beyond the faith communities. There are bishops in the House of Lords. Like Iran, Britain has ordained, unelected clerics in the legislature. There is no government department dealing with religion but nearly all government departments – education, communities, defence – have remits that incorporate the world of faith in some form.

I will refer briefly here to four specific areas in my beat.

So many stories have been written about the concern over sexuality and the weight which it carries in the broader split between the liberals and the evangelicals. In many respects, the church is a strange place in which to find what appears to the secular world to be virulent homophobia. Inside the Church, it does not look like homophobia. Conservatives draw a distinction between homosexual orientation and practice, justifying it by biblical texts. While liberals believe that the Church should be a haven of tolerance for this and other manifestations of the human condition, it has to be faced that in history it rarely has been. Sexuality has become a defining issue. Many churchgoers resent that their views on sexuality, which they consider a secular concern, should somehow have become central to the definition of their faith. For a religion correspondent, this is of course rich and fertile ground for reaping rows upon rows of news stories. I am aware that this is all grist to my professional mill. But as a 'practising' Anglican, this also causes me concern at a personal level.

There is the related debate over women's ordination. At the first service to ordain women priests at Bristol Cathedral in 1994, one of my colleagues sat through the service reading a well-known novel which fictionalised an Anglican theological college with a decidedly camp reputation. He was perusing it very publicly. This heat remains in the debate to this day, even though it has moved on towards the newer disagreements about women's eligibility as bishops with the extraordinary development, thanks to Pope Benedict XVI, of a new ecclesial haven being set up for what might be styled 'Prayer Book Catholics' in England. Is this a new schism or a step to a new unity? It is too early to say, but I will probably have to produce hundreds if not thousands of words for *The Times* attempting to do so.

Then there is the rise of passionate atheism from Richard Dawkins, Christopher Hitchens and others, yet another development that has brought religion to the heart of the news agenda. The problem with Dawkins is that he seems to have appropriated exactly the kind of certainty, even intolerance, that he castigates in others. He would say he is using science, yet this is remarkably unscientific because it does not take proper and careful account of the evidence. In *The God Delusion* he acknowledges that faith gives comfort and succour to believers but he seems intolerant of the necessity for belief in so many, although not all, humans. For many of us who do believe, we would argue empirically that it 'works'. The evidence is in the outcomes of issues aided by prayer in our daily lives. This is not saying that prayer brings cures from illness or secures parking spaces. For me it operates on a different level entirely. I tell the many enquirers who ask me about my own faith that the only thing I know for absolute certain about God is that I am not 'it'. Or 'Him' or 'Her'. Putting it as simply as possible, for me it is saying that acknowledging this facilitates a manner of 'being' which offers far more than comfort and succour, but a way of coping with life's 'triumphs and disasters', as Kipling writes, to 'treat those two imposters just the same'. Dawkins has done us all a terrific service in taking this debate to a higher level.

Islam is the other big story that took off after 9/11. There are the vast majority of good, peaceful faithful Muslims in Britain, producing increasing amounts of copy with a positive impact, such as the growing number of converts, many disillusioned by the hedonism and spiritual futility that life as a secularised Westerner can sometimes seem to be reduced to. And then there is, of course, the fall-out from Islamism and the public response to the extremist minority, in this country and abroad, with terrible atrocities still being committed, ostensibly in the name of religion.

And, of course, there has been the scandal, and its apparent mismanagement, of clerical child abuse. One of the aspects of my job I love most is that I am privileged to spend so much of my life with men and women of the highest possible ideals. These are good and godly people doing good and godly works. This means that when they 'fall', as in the case of child sex abuse, they fall farther and harder. Clerics sometimes complain that most abuse takes place in the home and they express bafflement that we in the media focus more on them. That is because clerics, like the saints they follow, are expected more than others to live exemplary, holy lives. It is not the number of child abusers exposed in the priesthood that has made it shocking, although in fact that has been shocking. It is the fact that it has happened at all, that there has been even one.

My husband Alan Franks, a prize-winning poet, has reflected on how the observing of faith can be obscured as well as assisted through symbolism.

THE STAIN
Faith in a sobering time,
Can't see the Lord for the lime.
A life cut short is the model,
Can't see the clues for the riddle.
I waken myself through sleeping,
Can't see the wound for the weeping.
Rivers of grief to swallow,
Can't see the bank for the willow.
Verses queue to be chosen,
Rhyme draws a veil round reason.
Light falls in waterless rain,
Can't see the glass for the stain.
A world there for the mending,
Can't see the life for its ending.

Alan is an agnostic but he is as spiritual, if not more so, as many believers I know. This is an agnostic poem dealing with matters of faith. The 'stain' is about the difficulty of belief. His poem is deliberately perplexing, about the confusion that can arise from contemplating images of faith. The stain is everywhere; it is the blood, the decoration on the glass that also obscures the clarity of the view. For me it is the stain of guilt on the conscience, the paradoxes that arise when you set faith and reason side by side.

Chapter 7
Networked Religion

Charlie Beckett

Summary

Religion, Charlie Beckett argues, receives a comparatively good deal from the news media, with a fair amount of coverage, much of it sympathetic. Responding to the perceived level of religious illiteracy among journalists, Beckett compares the situation with science journalism, particularly in relation to climate change. Journalists do not have a comprehensive understanding of climate change; their role is 'to translate complex reality into something the public can understand', and to do it quickly and with limited resources. This role demands the use of 'formulae to simplify and conflict to animate an issue'. Beckett's point is that the coverage of religion is neither more hostile nor more deficient than the coverage of other subjects.

Beckett also argues that online networks have radically changed the public's consumption of the news, and that the internet provides a massive opportunity for 'counter voices' which challenge conventional media outputs. He further suggests that 'networked religion' is changing the nature of membership in faith traditions: believers will seek greater levels of interactive participation and will be less inclined to be appreciate 'one-way sermonizing' by their religious leaders.

Introduction

Is there a crisis in the relationship between organised religion and journalism? Or is there actually a common communications crisis for both faith bodies and mainstream news media? In this chapter I will look at the key dynamics that are creating both problems and opportunities for those involved in the mediation of religion in the UK in this digital age. I hope that it will at least be stimulating and while some may find it provocative, it is supposed to be a positive and respectful contribution.

Certainly, the reporting of faith matters. There is some evidence of the growing secularisation of the UK. Church going appears to be falling. Minority faiths are showing signs of integration. But this is not simply about numbers, it is about significance. We are in a globalised society and across the world issues related to faith are becoming more, not less important. In a multi-cultural society, how we understand the world may be the way we understand our neighbour. In a multi-faith and non-faith population it is important that we understand and respect differences in belief as well as ethnicity. It is media that facilitates – or militates against – that understanding. We live in a society where moral and ethical values are increasingly important to citizens trying to make hard choices on difficult issues. Identity increasingly defines our politics as we seek to define our place in our communities and the world in general. Faith and religion are part of the discourse around those debates.

There are many people of faith in the UK who think that the news media are at least deficient if not positively pernicious in their representations of their beliefs and activities. They perceive hostility from journalists to organised religion, and scepticism about faith manifested in aggressive, distorted and inaccurate reporting of their values and actions. But are their complaints any different from those of anyone who has been subject to media attention? Is it simply the natural reaction to being put in the spotlight? You could easily argue that reporting of the lead up to both the economic crash of 2008 and the war in Iraq were also inadequate. As we shall see, other groups such as scientists also feel they have a collective grievance about the media. Or is there something particularly concerning about the way that faith is reported?

One good example might be the bizarre period in 2006 when for about six months the British news media became obsessed by Muslims. Understandably, there was huge interest in British Muslims in the wake of the July 7th bombings of 2005. Press attention was rightly focused on the Islamic communities of this country as it investigated the causes of that attack by British Muslims on London. But after a period of relative press restraint in the wake of the bombings the resulting coverage became a febrile stew of prejudice, ignorance and distortion. At the time I presented a BBC documentary on the issue.[1] It involved talking to a range of journalists and Muslim leaders as well as activists. It was clear that the British journalistic values of aggressive, competitive reporting were making a delicate situation worse. It was also admitted by many journalists that they lacked the intellectual and other resources to cover such a novel and complex story with the requisite authority and sensitivity.

However, the point is that the coverage did improve in many ways after that period of frantic scare-mongering. The news media learned lessons. This does not excuse its failings of course, much harm was done. But, for example, news organisations realised they had to hire more Muslims, or at least people who knew about those communities. Muslims also realised that they had a real problem on their hands: it became clear that they had to work harder at building continuing relationships with the news media rather than only dealing with journalists when things go wrong. Many acknowledged something in public that had previously been swept under the carpet: that in an open democratic society many of their coreligionists were, indeed, worthy of media scrutiny and that those with power in mosques should be held to account. They belatedly understood that they were too isolated and overly reluctant to respond to legitimate media inquiry. Even at a

---

[1]   BBC Radio 4, *Analysis* 'Telling Muslim Stories', broadcast on 28 December 2006.

practical level, their imams were often too conservative, out of touch and unable to speak English, to represent their community in the media. Some journalists, such as Martin Bright, went on to reveal serious failings by some parts of British Muslim communities in working to resist extremism.[2]

I argue that the Christian churches have a similar problem in relation to the media. Despite the well-oiled public relations machines at the heart of the main Christian churches there is a tendency to blame the messenger instead of recognising real problems, internal conflicts and specific faults. There is still a defensive public relations strategy that seeks to suppress or deflect criticism instead of a communications approach that welcomes open debate.

A science lesson

Some people of faith would claim that their situation has become analogous to media coverage of science, especially around an issue like climate change. I agree there are some parallels, but not all of them are entirely flattering to the churches.

Certainly, there has been some appalling reporting of climate change. Journalists are not scientists, quite the opposite. Especially in the UK they are – largely – arts graduates with little grasp of the physical laws of the universe, principles of logic or statistics. This is partly because a news journalist's job is to tell stories about our world and do so very quickly with limited resources. The journalists' daily task is to attempt to translate complex reality into something the public can understand and that they can be bothered to pay attention to. So journalists use formulae to simplify and conflict to animate an issue. In the preparation of the first draft of history the language must necessarily be compelling rather than detailed and comprehensive.

So with climate change we have seen the news media struggles to put the 'deniers' in proper perspective. How many times have you seen Nigel Lawson put up against a scientist in a TV studio to debate climate change? Lawson is there in the interest of 'balance' and yet by any objective measure the weight of his evidence is tiny compared to that of the global scientific community. On the other hand we have seen many journalists fail to critique scientists. We now discover they are much more divided about the nuances of policy and outcomes than the environmental lobby might let us believe. Sometimes even the scientists are wrong. Despite relentless media coverage, polling appears to indicate that both the climate change community and the politicians have failed to convince the public and they cannot just blame the journalists.

There is a vast lobby on behalf of science and in the UK there is even a special centre that works on behalf of scientists, devoted to influencing and training journalists. It has been marginally successful and I suggest that science reporting is much improved, albeit subject to the economic pressures that face all the news media. I do not think there would be any harm in setting up something similar for

---

[2]   Channel 4, *Who Speaks for British Muslims?*, Martin Bright broadcast on 14 July 2006.

religion. However, anyone who does so should not confuse faith with science. From a news perspective, science is essentially an activity that falls under the journalistic framework that deals with facts, such as economic reporting. Reporting faith fits much more with the kind of journalism that covers ideology, not empiricism, such as political analysis. In contemporary society the media is a forum, not a pulpit, for faith where its values must be openly contested as well as critiqued or celebrated.

The end of the fortress estates?

Religion actually gets a very good deal from the media. It certainly gets a lot of coverage, much of it sympathetic (as explored in chapter 2). The approach is often far more respectful than that accorded to, say, elected politicians. Despite scandals such as child abuse within the Catholic Church and bizarre contradictions within the Anglican Communion over issues such as women and gays, religious figures are automatically given a privileged position in debates on moral issues. However, as the mainstream media changes, that relationship between religion and news organisations is increasingly coming under strain. This is true of all aspects of society and media. The old settlement had media as a discrete entity interposed between the citizen and government or other social institutions such as churches. But as the BBC's Peter Horrocks has written, the fortresses of journalism are cracking and the idea of the Fourth Estate is being redefined as a network. It is time that those who wish to mediate their faith to do the same.

At the moment I think there is a collective failure on the part of those within religious institutions to understand how the news media is itself changing. It means that people of faith are missing an opportunity to enhance their dialogue with the rest of society. And by dialogue I mean a conversation where those in organised religion are able to listen as well as preach. Too many people in churches see new media platforms as just another opportunity to evangelise and a space to colonise. This attitude is not entirely surprising. Political parties are just as bad and they are supposed to be masters of the arts of communication. This is because adapting to the new media environment is about more than creating a website or signing up for a Twitter account. Certainly there are some good examples of religious individuals or organizations that have created interesting social media projects. For them to succeed as networked media and as a social project, however, faith institutions must embrace a much more thorough shift in the way that citizens wish to communicate. Part of accepting these new terms of mediation involves sharing power. Media barons and editors are finding that tough and so will religious leaders.

Networked journalism

This is not just about the many citizen journalists, independent bloggers or people using Facebook who air their views on religion without waiting to see what the authorities say. That 'blogosphere' or social media is significant in itself. It is forcing the mass media to change how it works. What I want to focus on is how mainstream journalism is becoming more participatory, transparent and interactive. It is learning to share journalism with the public and I hope that can create a more intelligent, diverse and trustworthy news media. I will show what I mean with the example of the work of Ruth Gledhill who is, appropriately, the religion correspondent for *The Times*.

The post of religion correspondent for *The Times* used to be one of the most establishment fixtures of British journalism. Yet the current incumbent Ruth Gledhill has transformed her impact through networked journalism. In addition to her newspaper and online articles she uses the micro-blogging site Twitter. She promotes her work and herself through Twitter but it serves as more than just a marketing tool. Gledhill uses Twitter as another portal for her to pick up information, commentary and reaction from the public and experts to stories as they break and develop. She also links through Twitter to the work of a variety of other journalists. At the time of writing she follows and is followed by 27,649 and 28,771 people respectively on Twitter. Her Twitter account is therefore the hub of a rich and varied specialist news network.

In addition she uses her blog to link to primary information that provides vital background material for the often complex issues she handles. It uses video particularly well to give the reader access to international broadcast news, original interviews and religious groups' own output. Gledhill is aware that this is changing her relationship to her readers in a profound way: 'Breaking the boundary between audiences and journalists helps to increase understanding, and lets audiences go beyond "my interpretation" of a story.'

The interactivity that allows her readers to comment and contribute is not without problems. Initially there was more heat than light in reader comments. Now the reader contributions have retained their commitment but they are becoming more civilised because that is what gets attention online, she says: 'Rants don't engage people – passion does.' Gledhill has a particularly informed and concerned audience and the quality of the responses reflects that.

Another consequence of this connectivity for the individual journalist is that their stories go beyond national boundaries instantly and then stay online permanently. The story that Archbishop Sean Brady was a notary at an event at which two children were sworn to secrecy about sexual abuse allegations was reported by the *Sunday Mirror* 10 years ago, but now that it is being brought up again it can have a bigger, broader online life. Rowan Williams' comments on the Irish Catholic Church, described in more detail by Christopher Landau in chapter 4 of this book, went around the world immediately after being reported in the UK. The internet brings that all together and into the open.

Gledhill retains a strong sense of her more traditional role as a newspaper journalist. She says that meeting people is still the best way to get new stories. She also insists that she retains overall editorial control and that ultimately the agenda is set by the newspaper not the readers. As is clear from her chapter (chapter 6) in this book she also welcomes *The Times*' paywall plans as a way of setting some kind of boundary to her work. However, there is a danger that the subscription barrier might restrict the kind of reciprocal public involvement that has boosted her work.

In a sense, Gledhill is simply a very good blogger who happens to write for a newspaper. But she uses the institutional capital and the legacy audience of *The Times* to create a network that collectively produces more 'quality' journalism than would have been possible working in traditional ways. Gledhill is by no means the only correspondent doing this kind of work. There is evidence that this networked journalism is becoming standard.

Faith in a networked world

People of faith who want better mediation of their lives and beliefs need to be part of that sort of networked journalism – and not just with religion correspondents. Those within the religious institutions need to make their communications just as transparent, participatory and connected. This is a practical and an ethical imperative. This is a wonderful time for people who think media can promote understanding. There has never been more media and much of it has global reach thanks to the internet. People are more educated and equipped to engage if given the opportunity and incentive. But this is a dreadful time for people who think the media is there to promote only what they think. There is more competition for people's attention than ever before. So if you want to be heard you have to be where people are talking, rather than expect them to come to you. That is what networked journalists like Ruth Gledhill have learnt. As a priest recently told me, this is what Jesus did when he took his message (the Good News) out to where ordinary people lived. The rabbinical tradition is also very much one of interactive dialogue rather than one-way sermonizing.

At the technical level it is easy to do this. Anyone can blog or Twitter, but to use it well is more complex. The issues in people's lives are now more complicated and how they mediate them is too. Communication is now multi-layered, interactive, creative, passive and active. It is participatory and multi-platform, often involving multi-tasking (Have you got music on while you read this? That's multi-tasking). There is a much greater diversity of media sources, although often people cluster online. People want news that is much more relevant to their lives and delivered in a way that suits them. If it is not then they will quickly click away to news that is. The public are also finding new ways to find out about their world for themselves by getting information direct from organisations or other citizens.

So institutions like organised faiths also have to learn to be networked organisations. They will now have a different relationship with mainstream media but they can also have a direct relationship with the public, too. They can be media organisations creating their own channels and content, but just like mainstream media they have to go where the public is and that usually means social networks and non-news programming. They have to be more open, engaged, literate, and interactive.

Conclusion

So ultimately, my injunction is 'don't get mad, get media'. Stop complaining and do something about your coverage. Start connecting. Most faiths are natural networks but I think they have atrophied or been allowed to become closed systems. If all you do is connect with your followers online than obviously you are simply rebuilding ghettos in cyberspace. Newspapers initially made the mistake of thinking that going online meant replicating their newsrooms and their pages online. They thought they could control the communication process and continue with the same editorial assumptions. Now they realise that their whole business model, their production processes and their relationship to the citizen must be re-thought and re-shaped. There has been a shift from a fortress mentality and fortress institutions to networks. In response to the Internet, people of faith must do more than simply build digital churches or mosques. They must create real networks and part of that process will be a new relationship with networked journalism.

Chapter 8
Religion and the Specialist Press

Catherine Pepinster

Summary

In Chapter 8, Pepinster tackles the problem presented by the public good of journalism as uncovering the truth. For one thing, journalists are keenly aware of their target audience, and frame their stories for them, but this framing is not always in the interests of objectivity – a problem Pepinster explores through looking at the example of coverage of the abuse scandal in the Roman Catholic church. This chapter was written before the Leveson enquiry (briefly discussed in chapter 1 and the conclusion) was established. Nevertheless, the issues raised remain topical. In religion reporting, she argues, depth and discursive analysis are often sidelined in favour of covering 'spats', thus distorting the significance of what might otherwise be marginal disputes. Pepinster offers an intriguing explanation for this lack of depth: virtue is harder to talk about than utilitarianism, and whereas the one characterises religious discourse, the other has the monopoly on journalistic accounts.

Fourteen years ago, the Nolan committee was set up to oversee standards in public life and provide advice to the Government on ethical standards. It recommended that office-holders should have seven principles of public life. These were: selflessness, integrity, objectivity, accountability, openness, honesty, leadership. Since then, of course, we've found that MPs – the very people whose behaviour was first looked at by Nolan – have been found wanting yet again. In 1996, then, the issue was cash for questions; more recently it was MPs' expenses. But what of the very people who discovered these shocking aspects of MPs' behaviour – the journalists? Does their behaviour bear scrutiny? Journalists are not always ethical – is it appropriate, for example, that they spend money buying information? A lot of us would find that unacceptable in theory. Yet the very journalists who revealed the scandal of MPs' expenses did just that. Without their cash, we would still be in the dark about MPs.

This example highlights how difficult it is to have rigid rules about how to behave ethically as a journalist. But some basic guidelines such as Nolan's – selflessness, integrity, objectivity, accountability, openness, honesty, leadership – can help. And at a time when the world seems to be losing its moral bearings – consider, for example, not only MPs, but what we've learned about the City in the last few years, and what we've discovered about the Catholic Church and sexual abuse of children

– journalists need to be rigorous in their challenges to institutions and to report on the world with integrity. Unfortunately, not only do many journalists often devote their considerable talents to the trivial or the unpleasant, both usually involving celebrities, but even serious discourse is increasingly coarse and unpleasantly recriminatory. (Not that I wouldn't endorse the view of the late Nick Tomalin who recommended that journalists require rat-like cunning, a plausible manner and a little literary ability. Journalism has always attracted rogues, cheats and liars and they do a splendid job finding their own kind elsewhere, be it in the House of Commons, in the City of London and even in the Church.)

The justification for spending money on information is that wrong-doing is exposed and the public gets to know the truth. Truth seems a straightforward enough issue when discussing the point of journalism. Or is it? Think for a moment of a situation where you would expect to find out the truth – in a court of law, spoken, under oath. You would expect the facts to be spelt out, but there might be different evidence about the case from different witnesses. You might suggest that the truth is what corresponds with the facts, then, as outlined in the case. Or you might say that something is true if those who had experienced it endorsed it. Or you might say that truth exists if the facts, or someone's beliefs, fit together and are coherent. Truth-telling is more complicated than one might at first think. It becomes even more complicated if you not only can communicate with your immediate neighbour but if you have access to communication with all manner of people – when you have immense power to carry out truth-telling, or indeed lying, through the media. So how does the media go about communicating? Is it there to tell the truth? Or is it there to do something else? And in what way does a journalist serve society?

I have spent the past twenty-odd years working as a journalist and for much of that time I would say that the emphasis has not been on truth-telling, but on telling stories. That is the reason for what we do. 'Is it a good story?' is a question journalists ask time and time again. Not that we are there to relate fiction, but real stories. Stories which are then, in effect, true, and sometimes important. Sometimes they are not important at all, but they are interesting. Sometimes they are both. For example, you would say that it is important to tell people who won the general election, and it is also interesting. But it is not very important, but quite interesting, to know that the election's vote counters are recruited from banks because they can count very fast and so have very nimble fingers. And it is really not very interesting but terribly important that all ballot boxes are sealed up after the polls close.

These criteria then – is it important? is it interesting? – are vital to journalists' work and their relationship with the truth, but what is interesting and important depends on where you read the material or who you listen to. So the story that is important to the *Oxford Mail* is probably very dull to people living elsewhere. What matters to the readers of *Dental Hygiene* is irrelevant to the readers of *Amateur Gardener*. It means that certain stories get a particular slant according to their audience. That, in turn, I would say, affects the truth of a particular story.

A hypothetical story would explain this more clearly:

A house burns down in Oxford, causing disruption to the traffic on the Cowley Road for hours. It contains a dental surgery on the ground floor, where a world-famous dentist has worked for years. His wife, a prize-winning gardener, sees her life's work trampled underfoot by the firemen. The *Oxford Mail* runs the story, covering the loss of the dentist's surgery, the garden and the traffic disruption. The readers of *Dental Hygiene* only get the account of the loss of the surgery, and *Amateur Gardener* readers only hear about the loss of the prize-winning dahlia collection. Each of the stories is true in its way, but each does distort the truth because of the emphasis. Are they, then, not really true, but dishonest? While this is a trivial example it give some insight into the way in which what might seem simple – telling what is true – is not necessarily quite so straightforward. You can see that the way journalists write stories – the narrative requirements – can in fact distort the true picture.

The demands of news desks also serve to colour and shape the news that we read and hear, including news about religion. And with the advent of 24/7 television rolling news programmes there is an even greater desire for drama, personality and developments in stories. The leading media sources of information – newspapers, TV and radio, and websites – are dominated by drama and especially political drama. Political news is characterized by rows, fallings out, failures, sackings, scandal, what's in it for the reader, and to a lesser extent, policy. In other words, political news is about success and failure. It is rare to find ideas or beliefs explored in depth.

This approach is also colouring the one that news desks frequently take to religion. Religious news in the non-specialist, national media is about new appointments, speculation on future appointments, rows, sackings, controversial statements, perceived attacks on other groups, be they non-believers or members of other religions. Newspapers, particularly tabloid ones, love stories that combine sex and religion – either condemnations of the teaching on it, or scandals involving it. In many ways all these approaches are entirely justified. It is understandable that readers will want to know who is likely to be the next Archbishop of Canterbury, or if a bishop's in trouble, or the Chief Rabbi has warned anti-Semitism is on the rise and blames a growing Muslim population, or if a priest is being prosecuted for child sex abuse.

However, the way in which feuds are reported can make for distortion. For example, in February 2009 BBC Radio 4's flagship *Today* programme invited me to comment on the row that had developed over the Catholic Church trying to draw back into its fold a highly traditionalist group, commonly known as the Lefebvrists, whose bishops included Briton Richard Williamson, who has known anti-Semitic views. At the last minute they dropped me because they decided it would be more balanced to have a debate between a Jewish academic and a Catholic with a strongly different view. So they invited a Catholic who told listeners that the Pope was being compassionate to the Lefebvrists and that Williamson was really only a little local difficulty. Instead of being balanced this was distorting, because the majority of Catholics are horrified by Williamson and his anti-Semitic views.

Broadcasters, and you see this particularly on the *Today* programme, not only want balance, as in having two sides of the argument, but they want a spat. A courteous discussion is dismissed as dull radio.

Meanwhile, the realm of ideas remains unexplored, as does church teaching. For example, when the Pope visited Africa in 2009, a few comments that he made on the use or non-use of condoms in combating the spread of HIV were covered widely in the press. Coverage highlighted both the focus of the media on sex and its narrow perception of morality – that moral matters equate to sexual matters. This then enables secular commentators to suggest that religion should keep its nose out of the bedroom. But certainly in the Catholic Church, through the body of teaching known as Catholic Social Teaching, morality also encompasses the eradication of poverty, climate change and the treatment of migrants. But later comments made by the Pope during his African trip about all these matters, as well as education and women's rights, were ignored by the press. This highlights how faith communities, who are often advocates for change, are given little credit for this by the media. (Interestingly, politicians, if not the media, have noticed this. They court faith groups because they can either influence voters, be vehicles for change, or can provide services. The Catholic Church's role in helping promote the Millennium Development Goals, for example, was a key reason why the British Government asked Pope Benedict to visit Britain.)

Another example of the media's lack of interest in ideas was evident in its coverage of recent teaching documents (encyclicals) published by Pope Benedict about love in the wider sense (*Deus Caritas Est*) or the morality of the markets (*Caritas in Veritate*). These got at best a downpage slot on an inside page or a few seconds of airtime.

The specialist religious press has a somewhat different role, as journals of record. Journals like my own, *The Tablet*, and *Third Way* provide far more space to explore ideas and beliefs. Yet we too cover the rows, the speculation and the scandal, because they do form the warp and weft of religion as well. But the treatment of scandals tends to be more sober, and, I hope, fairer.

So what has particularly influenced the way that religion is perceived today? I would suggest that three notable historical changes since the start of the twenty first century have had the most significant effect.

These are:

- 9/11 and the rise of Islam
- The new atheism and aggressive secularism
- The ever-faster speed of scientific development, particularly in the biological and medical sciences, with ethical consequences. This affects the reporting of issues such as assisted dying and stem-cell research.

9/11 caused a renewed interest in religion – but it also meant that faith is sometimes perceived through a fear of religion, particularly Islam, as a malign force. Religion is also seen by some publications as part of race relations, seeing members of particular faiths affected by hatred which is viewed as racism. Other journalists focus on religion as something which is tied up with international conflict, particularly in the Middle East.

Interest in religion is also influenced by the rise of hostility to faith, which ranges from a desire for political correctness that leads to the removal of perceived special treatment of religion, to scepticism about faith's claims, to the dismissal of believers as idiotic fools and downright hatred of religion. The most extreme loathers of religion – what one might call members of the Dawkins school – like to caricature believers as unthinking, craven, with no room for doubt and sometimes as rabid creationists.

In recent times some of the most savage criticism of religion has been saved by atheist commentators not for Islam or Judaism, but for Christianity, and Roman Catholicism is a particular pariah. This approach was evident from the way the press regarded the visit of the relics of Therese of Lisieux to Britain in 2009. This is Matthew Parris in *The Times* on 17 September:

> 'Don't "respect" this credulous folly! Don't let the madnesses of these faith minorities go by default! Stop our politicians kowtowing to nutters!'

Or Minette Marrin in the *Sunday Times* on 20 September:

> 'The bamboozling of frightened, suffering, suggestible people by Christians'.

Or Simon Jenkins in the *Guardian* on 17 September:

> 'The credulous classes, the brainwashing of unreason'.

These writers were all polemicists and opinion is their meat and drink. But should not opinion be based on fact? All three claimed that the Catholic Church was promising cures and miraculous healing through the tour of Therese of Lisieux's relics. There was no evidence of this at all. Rather, the Church suggested that the visit would be a time for prayer and a deepening of faith. To be fair to the *Guardian*, it did allow the debate to be explored further through its website, with Theo Hobson and Fr Stephen Wang, a seminary lecturer, countering Jenkins' opinions.

The religious news story which has – understandably – received the greatest coverage from the general media in the last two years has been the child sex abuse crisis in the Roman Catholic Church. Since the first revelations by the *Boston Globe* in 2002, there have been disclosures in the United States, Ireland, the United Kingdom, Australia, Germany and France of sexual and physical abuse by Catholic priests. The incidents ranged from gropings to rape, the victims were both male and female, and the abuse by one individual has sometimes involved occasional assaults on one child, regular activity involving several children, or extraordinary systematic abuse of many children over many years. While there have been no revelations of paedophile 'rings', it has become apparent from international press coverage that church authorities often knew of the abuse, but their interventions commonly involved moving priests around. This served to enable the abuser to target new victims elsewhere. The Catholic Church used its own canon law as a basis for action rather than co-operating with the police. Revelations about abuse go back decades.

The media's way of dealing with this has made me proud to be a journalist. In various countries, but particularly in the United States and Ireland, it took the media's involvement to reveal patterns of sexual abuse and misgovernance by bishops, who not only failed to tackle the issue but made it worse by recycling abusers into church ministry and failed to come to grips with the psychosexual problems of their pastors, their criminal activity, and the collapse of discipline. Their consequent failure to care for victims was also deeply shocking.

But the story which made me ashamed at times to be a Catholic has also made me deeply concerned about my profession too. It has been seized upon in such a way by some journalists to attack the Catholic Church as if it is the epicentre of child sexual abuse. Abuse of children occurs in families as well as schools, care homes and youth organisations run by other denominations and by secular authorities. But the media's portrayal is of a vast ecclesiastical conspiracy with little reference to the fact that the cases are decades old and that attempts have been made in countries such as Britain to tackle the crisis.

This became particularly clear in the spring of 2010 when media across the globe turned on the Church, suggesting that Pope Benedict was party to a vast church cover-up. In Germany, where cases shocked devout church-goers, *Der Spiegel* called for the Pope's resignation and there were similar demands from the press in Ireland, where some of the most appalling abuses occurred, finally documented in a series of devastating reports.

The New York Times has been one of the Church's most trenchant critics on this issue, regularly revealing incidents of abuse and cover-ups. On 25 March it ran a front page item on a case in Milwaukee where it claimed that the Pope, in his previous role as Cardinal Joseph Ratzinger, Prefect of the Congregation of the Doctrine of the Faith, had prevented sanctions against a priest who years before had abused 200 deaf children in his care. The case was deeply shocking but there appeared to be no solid evidence of such a malign cover-up by Cardinal Ratzinger.

Like most bishops, the then Cardinal Ratzinger seemed not to understand the scale of the sexual abuse crisis when he first learnt of it. But closer study of his response suggests that he did start to understand it, and far more than his fellow clerics. As head of the CDF, he read files on the abusive priests: just days before he was elected pope, Cardinal Ratzinger spoke of the 'filth' in the Church. While papers like *The New York Times* give him little credit, there are smaller voices, some of them unexpected, who have cut him some slack. Blogger Thomas Reese, a former editor of the Jesuit weekly, *America*, and my own journal, *The Tablet*, long a critic of Joseph Ratzinger in his time as head of the CDF, have pointed out that he supported the American bishops when they advocated a zero tolerance approach to abusive priests, refusing to allow them to return to ministry; that he took action against Fr Marcial Maciel, a notorious abuser who founded the Legionaries of Christ order, and funded the Church, after John Paul II did nothing about him.

Examination of one case from Britain serves to show how newspapers can distort in order to produce a scandal where there is none. In August 2009, the *Sun* ran a front-page headline, 'Devil in a dog collar', about a Catholic priest who had been convicted of several sexual assaults on children. The priest, Fr David Pearce, was a monk who had been the headmaster of the junior section of a boys' public school, St Benedict's, in Ealing, West London. The headline came from an anonymous figure quoted in the story, and was then used as a headline in other papers, including the *Independent* in its story of Pearce's sentencing to eight years in jail two months later in October. Abuse of children is always a serious matter and all the stories reported conveyed the sense that the incidents involving Pearce were utterly revolting and the very worst that someone might imagine. After approximately 350 words the *Independent* story did quote the judge saying that they were not at the more serious end of the scale. Noticeably, none of the national papers that reported the case later reported that the sentence was halved on appeal by higher judges that criticised the trial judge for his response to the case.

The Times went far further than other papers in its coverage of the Pearce case, with a front headline on 10 April – 'Britain's top Catholic "protected" paedophile' – with an attempt to implicate a senior churchman. The story suggested that the Archbishop of Westminster, Vincent Nichols, was responsible for Pearce's abusing victims over a period of years because Archbishop Nichols had chaired the Catholic Church's child protection committee in 2001–2008. In fact, Pearce's main activities took place before this period; he was a monk who was the responsibility of his abbot, and the Archdiocese of Westminster was informed of his case in recent years, but Archbishop Nichols was at the time in Birmingham, not Westminster. He was not told the full details of the case until he moved to Westminster. The newspaper report gave no reason why he should have been accused of protecting Pearce, even if the word was in inverted commas. But the innuendo was there. *The Times* then repeated the smear by reproducing the headline in a cut-out of the story, used to illustrate another story about Pearce and an investigation into the handling of his case by his monastery, Ealing Abbey.

A story of child abuse, which was basically a story of how a charming man used his position of trust to indulge in undoubtedly distressing but not the worst kind of assaults, was ramped up to try to damage the reputation of someone with no responsibility for the perpetrator.

The sex abuse scandal in the Catholic Church highlights how vital the press is. If it hadn't been for journalists in newspapers such as the *Boston Globe*, where victims of sexual abuse turned for help when their experiences were either being ignored or covered up by the Catholic Church, then we probably still wouldn't know how devastating that abuse has been. But the healthy scepticism of the press has all too often been replaced when it comes to religion, with a marked degree of cynicism and a desire to make the story fit a particular frame. This is notably the case with the child abuse scandal, as the story cited above shows. In this case, the frame was that all senior Catholic clerics have been involved in covering up or protecting paedophiles.

The frame of a story can be provided via those who write the headlines and the standfirsts; it can be set up via a publication's editorial policy. It can sometimes emerge through the influence of people in positions of public influence. This kind of frame is particularly evident in the reporting of medical and science stories with a particular ethic. To a great extent the frame of reporting on these kinds of stories was set some years ago with the hugely influential Warnock report on IVF. And that frame, or perspective, was utilitarian. And so it has stayed: reflecting on these developments with the idea that what matters is the greatest happiness for the greatest number.

But if journalists just accept that line, are they, first, really questioning and examining the issues as thoroughly as they should, and will they understand that there are different ethical and religious views on such issues, or at least take them into consideration and research them more thoroughly? So, to take stories on assisted dying: a journalist, if he/she is to do a thorough job, needs to question different ideas about life and its value; the extent to which we should intervene to end life or prolong it; who should make the decisions about whether a patient should have that kind of autonomy; the role of the doctor and his professional codes of conduct; the extent to which you would harm the community as a whole to which the person concerned belongs. Some of those differing views about assisted dying come from those with a religious perspective. But how much do journalists know about religion?

Anecdotal evidence suggests there is a growing ignorance of, despite growing interest in, religion. When City University made religion a special subject as part of its postgraduate journalism training course, it became hugely popular with students, who said they knew nothing about religion and about the major faiths. Certainly, we can never assume, or so the BBC thinks, that people know the first thing about religion. When making *Thought for the Day* for BBC Radio Four's *Today* programme a producer told me that I could not assume, for example, that anyone listening would ever have heard of Advent or know what it is.

To sum up: Coverage of religion in the news often lacks discursive analysis and suffers from over-simplification. One of the difficulties with the reporting of religion and ethics is that journalists inevitably find it easier to report on an ethical framework that's about acts and decisions, but much of ethics linked to religious belief is about character. So the utilitarian will ask 'what should I do?', which translates easily into reporting the issues as stake, but those who are concerned with virtue – and virtue ethics is highly influential in Christian thinking at the moment – would ask 'what sort of person should I be?' That's far more opaque and harder to connect with a report on, say, stem cell research.

Given the interest in religion, which is evident in the rising numbers of young people taking GCSE RE and A Level RE, Philosophy and Ethics, and the audience figures for programmes like *The Monastery* and events such as Pope John Paul II's funeral, there would seem to be more of an appetite for religion than newspapers and broadcasters think. Websites have broadened coverage but there are also deeply disturbing blogs full of hatred and bile which shame people of faith.

I would hope to see in future:

- Fuller debate about issues and ideas in the general as well as specialist media
- More space given to spirituality.

Religion and the news do make for uncomfortable bedfellows. Many of those in positions of power in religious organisations are suspicious of the media's liberal thinking, its belief in freedom of speech, and its perceived challenge to authority while thinking they themselves have a special relationship to the truth. But in a church like the Catholic Church lay people have little by way of any official or recognised forum. That is why ideas and opinions should be expressed through the media. That is a way of bearing witness.

Nolan cited selflessness, integrity, objectivity, accountability, openness, honesty and leadership as principles for public life. They are suitable principles for journalists too. But unlike those in public life, journalists reporting on religion are not dealing with democracies. Their responsibilities, which include dealing with organisations where secrecy is the norm, making them vulnerable to misunderstanding and hostility from the secular world, are even greater.

Chapter 9
Cumberland Blues

Andrew Brown

Summary

The growth in religion and in religious news over the past twenty years has defied expectations. But, as Brown dryly observes in this chapter, parts of the press now face the very demise that was predicted of religion twenty years ago. Circulation of newspapers has dropped, partly due to the rise of the internet, which has not yet yielded a reliable revenue model to replace that of print media. This raises a profound question, addressed by Brown, namely: what are the skills offered by journalists which are threatened not only by the looming cutbacks at the national newspapers but also by the technological innovations of blogging and instant online comment? Ultimately, his question is: what is the future for journalism? An intriguing answer, which he explores, is that journalists online may well 'march into the church's territory, and establish themselves as some kind of voluntary community, requiring and rewarding more commitment than the simple exchange of money'.

The question at the moment about the future of religion and the media is whether the media will still be around in any form we might recognise in twenty years' time. That makes a neat reversal from the default assumption 20 years ago, which was that the question would be whether religion would last until today.

Now, 'religion' and 'media' are both terms rather too large to be useful. So I'm interested in newspapers, primarily, and Christianity because these are the things that I know something about. I once heard a newspaper executive ask an archbishop whether either of them headed organisations which would still be there in 20 years' time. The Archbishop thought that schools would pull the Church of England through. Unfortunately, the newspapers do not sell anything as useful as education. So we are in trouble.

In the last decade, the quality end of the national press has lost about 20 per cent of its circulation. This isn't entirely down to the internet, but it is the internet which has persuaded everyone that print revenues will never recover. In the autumn of 2009, the financial position of the national press was just awful. This is true in the USA as well, but the figures I know come from here. The *Guardian* needs to save about £20m this year, out of operating costs of about £80m. There will be redundancies in the newsroom, not all voluntary. The *Independent*, which twenty years ago was nudging 400,000 sales, now sells 96,000 copies a day at full price. *The Times* and *The Sunday Times* are expected to lose £50m between them. The *Telegraph* is not in any better shape financially. No one knows the way out of this hole. The revenues available from an ad-supported model online are wholly insufficient to maintain anything recognisable as a newspaper, since the overwhelming share of the money from ads online goes not to the media owners, but to Google.

This redirection of ad revenues is a more subtle point than the obvious one that Google makes news into a commodity. But it does that, too: if you look up a reasonably large story, like Pope Benedict's opinions on condoms, Google will list more than a thousand stories on it. Most of these, of course, simply repeat wire service analyses, and are entirely interchangeable. So if all you want is the facts, there is no reason whatever to pay for them. But even if you want first rate analysis, there is a lot of that available for free, though Google won't tell you where to look.

In the summer of 2009 I was at an international press jamboree in Helsinki where we talked a lot about this. The only people who were remotely optimistic were the Finns, but they have both a small language and a small, coherent, determined ruling class. But the presentation I remember came from Jacob Weisberg, who founded *Slate*, one of the first web magazines, now owned by the *Washington Post*. Paper newspapers, he said, will persist, but only as a boutique product, for older readers.

These are the facts, the attitudes, and the expectations that explained Rupert Murdoch's decision to try to start charging for content online, and to challenge Google's right to grow fat on the labours of his employees. I'm writing before we know whether this will work, and the constraints of academic publishing mean that I have to. The preliminary figures suggest that with only 100,000 or so subscribers, of whom perhaps half are paying the full fee of £8 a month, the experiment has failed. Certainly the paywall killed Ruth Gledhill's blog stone dead. When it was free, it was widely read and influential. As soon as it vanished behind the paywall the readership, and the comments, collapsed. Now she has moved her efforts onto Twitter, which cannot be charged for.

Thirty years ago, the introduction of digital typesetting destroyed the business of printing newspapers. Around ten years ago, digital photography destroyed the profession of newspaper photography. So if the digital distribution of words destroys the trade of journalism we can hardly complain that this was an unprecedented injustice. Now, the normal reaction of journalists, when faced with this prospect, has been to say that you'll miss us when we're gone. I'm not at all sure that you will. Looking around at all the people who have already abandoned newspapers, news, and television, I do not see them notably less happy or well informed.

In the long run, journalism does provide a useful, in fact indispensable, service, but it is not useful and indispensable to society, or only in a second order way. It is useful and indispensable to people who have to make decisions and to know things. No one would suggest that most citizens in a modern democracy fall into either of these categories and if anyone did, I would direct them to the voting figures in elections.

So before getting onto the question of why no one is paying now, which has social as much as technological answers, I think it is worth asking what it is that anyone might be prepared to pay for that journalists do. What are the core skills? There were a couple of answers both popular and profound, as journalistic clichés ought to be, when I was learning the trade. One was Claud Cockburn's observation that journalism was some mixture between advertising and entertainment. All a journalist had to do was to decide what, or which cause, he was advertising, and whom he wanted to entertain, and then the stories would appear. Cockburn himself was said by Graham Greene to be one of the best journalists of the twentieth century. He was certainly a very good writer of marvellous, self-concealing autobiographies. He worked for everyone from *The Times* in Wall Street before the last great crash, in 1929, to *Private Eye*, which he helped to found. He knew what he was talking about, and he had a very low view of the pretensions of our trade. The other was Nick Tomalin, killed on the Golan heights, whose most famous phrase, also quoted earlier by Catherine Pepinster, was that 'The only qualities essential for success in journalism are rat-like cunning, a plausible manner, and a little literary ability'.

But Tomalin went on to say that these weren't the qualities for which journalists were actually paid. In his view, writing when it was one of the most enjoyable and well-regarded trades in England, at least at the top, the thing you really needed was luck, and preferably connections. The essential point was that many people could do the job of the lucky few as well as they could themselves. I'm not sure this is entirely true. But it is truer than we would like. All journalism is in one sense a struggle around Beaverbrook's Law, which states that 'any journalist may be replaced by any other journalist'. Managers are constantly trying to prove this law true; journalists that there is at least one exception.

I think that the core skills of journalism, the things that we actually get paid for, are twofold. Reporters find things out, and editors leave things out. These are morally neutral skills: the *Daily Mail* excels at both. It is no coincidence that it is also profitable. But they are both things which the new media are notoriously bad at doing. There are technological reasons for this as well as social or human ones: the existence of essentially unlimited reading matter on the net does change the rules. Even if my newspaper does not find things out, it does not matter, because someone on the net will have done; similarly, there is no point in my leaving things out, if someone else will put them in. But neither excuse gives anyone any reason to prefer my offerings, and still less to pay for them. And unless journalism of this sort is paid for, it won't get done.

Google, as we know, destroyed the economic basis of journalism by making a more direct link between advertisers and readers. Tomalin in all his glory knew very well that the classified ads were the point of the paper economically, and said so. 'The most valuable lesson a small local newspaper can teach an apprentice is that its most interesting contents, which sell the paper, are the classified advertisements.' But he gave no thought for the day when they would disappear. Neither, of course, did anyone else, and that was one of the things which made the industry so vulnerable to Google.

In important ways, the papers spent the ten or fifteen years immediately before the internet hit them making themselves as vulnerable as they could. You could say they were merely maximising their profits, where the profits were to be found, but I blame Andrew Neil. His *Sunday Times* was a model for the paper that found little out (despite all the fuss made of the Insight team) and left almost nothing out. This made it vulnerable to Google. If you have eleven supplements, all crammed with advertising, the one thing certain is that most readers will throw at least eight away unread. Google spared them this trouble. But the car ads in the unread motoring supplement were what paid for the languid Tomalins whom everyone read in the feature pages. 'Everyone' was not perhaps the word we thought it had been.

It wasn't just the economic model that made Neil-type papers vulnerable to the internet. There was also the style of journalism they promoted. Every story had to tell the readers they were smarter and better informed than the people being written about. The tone of snark and condescension was nicely summed up in Neil's remark that he did not want his specialists to be 'fans with typewriters'. But it turns out that what the fans want to read are other fans: people who care. And while we may sneer at the fans of anything, the readers who do not much care what they read won't pay for any of it. The internet was first colonised and, to the extent that it has been, first civilised by fans at keyboards. Whatever their other faults, they cared, and that's why people read them.

I do not want to suggest that this attitude is unique to newspapers. Smirking and snarking are far more common in mainstream television, but I cannot bear to watch that, so I have no particularly well-informed opinions on the matter. It is no coincidence, though, that Diarmaid McCullough's serious *A History of Christianity* could only be broadcast initially on BBC4.

So where might the skills of journalism be exercised in a digital future, and who might pay for them? I think there is very clearly a market for niche, or trade, journalism. If you work in a particular industry, then news about it is of the first importance to you, and supplying it will always be a specialised trade. There is scope both for finding things out, and for leaving things out. But this does not apply to all industries, by any means. You might think that the *Guardian*'s massive Society and Education supplements represent the importance of these sectors to the economy and the interest that people who work in them have in the news. But the connection is indirect. It is because these are important industries that they must advertise a lot, and because the *Guardian* is the preferred place for these jobs to be advertised that it finds so much to write about in those fields. If, as now seems so sensible and so cheap as to be almost inevitable, this advertising moves out of the newspapers and onto government websites directly, there will be a lot less coverage of their news in the paper.

By analogy, if the *Guardian* had the *Church Times*' classified market, its treatment of religion would be very different. But there is no obvious reason why even the *Church Times* should continue to enjoy its dominance of a specialised kind of job advertising. One bishop told me the other day that he had had one job application from a young man who neither wrote nor sent an email to indicate his interest. He simply changed his status on Facebook, and took for granted that this would communicate with his potential employers.

But let's suppose there is a market within every significant niche for news. There are some newspapers which bundle all kinds of disparate news of this sort into the one thing. But there is no single paper in Britain today that is best at all the niches that it attempts to cover. The idea of a newspaper of the record was that it should do so. But there aren't any newspapers of the record left. It is extremely common among people who still buy different papers that they read them on different days for their different strengths.

The only exception to this that I know is the *Financial Times*. That has a very wide range of niches covered – its foreign news and even its culture are remarkably good. But the *FT*, I think, is also in some sense a trade paper. The trade it caters for is that of governing, or managing as it is now known. This, too, is a small market. The paper is shrinking like all the others, though less quickly, and it is quite successful in charging for its content, because both what it finds out and its decisions to leave certain things out convey valuable information to readers who can act on it.

So in that sense the *FT* remains one model of what we believe a newspaper should be; and the fact that it can charge for the use of its website suggests that there will continue to be a market to support its work, even if a smaller one. The same, I suspect, is true of the *Economist*.

But it is an important point about the web that there is very little point in being number two. The names we know, and use, are those which dominate their fields almost completely – Google, not Yahoo; Amazon, not Barnes and Noble; Ebay. It seems to shape itself naturally into a series of winner-take-all games. That does something to explain the energy with which the papers have thrown themselves onto it. At first nobody wanted to be left behind because it was the new thing. Now we are frightened of being left behind lest the wolves eat us. This is especially true among English-language newspapers because our market is potentially so immense. Anyone who could come to dominate it would really bestride the globe. Finnish journalists to whom I have spoken about this are much less worried. They will always have to compete only with other Finnish papers.

Religious news may not be part of this winner-takes-all world. I honestly do not know. There are arguments for both sides of this question. Some stories, like the Anglican schism, are clearly global. I do not believe it would have happened, or could have done, without the internet. If outrage excites you like Spanish Fly, then you will naturally want to read the site which gathers the greatest possible amount of outrage from all around the world. What's more, the English-speaking forms of Christianity do form a more-or-less coherent whole, irrespective of their denominational divisions. Their international expressions are all largely funded by Americans and driven by American concerns. This is obvious in the history of the Anglican schism, but it is also true of the Catholic culture wars.

But these international stories are quite rare, and most believers just do not care about them at all. So you might argue that all religion is local and inculturated, and that for most people the only sort that matters, and which they can understand, is the kind that they practise themselves. In that case, religious journalism becomes an environment with a much greater carrying capacity, one in which there are countless niches: many journalists could then hope to become trusted and vital providers of important news, if not for fifteen minutes, at least to fifteen other people. I'm not sure this is a hugely hopeful prospect, but it might be better than the alternatives.

In both cases, though, newspapers must make the case that they are right homes for the authoritative sites. Especially in conditions of conflict and schism, actual reporting is much less in demand than bloviation and the confirmation of existing biases. The business of finding things out and leaving things out works in many ways, and it is just as easy, and often more effective, to make a story by leaving out the wrong things as by finding out the right ones. Dishonest and propagandist sites do not flourish despite their vices, but because of them. So while they might fulfil both Cockburn's and Tomalin's criteria, they are not really bringing reliable news of the sort that newspapers ought to aspire to. There is still a niche there. We do not know if anyone will pay for it.

Another possibility is that the news of the future will be much more interactive. This is only completely possible through computers, though I suspect that a thoroughly localised local paper already represents a good model of interactivity. But the idea is that readers, through their reactions and comments, can shape and contribute to the news. This is not an entirely new or revolutionary idea. It is implicit in the most local and unglamorous forms of journalism, where you are taught that there is a story in everything, and everyone is a potential source. But that has not been the way that metropolitan newspapers have operated in the last fifty years. The whole apparatus of public relations has functioned to make it less necessary and less possible for journalists to talk to real people, especially unimportant ones.

On the other hand, the technologies of digital communication allow churches to bypass the commercial media almost entirely with their internal communications. A bishop with a blog and a twitter stream can say exactly what he wants and when he wants without having it subbed or sharpened by anyone. He needs neither a PR consultancy nor the nasty mainstream media that the PR consultants are meant to manage. We're out of the loop.

In fact it is worse than that. The people we write about need no longer talk to us, while the web has made it vastly easier for readers to do so. Almost everyone in the business believes this was a disastrous mistake, but officially, almost everywhere, we are meant to welcome readers' comments and opinions.

Alan Rusbridger, editor of the *Guardian*, has a slide used in many presentations in which a man is holding a newspaper in front of his face to read it – but there is a hole cut in the middle so he can look through it and talk to the startled journalist beyond. This is an interesting idea. In practice, of course, when the journalist looks through the hole they do not often see a reader's face, but an anonymous flasher pleasuring himself.

Jacob Weisberg, of the online magazine *Slate*, whom I quoted earlier as saying that printed newspapers would persist only as a boutique product for older readers, also says that one of the important decisions made early on by *Slate* was to arrange the comments so that they could not be seen at all by most readers and to make it easy and natural to read the site as if only paid and edited people wrote on it.

Is this necessary? The idea of interaction with readers is attractive, as well as in some sense noble. On any given story, the journalist will know more than about ninety-nine per cent of the readers, but the other one per cent will know more than we do. If their knowledge could be harnessed or harvested, we would all benefit (assuming for the moment that they want to share it; something by no means obvious and often entirely untrue). So we dream of stories which are improved by the addition of pertinent facts and accumulated knowledge. Let's face, it, any story could be. We never know enough, nor have enough time; otherwise we would be historians, not journalists at all. This happens in some places online. It does not, by and large, happen on newspaper websites. Still less does it happen on the BBC talkboards. Cracking that problem is, I think, a great challenge.

You can look at it from various angles. Some of them are technological, and some are organisational. Technologically, the important fact is that email is easy; many sites, crazily misguided, have tried to make it as easy as possible to comment. You read at the screen, and respond at once. It is almost like a computer game. It is certainly not like the old-fashioned procedure where you had to find paper, an envelope, and a little time to write in, before spending money on a stamp and walking to the post office, or at least summoning the butler to bear the letter away. Email requires no more effort or consideration than shouting at the radio. Usually it produces no deeper thought.

The obvious organisational answer to this problem would be to employ lots of people to read and edit the incoming feedback. *The Huffington Post*, which pays no writers anything at all, employs 70 people, paid, to read and filter the comments, almost in real time. I cannot say I think their efforts are worthwhile, but that gives an idea of the size of the problem.

Most British newspapers do not even try. They do not do it now because they cannot afford to. They did not do it when they could have afforded to, in a time of fewer comments and higher revenues, for two bad reasons. The first was a strain of techno-utopianism among the early adopters of technology in the newsrooms. Farcical ideas about democracy and free speech meant that people were very reluctant to 'censor' the incoming comments at all. This exaggerated apparent respect for the opinions of our readers in theory was matched in practice with an equally exaggerated, though concealed, contempt for them. We could not expect anything better.

This was the final poisonous legacy of Andrew Neil-ism: the idea that 'content' was an undifferentiated sludge without quality, and only the width of it mattered. 'User generated content', in the BBC's unlovely phrase, was just as good as anything else but it was free. The underlying assumption was that advertising would always expand to cover any content we might have. Well, it does not, and even when it does, it is Google that profits, not the newspapers.

But there is another factor involved, beyond the technical and the organisational, which has been around a lot longer than even the telephone or the telegraph. The fundamental problem is that the opinions worth having are those of the people who do have better things to do with their time; the opinions we tend to get are those of the people who have nothing better to do with their time than to opine. In fact the best description of their condition is found in Hazlitt's *Essay on Coffee House Politicians*, published in 1821:

> It sometimes gives one a melancholy but mixed sensation to see one of the better sort of this class of politicians, not without talents or learning ... waving his arm like a pump-handle in sign of constant change, and spouting out torrents of puddled politics from his mouth; dead to all interests but those of the state; seemingly neither older nor wiser for age; unaccountably enthusiastic, stupidly romantic, and actuated by no other motive than the mechanical operations of the spirit of newsmongering.

I can think of half a dozen people online who would fulfil this description to the letter. Still more will answer Hazlitt on this one:

> A dearth of general information is almost necessary to the thorough-paced coffee-house politician; in the absence of thought, imagination, sentiment, he is attracted immediately to the nearest common-place, and floats through the chosen regions of noise and empty rumours without difficulty and without distraction.

Hazlitt even understood the charm of reading, without contributing to, these discussions: 'We may happily repose on dulness, drift with the tide of nonsense, and gain an agreeable vertigo by lending an ear to endless controversies. The confusion, provided you do not mingle in the fray and try to disentangle it, is amusing and edifying enough. Every species of false wit and spurious argument may be learnt here by potent examples.' But the coffee houses made their money selling coffee.

Attempts to get people to pay for the pleasure of idle conversation on the web have all failed. Sociability has been hugely popular: look at Facebook. But Facebook even more than Google makes money from the things that its users tell it about themselves, even when they do not intend to. No one pays for an account there; even if they could be persuaded to do so, I do not think that newspapers could compete with Facebook, because it offers 'news' which is entirely personalised.

This is a pity, really. If the *Guardian*'s website could become the place to learn what Guardian readers were up to, we would surely be able to make a profit sufficient to keep the newspaper going indefinitely. But such a site would be a very different place from a coffee house exchange of opinions, expert or otherwise, or even from news. News is what's interesting about lives; but what we find interesting about our own lives is only news to others if we are thoroughly unlucky.

As a general rule, no one cares very much about anything in the papers that they have not written themselves. That is why journalists care about the bylines, and readers care about sudoku and the letters to the editor. If comments on a site are carefully edited it is possible that they become something that shows the readers themselves as they wish to be, or at least a bit brighter and nicer than everyday experience would suggest.

I suspect this would only work with quite small groups. Just as news will become an affair of niches, or fandoms, if newspapers get into the business of running online communities, these will be aggregated out of many smaller ones. The same kind of dynamics operate here as in church growth: any group of more than 120 or 150 people starts to feel impersonal. Now, 120 or 150 regular posters could represent ten or a hundred times as many readers; my own rough comparative analyses of the number of comments on any article versus the number of readers who show up in our statistics shows that it is only a very small number who comment, and that if there are twenty commenters in all, the top three or so will post half of all comments, while half the commenters will only post once. The challenge is to make them come back and read what other people think.

All this makes it sound as if the only future for newspapers online is to march into the church's territory, and establish themselves as some kind of voluntary community, requiring and rewarding more commitment than the simple exchange of money. I really do not know that this is possible. It could just as well happen that expert journalism retreats entirely from the mass market. There is always a demand to know what is really going on, from the people who have to deal with the consequences, and a good journalist will be better informed than most of the people that he writes about. That is a skill for which someone will always pay. But that someone could very well be a think-tank, a large company, or a government. There is nothing at all to say it needs be a newspaper, or a website operated by a media company.

I hope I am wrong. I hope there is some aspect of the situation I have missed which upsets all my carefully reasoned pessimism. But all I can say is that I cannot see it; should it turn up, as I hope very much that it will, my defence will be the time-honoured one of my trade: the story was true when I wrote it.

SECTION 3
Representing Religion and the News

Figure 11   A crowd of pilgrims, spectators and others in St Peter's Square,
Rome, close to a large television screen showing Benedict XVI and
Cardinals during the beatification of John Paul II on 1 May 2011.
Giuseppe Fucile / Shutterstock.com

Introduction to Section 3: Representing Religion and the News

In this section, representatives of major religious groups in the UK address the relationship between religion and the media. All the contributors to this section have experience of engaging with broadcasting media in the UK, whether as an occasional contributor to discussions, or as a seasoned presenter of religious programmes. This mix of experience produces an intriguing variety of perspectives on the reporting of religion.

Monawar Hussain and Indarjit Singh voice some of the frustration that religious representatives feel when their community is the subject of unbalanced, sensationalist reporting or misrepresentation in the media, but they also acknowledge ways in which religious leaders and communities could engage more fruitfully. Jonathan Romain provides personal reflection on some of the ethical difficulties faced by religious leaders who engage with broadcasting media – issues of personal integrity and representation. Roger Royle, drawing on over twenty years of experience in religious broadcasting, discusses how humorous or 'light' approaches to religious topics and news can be a helpful way in to discussing more serious and complex issues. Ruth Scott considers an issue central to all the contributors to this section – the question of balance in religious reporting, and whether and how it can be achieved.

Chapter 10

Islam and the News

Monawar Hussain

Summary

The 'media says that Muslims spend their time killing people', so wrote a school pupil to Hussain, quoted in this chapter. The frustrations of representing Islam in the media are made apparent by Hussain: interviewers are not interested in vital interfaith work but ask instead about 72 virgins, suicide bombings, jihad, women Imams, honour killings and sharia. The problem is not just that of getting past these questions to something more meaningful, it is that these questions perpetuate an image of Islam as being 'inherently violent, intolerant and monolithic'. The notion that Islam has richly diverse cultural traditions and theological interpretations is lost, buried by toxic media tropes. Hussain tracks the way that 9/11 and 7/7 changed the way Islamic representatives have been treated even by local media, which had been helpful and fair until the terrorist attacks. The portrayal of Islam in the news is not only dominated by violence but also by the 'cultural threat' that this faith poses. Hussain makes this clear by relating the story of the 'call to prayer episode in the city of Oxford' in August 2007.

The British Muslim community, being a young community, is for Hussain at an 'economic and educational disadvantage'. The consequence of this is that there is scope for reforming the training of Imams so as to provide Muslim leadership that can engage more effectively with British culture and the British press. Hussain concedes this, though, in the context of calling for better media leadership. He quotes several wildly misinterpreted passages from the Qur'an and demonstrates that the broader scriptural context belies the media's use of such passages to generate fear and a sense of threat. Offering a final reflection on the diversity of media outlets brought about by rapid technological developments, Hussain urges caution. While this media diversity offers the space to counter stereotypes, it also harbours the danger that individual and group prejudices can be reinforced by remaining unchallenged in different media streams.

My aim in this chapter will be to draw on examples from my personal experiences of the media locally and nationally; to provide some clarity around certain aspects of Islām reported in the media and also offer some suggestions as to how the media might better report stories relating to Muslims and Islām. I hope that through this the relationship between religious leaders and the media might be strengthened.

I write as a British Muslim, an Imam, a community worker, an educator, and an interfaith advocate.

I thought I should commence my chapter with insights I have gleaned from my interaction with young Muslims. Last year I began an educational programme that sought to engage school pupils from various faiths or from none within a local secondary school in Oxford. My aim was to challenge stereotypes of Muslims through engaging the whole school community in assemblies and in classroom. I also sought to create space within the school dedicated to addressing issues of particular concern to young Muslim pupils growing up in the United Kingdom. When asked what the major issues of concern to them were – the media was consistently in the top five. They found the portrayal of Muslims in the news as deeply inaccurate, Islāmophobic, disempowering and leading to a feeling of alienation. One of the feedback comments from a pupil read:

> He teaches us things that you don't hear in the media ... the media says that
> Muslims spend their time killing people.

This attitude is borne out by a number of reports on Islāmophobia. For example, Ken Livingstone, the former Mayor of London, in a foreword to a report commissioned by the Greater London Authority entitled, *The Search for Common Ground*, states:

> One of the most startling findings of this report is that in one typical week in
> 2006, over 90 per cent of the media articles that referred to Islām and Muslims
> were negative. The overall picture presented by the media was that Islām is
> profoundly different from and a threat to the west.

As a consequence, the violent extremists from within the Muslim community exploit this pool of alienation, disillusionment and disempowerment with mainstream society to recruit vulnerable young Muslims, who are seeking a sense of identity and belonging, to a virulent and violent extremist ideology. Conversely, the far right extremists exploit media's stereotyping of Muslims and Islām to create an environment of fear of the 'other', this enables them to generate hatred against and even violence towards Muslims and their places of worship. Many Muslims find it deeply offensive to find leaders of violent extremist groups being portrayed by the media as being representative of Muslims in general or Islām in particular.

But what can the media do? I will outline some real-life experiences that I have had with the media and propose certain steps both media and religious leadership can take to ensure a more representative and balanced coverage of Muslims.

Local media

My first contact with local news began in my late teens and revolved around seeking publicity for local cultural/interfaith events in Oxford, aimed primarily at drawing people of many faiths together for conversation over a buffet curry meal, or a music event or both. The local radio stations and print media were great; they would interview me, ask relevant questions and this enabled us to communicate our message. However, in the post 9/11 and 7/7 world, there has been a tangible shift even in the way local news is reported. The landscape has become far more hostile. For example, after well over a year of striving, collaboration and genuine desire to establish a platform for the diverse faiths of the city of Oxford, we launched the Oxford Council of Faiths (OCF). When a local radio station invited me for an interview about the launch, I accepted. Some 8–10 minutes into the interview, what I call my 'shock and awe' moment occurred. The interviewer suddenly and abruptly changed the topic of questioning, from the OCF to the wholly different area of the 72 virgins in paradise, suicide bombings, jihad, women Imams, honour killings, and sharī'ah. Time seemed to stop; the verbal assault was consistent and sustained for what felt like an eternity. I felt deeply aggrieved at the manner in which I had effectively been set up.

What was rather distressing about this incident was that I had not been forewarned that the interview would be far broader than the launch of OCF. But this also illustrated the inherent unfairness in the way that parts of the media can work. The set of questions was rooted in a set of assumptions about Islām that presume it is inherently violent, intolerant and monolithic. In reality, however, there are multiple interpretations within the schools of law, theology, and Sūfism. There is great cultural, ethnic, linguistic, artistic and literary diversity within the Muslim community. All this is lost in an attempt to extricate soundbites or simplified answers to issues that often involve vigorous debate and discussion within the tradition.

Having said that, I believe it is essential that faith leadership and local media actively work to build relationships based upon trust, strong knowledge of the local community, and have conflict resolution mechanisms in place for when things go wrong. The reality is that faith leadership needs local media and conversely a sizable proportion of local media consumers will be from the faith communities, so it is a relationship that is mutually interdependent. Broadly speaking, other local radio and print media have often been sympathetic towards the efforts of local faith leaders in bringing communities together and have generally provided a fair representation. The secret, I think, has been the building of trust and a working relationship.

National media

Another incident that is a good illustration of the national coverage is the famous, or should I say the infamous, 'call to prayer' episode in the city of Oxford. One

Friday a retired Christian priest, who is also a friend and an interfaith colleague, suggested to our Imam that we should institute a call to prayer from the minaret. Both asked my opinion and I informed them that in the present climate this should not even be contemplated. A couple of weeks later I left for the Hajj. On my return, I discovered to my shock that this was now national and international news:

> 'Mosque call outrages Oxford' – the *Sun*, 27 December 2007
> 'Loudspeaker plan re-ignites "call to prayer" row' – the *Telegraph*, 14 January 2008
> Mosque's plan to broadcast call to prayer from loudspeaker 'will create Muslim ghetto' – *Daily Mail*, 14 January 2008
> 'Oxford Clergyman attacks Muslim plan for calls to prayer' – *The Times*, 30 January 2008.

A number of my interfaith colleagues representing various faiths, who had worked over many years to build trust, friendships and understanding in Oxford, now suddenly found that much of the work was being dismantled before our very eyes. Interestingly, those we'd never heard of or who had never participated in any interfaith initiative were exploiting the story to progress their personal agendas. The image of Christians and Muslims at loggerheads with one another was just blatantly untrue. What was worse was that a report in the *Daily Mail* had even conflated the mosque in question with the new Oxford Centre for Islāmic studies. The article displayed a picture of Prince Charles with the caption reading 'Prince Charles is backing the plan for the Oxford mosque', implying that His Royal Highness was in favour of the 'call to prayer'.

In response we decided to hold a public meeting under the aegis of the Anglo-Asian Association. The Bishop of Oxford, John Pritchard, and I spoke at the meeting, which was well attended and where our input was very well received. The headlines in the *Telegraph* read:

'Bishop's death threats over mosque plan' – the *Telegraph*, 11 March 2008.

The report excluded any reference to the wider speech by the Bishop or any of the other speakers; the newspaper had defined the whole meeting, including the discussion, the questions and answers, by extrapolating two words – 'death threat' – from one and a half hours of an excellent, well-informed, well-attended public meeting.

One (of many) other examples that come to mind is when I took part in a documentary for one of the mainstream television channels. I was followed by a crew for over a year at almost every public speaking engagement, including the Universities of Oxford and London, the College of St George, a number of leading public schools and our local mosque. In total the TV crew had filmed many hours. When I attended the viewing of the first part, I discovered that they had included a conversation I had with one of the elders in the mosque. I recall our conversation had been a lengthy one during the month Ramadhan (month of fasting), and revolved around the transient nature of our lives and of existence.

This man had uttered something to the effect, 'Muslims love death more than life', meaning that death was the meeting with the Beloved, the goal and end of all spiritual quest. However, I reminded him that he was not going to be understood in that manner. That is precisely what happened.

Something far more distressing was the fact that we were filmed conducting a funeral of a year-old child. When the undertakers were about to place the coffin in the grave, they accidently dropped the coffin sideways. I asked the editor to cut it from the final version but sadly his retort was that this would be seen as Muslim favouritism. So this clip was included.

So what can we deduce from these experiences?

It is important to remember that many parts of the media do not just target Muslims but are often hostile to other religious traditions too. This is a point that is often lost on Muslim audiences. I noted above the case of the Bishop of Oxford but the 'Sharī'ah' controversy and the baseless attacks on the Archbishop of Canterbury or the misuse of the child abuse scandal to caricature the entire Catholic Church are examples of other traditions receiving their fair share of negative media coverage. However, where it affects disproportionately the lives of Muslims is the sustained coverage, on a daily basis, of violence linked to Islām. It portrays Muslims as violent, irrational, intolerant and lacking any appreciation for human rights. This functions to perpetuate the myth of a violent, intolerant and monolithic Islām. One way of addressing this may be to share stories of Muslim victims of extremist violence. Another would be for the media to provide agency to the voices of mainstream Muslim religious leadership who consistently condemn such violence, highlighting the marginality of violent extremist groups within Islāmic societies. A Gallup world poll representing the views of some 90 per cent of 1.3 billon Muslims has shown some fascinating data. Such a source should be utilised by the media to understand Muslim opinions rather than second guessing them.

There are also important lessons to be drawn for both Muslim and media leadership.

Muslim leadership

The British Muslim community is a young community compared with, for example, the Jewish or Catholic communities. It is at an economic and educational disadvantage. In recent years some government funding has been made available to train Imams and Islāmic scholars in communication skills (primarily improving their English language), but other training, particularly relating to British culture and history, the nature of the media and effective media handling skills, is also absolutely essential in the contemporary world.

In the case of the 'call to prayer' there was effectively no legitimate elected leadership in the mosque. As a consequence the 'elders' who lacked understanding of the media played right into the hands of the sensationalist media. Had they issued a statement, as the properly elected committee later would, denying any plans for the 'call to prayer' the whole episode would not have been exploited by the media and others.

I would also suggest that Muslim leadership review the Islāmic curriculum for Imam training in the United Kingdom with the intention of reforming, adapting and expanding it so that it is 'fit for purpose'. The aim of such an endeavour should be to produce Imams in the UK who have a deeper understanding of Western philosophical and secular thought and are at the same time sufficiently rooted in their Islāmic tradition so that we may witness the emergence of a distinctive 'British' Islām. In addition, we will have a religious leadership that will be able to articulate Islām in the global media age and also challenge robustly extremist interpretation of the primary sources – Qur'ān and hadīth.

Media leadership

This brings us to an area that I find the media has to a large extent allowed itself to be manipulated by savvy Islāmophobes and Muslim extremists by quoting verses of the Qur'ān out of context. I cite below examples of such verses and a contextual interpretation which I hope will provide the media leadership with the knowledge to challenge those who quote these verses incorrectly and go unchallenged because of a lack of scriptural understanding.

However, before I cite these I would just like to add here that there is no one monolithic 'Islām' or 'Islāmic' community. There are many diverse Muslim communities, constituting a richness of culture, ethnicities, nationalities, languages and each with its particular customs and norms. Broadly speaking Islām is based upon three dimensions – Islām, Imān, Ihsān. Islām relates to the outward practices of the faith – the orthopraxis as it were, which is represented by the five schools of law – four Sunni and one Shi'i. Imān relates to theology, of which there are two mainstream schools. I have argued that it is within this dimension that we could scrutinise the theology of the violent extremists and defeat it! Finally Ihsān, or Sūfism, with numerous spiritual orders. There is tremendous diversity, with multiple interpretations and a deep and rich spiritual tradition that is hardly ever reported.

On the issue of Jihād it is worth pointing out here that Muslims have divided Jihād into the 'greater' and 'lesser' Jihād. The 'lesser' Jihād relates to the conduct of war. Despite the efforts of violent extremist ideologues, warfare in Islām is not a perpetual state but a means to be employed only as a last resort. Islām restricts war, promotes peace, prosperity, justice, freedom, mutual co-existence and cooperation between nations and peoples.

The 'greater' Jihād is:

- To cultivate virtue, such as prayer, sincerity, humility, forgiveness, love, generosity, patience, honesty, loyalty, moderation, self-restraint, discipline, courage, justice, tolerance, wisdom, good speech, gratitude, contentment, etc.
- To struggle against one's selfish desires.
- To discipline and reform the soul from harmful characteristics, such as forgetfulness of God, anger, deceit, envy, pride, laziness, etc.
- Any struggle or effort in the way of God, such as to fast, perform Hajj, to rise at dawn for salāh (five daily prayers), to serve one's parents, community, society, generally to bring about positive change within and without.

The 'Greater' Jihād is the domain of the Sufīs and it is high time that there was a sustained effort to highlight this vast and rich aspect of the Islāmic tradition, thereby creating a counter to the violent extremists in all their various guises.

So when journalists pose questions about Jihad, the 72 virgins in paradise, honour killings, and so on, they are reducing the whole discourse of a great and vibrant tradition to issues related to war, violence, sensuality and barbarism. These kinds of questions, drawing on a limited understanding of Jihad and the rich Islamic tradition, reveal some of the negative assumptions that journalists carry with them to a story; there is nothing about the ethical, theological, theosophical, philosophical teachings of the Islamic religion, its rich culture, its architecture, art, music, love poetry, and vast corpus of literature.

Misinterpreted verses

Certain Qur'ānic verses are employed by violent extremists to justify wholesale killing of civilians in the West. For example, 'Slay them wherever ye find them' [Q. 2:191]. These are commonly also employed by journalists to caricature all of Islam as a violent religion. Journalists often overlook the fact that those individuals and groups who declare war on fellow citizens and the state are referred to as rebels (al-baghy) under the Islāmic law, so the very legitimacy that they appeal to from the Qur'ān and hadīth does not in fact exist. It is important to place the above verse within its wider context:

> Fight in the way of God against those who fight against you, but begin not hostilities. Lo! God loveth not aggressors. And slay them wherever ye find them, and drive them out of the places whence they drove you out, for persecution is worse than slaughter. And fight not with them at the Inviolable Place of Worship until they first attack you there, but if they attack you (there) then slay them. Such is the reward of disbelievers. [Q. 2:190–191].

From a cursory examination, once placed within the preceding and following verses we discover that the Qur'ān itself provides the context. In this instance the Qur'ān lays down rules relating to warfare, this verse specifically restricts the fighting to only combatants. Ibn Kathīr, a classical commentator of the Qur'ān (1301–1373 CE) states:

> This Āyah means, 'Fight for the sake of Allah and do not be transgressors', such as, by committing prohibitions. Al-Hasan al-Basrī stated that transgression (indicated by the Āyah), 'includes mutilating the dead, theft (from the captured goods), killing women, children and old people who do not participate in warfare, killing priests and residents of houses of worship, burning down trees and killing animals without real benefit'. This is also the opinion of Ibn 'Abbās, 'Umar bin 'Abdul-'Aziz, Muqātil bin Hayyān and others.[1]

According to this perspective Muslims have the right to fight to drive out the polytheists from the place that they drove them out – that is Makkah and the Holy Sanctuary. Muslims were not sure whether they were permitted to fight within the holy sanctuary; this verse permits them to fight back in self-defence and does not in any way allow for the killing of civilians as violent extremists interpret it. Another one of the favourite verses of both violent extremists (religious and far-right) to justify either violence towards non-Muslims and for Islāmophobes to show that Islām is a violent religion is:

> 'Wherever you find the polytheists, kill them, seize them, besiege them, ambush them.' [Q. 9:5].

Once again, when we examine the verse in context, we discover that it provides an answer for its critics itself. It therefore merits quoting at some length.

> A release by God and His Messenger from the treaty you [believers] made with the polytheists [is announced] – you [polytheists] may move freely about the land for four months, but you should bear in mind both that you will not escape God, and that God will disgrace those who ignore [Him]. On the Day of the Great Pilgrimage [there will be] a proclamation from God and His Messenger to all people: 'God and His Messenger are released from [treaty] obligations to the polytheists. It will be better for you [polytheists] if you repent; know that you cannot escape God if you turn away.' [Prophet], warn those who ignore [God] that they will have a painful punishment. As for those who have honoured the treaty you made with them and who have not supported anyone against you: fulfil your agreement with them to the end of their term. God loves those who are mindful of Him. When the [four] forbidden months are over, wherever you find the

---

¹   See http://www.qtafsir.com/index.php?option=com_content&task=view&id=234 (accessed 1 September 2010).

polytheists, kill them, seize them, besiege them, ambush them – but if they turn [to God], maintain the prayer, and pay the prescribed alms, let them go on their way, for God is most forgiving and merciful. If any one of the polytheists should seek your protection [Prophet], grant it to him so that he may hear the word of God – then take him to a safe place – for they are people with no knowledge. What sort of treaty could these polytheists make with God and His Messenger? As for those with whom you made a treaty at the Sacred Mosque, so long as they remain true to you, be true to them; God loves those who are mindful of Him. [Q. 9:1–7].

This is a rich passage that there is not space to consider in detail, but we note that the verse employed by violent extremists in fact appears much later and the preceding verses place it within its context of revelation. Through examining it within its context we comprehend its true meaning, whereas through isolating it from its context, it is clearly misinterpreted. The Prophet is to grant protection to those polytheists who seek his protection and also to transport them to a 'safe place'. When we study the biography (sīrah) of the Prophet we discover that in reality the conquest of Makkah was achieved without a battle.

Establishing the facts

Checking and establishing the facts about any issue should be a basic requirement of journalism. If this had been done there would have been no confusion between the Oxford Centre for Islāmic Studies and the Central Oxford Mosque. The fact that no application was submitted for the 'call to prayer', no effective management was in place and no consultation had taken place with mosque membership, a basic journalistic rigour would have stopped the whole episode in its tracks. In this respect it is worth adding that the closure to the 'call to prayer' took place through an excellent piece by a Muslim reporter based at the BBC *Today* programme. She understood the community, was able to gain the trust of a bruised leadership and produced a piece that was well balanced and thoroughly researched.

Finally, what are the consequences of a failure to ensure a more balanced media reporting of Muslims, away from simple stereotyping but rooted in a more sophisticated and nuanced approach? One of the consequences has been the emergence of a vast array of satellite and e-media channels. This is a positive development on the whole but there is a downside. It is now possible to access media that simply reinforces individual and group prejudices and could potentially lead to further polarisation. For example, the images that Muslim audiences may be viewing on Aljazeera will be far different from what their neighbours may be viewing on the BBC. My point is that this deepens the stereotypes of the 'other' on both sides and is not conducive to the development of a cohesive society based upon mutual trust, respect and understanding. It is for this reason that we urgently require broadcasters with integrity, who produce well-balanced and thoroughly researched reports and who may be seen as balanced rather than perpetuators of caricatures and myths.

Chapter 11
Speaking on behalf of God ...

Jonathan Romain

Summary

This chapter places issues about religion in the news into a broader communicative context. Offering an overview of religious programming, Romain expresses a slight concern that a 'disproportionate number of long-running religious programmes are comedies'. He concedes that incongruity and humour are powerful media tools, but adds a concern that humour should be used more to illustrate a serious discussion than to 'fill up the slot' in the broadcasting schedule. More positively, Romain points out that religious programming has made a significant effort to allocate time to religious minorities, which has helped to disrupt unthinking stereotypes of these minorities.

  Romain also offers personal reflections on the challenges of maintaining integrity as a faith leader in the media spotlight: confidentiality must be maintained; the re-packaging of one's message by editors is notorious; the lure of publicity at the cost of respect; the expenditure of time on promotion instead of ministry; the risk of being misinterpreted; the risk of offering a different religious message to that of the majority of your faith group. Perhaps the most striking insight is Romain's remarks on the effect on the individual of becoming part of an interfaith media community. The cross-fertilisation of faiths promotes harmony and understanding, but it can also 'undermine some of the certainties you once had'. This process is healthy and enriching, but the fact that it is also unsettling is made evident by Romain's remarks.

Let me start with an overview of religion in the media and then hone in on the news angle. I think it is true to say that God's spokespeople are experiencing mixed fortunes in the media stakes at the moment.

  It is ironic that those who blazed an early trail in the communications industry and were responsible for brilliant innovations such as the two tablets of stone and the Gospels, along with powerful parables and mesmerising sermons, are now finding it hard to make their voices heard. Ask most people who is the most famous cleric in Britain and there is a very good chance that they will come up with the Vicar of Dibley. Even those who realise she is a fictional character will struggle to name a real one. This may in part be an indictment of real vicars not being able to make their mark nationally, but it is not helped by the insistence of producers to use secular figures to front religious programmes – such as Roger Bolton on

Sunday or Melvyn Bragg in *Faith in Our Times* – rather than trust a minister to be engaging and challenging. Normally, a scientist presents a science programme and an historian introduces a history series, so why are religious professionals not allowed the same opportunity? This makes it even more astonishing that there is indeed one Radio 4 programme that does have a religious presenter – the Reverend Richard Coles, who fronts *Saturday Live* – which is very popular yet which has virtually no religious content at all. All credit to him for both being a successful broadcaster and insisting that his title accompanies him, presumably as a deliberate statement to show that one can be religious and interesting. Yet how sad that the BBC's one media vicar occupies a religion-free zone.

Moreover, look at the scheduling timetable and you will find religious broadcasting banished to the very early hours of the morning or the very late slot, with the clear assumption that if you are at all interested in religious issues you must also be an insomniac. Equally annoying is the habit of putting on religious programmes on Sunday mornings when those most likely to appreciate them cannot do so as that is precisely the time when they are at church. Can you imagine the outcry if *Blue Peter* were shown whilst children were at school?

There is also a propensity to assume that the best way to tackle faith is through humour. A disproportionate number of long-running religious programmes are comedies – *Rev*, *The Vicar of Dibley*, *Father Ted* and *All Gas and Gaiters*. Humour is certainly a powerful tool that many a preacher employs, but usually in order to illustrate a serious point, not to fill up the slot. To be fair, amid these frustrations, there is also much to praise about the media's religious output. There have been some excellent productions – from the everlasting *Songs of Praise*, to short series such as *Friends Who Disagree* in which exponents of different faiths who respect each other examine the issues that divide them. Ernie Rae's *Beyond Belief* is another example of excellence. *Monastery* needs a mention too. Even *The Vicar of Dibley* had its merits, because, despite a few hiccups, Geraldine is depicted as a warm, caring human being and a minister one can trust – a definite advance from the buffoonery of Father Ted or Derek Nimmo's limp handshake of a character. In fact, Geraldine was sufficiently credible to help front the Make Poverty History campaign. Personally I would not have minded a parallel series by the same script-writers on 'The Rabbi of Dibley'.

What has been outstanding, though, has been the extent to which radio and television have allocated time to religious minorities and have taken great interest in different ethnic cultures. The BBC in particular has led the way in recognising religious diversity in Britain at a time when others were still reluctant to admit the new reality. Rabbis, Imams and Sikh leaders are not only familiar voices on *Thought for the Day* but are also *de rigeur*, alongside vicars and priests, on any religious programme, with the key words for producers being 'balance' and 'representation'. One important effect has been the destruction of many stereotypes. Those who previously associated Sikhs only with militant violence in the Punjab have been forced to re-evaluate after being exposed to the gentle wisdom of Indarjit Singh. Those who imagined rabbis as bearded foreigners divorced from everyday life have had to cope with clean-shaven Oxford graduate Lionel Blue and his homely accident-prone insights. In fact, not only has the media reflected change but it has also been an agent for change: I have met more imams and bishops in the television studio and 'green room' than ever I would have done in the High Street. It has created an interfaith media community that has led to a cross-fertilisation of ideas and personalities that might not otherwise have happened.

Of course, there is always the backdrop of figures about falling church attendance or shrinking synagogue membership which may give the impression that religion today is on the wane, and therefore deserves less coverage. Not true. The growth in new religious movements, the high number of conversions from one faith to another and the yearning for New Age spirituality indicate that religion is not declining, but it is changing. The big questions still remain: Who am I? What is the purpose of life? Why do things often seem to go wrong? What will happen to me in the next world? The challenge for mainstream faiths is to answer such concerns clearly and coherently, and if the public do not come to the pulpit then, for clerics, the media is the best way to reach them. It would be a great mistake for faith leaders to retreat from mainstream broadcasting and seek solace in the religious channels that are more common in the United States. We are commanded to stay in the public arena. I am sure it says somewhere in the Bible 'Thou shalt not abandon the average viewer, nor his son, nor his daughter, nor his live-in partner and her children'.

The onus, though, is on faith leaders to give a message that is worth hearing. We cannot expect the media to do our job for us and cannot expect broadcasters to push the faith on-air that we are failing to sell outside the studios. Likewise, we cannot blame them entirely when the stories they do cover do not come out in the way we want. We have to take half of the blame: for not briefing properly and for not getting our view over in a sympathetic or dynamic way. We have to recognise that if we want the media to be involved in our stories, it is part of our task to make their life easier. Let me suggest three ways in particular. First, it means accepting that there is no special pleading for religion – if we want coverage we have to earn it, through stories that are newsworthy and of genuine interest to the wider public. A press release on a new interpretation of a verse in the *Gospel of St John* that could dramatically advance biblical scholarship may be wonderful for those who devised it but is of little relevance to anyone else. However, a release on why there are strong religious reasons for legalising brothels, or what faith has to say about the possible discovery of intelligent life in space, may well deserve column inches or radio time.

Secondly, it also means accepting that religion does not have a deferential place – our stories have to stand up to the same journalistic criteria as all other types – and reporters who are rigorous about analysing political or economic news will rightly apply the same standards to faith matters. That includes pushing aside bluff, hypocrisy or double-speak. In turn, we should not resent such attempts and regard it as the media being 'out to get us', but view it as a natural part of investigative journalism. If our stories do not stand up to scrutiny, then we should not put them out in the first place. By way of example, Chief Rabbi Jonathan Sacks was very embarrassed when he was lambasted in 1997 by both the Jewish and non-Jewish press after it came to light that he had written a private letter attacking the much admired and recently deceased Reform rabbi Hugo Gryn. Sacks had not only described Gryn as 'among those who destroy the faith', but had done so shortly before he was due to speak in praise of him at his memorial service. It was a religious own-goal that deserved to be exposed. Many believe that he was being duplicitous and got found out. He has since apologised and moved to establish better relations with Reform synagogues.

Thirdly, it also means framing our stories in a way that is comprehensible – given the level of ignorance about religious detail either among some journalists or in the audience for whom they are catering. For instance, in a talk I delivered a few years ago I mentioned The Last Supper and was asked whether that meant the final meal before a nuclear war! I have long given up referring to the bread and wine which Jews have on the Sabbath eve as being akin to the Eucharist. It was obvious that people totally missed the analogy, and they either did not understand the reference or thought I was referring to a pop group, confusing it with the Eurythmics.

But while the media have been very good at representing a wide range of different faiths, what it has been less successful at is distinguishing between the different groups within each faith. It is a hard task, I admit, as many religious people are not sure either – but it is important to understand that the difference between Catholics and Protestants is not whether you like or dislike the Pope but, among other things, diverging views on the Eucharist and the nature of authority; or to know what divides Sunni and Shi'a Muslims, or to appreciate how Orthodox and Progressive Jews differ. In all such cases, it is not so much an exercise in theology but a way of understanding different trends that have social and political repercussions.

Still, if at this stage I feel an overwhelming desire to burst out with the cry 'Hallelujah', it is because it is so refreshing to have a media slot like this by invitation and not have to battle my way in and justify why a religious angle might be of interest. The reason it is often difficult for a religious voice to be heard in the general media is not only competition from so many other areas – such as politics, sport, and celebrity gossip – but because of two inherent media characteristics which are diametrically opposed to religious values. First, the media tends to concentrate on bad news – disasters, wars, skulduggery. Its key words are 'scandal' and 'horror'. In complete contrast, religion veers much more to good news: how people comfort or help each other. The word 'religion' comes from the verb 'religio', which has the root meaning of 'to bind together'. Our key words are 'enriching' and 'healing'. There is a major disparity of focus between the media and religion.

The second problem is that the central religious value is to love your neighbour as yourself, and not to throw stones at others, whereas the media thrives on confrontation and condemnation. It means that when the media does want a religious opinion, it instinctively goes for the most extreme – so as to provide sharp counterpoint – and therefore does us a double disservice: not only ignoring the moderate majority because we are not controversial enough, but also stereotyping religion as the preserve of the prejudiced. Even when vicars and rabbis who do not rant and rave get on air, there are serious problems to overcome. I will briefly list seven – the seven deadly media sins of Confidentiality – Prostitution – Energy levels – Hard calls – Hurting friends – the Voice of conscience – and Exposure.

Confidentiality: over time you come to know your colleagues pretty well, and I am sitting on some wonderful stories of clerical impropriety which would guarantee me front a page scoop in the *Sun* and even a demure mention in *The Times*. But I have to live with myself the next day, and also be able to have relationships with those around me based on trust and respect. I have a real dilemma coming up soon. I am writing a history of my congregation in Maidenhead. It will prove a good read for those living locally but frankly will not be of interest to anyone outside the area. However, if I include a chapter entitled 'Scandals', which would reveal some extraordinarily colourful stories to which I am privy, it would make the *News of the World* look tame by comparison and boost my sales hugely. Of course, I would change the names of those involved, but would it not still be breach of trust, putting marketing and Mammon ahead of communal harmony?

This leads to the second danger: Prostitution. There is a thin dividing line between helping the producers and editors package your message in a way that you feel is not quite you, but which they insist 'gets it across much better' – between that and acting in a way that becomes so alien that you are prostituting yourself and end up paying too heavy a price. I remember two instances of crossing that threshold: one was agreeing to be on the Kilroy television programme several years ago. It was on a serious subject: mixed-faith marriages, an issue in which I specialise, but it was reduced to vying physically for the microphone, with no real debate and just shouting slogans. When they asked me back some months later on another topic, I said 'no thanks'. One media scrummage was enough.

Even more squirm-inducing was the *Mail on Sunday*. I was doing some fund-raising for a lifeboat to be in memory of four Maidenhead boys who drowned during a school trip on the coast. I did an evening of sponsored religious jokes, which led to great hilarity and raised several thousand pounds. The media got hold of it, and while I was happy to retell a few of the jokes on television, the *Mail on Sunday* wanted to do a photograph with me on a bicycle balancing jokes books on my head and going cross-eyed – no doubt with a caption like 'Rollickin Rabbi's Heavenly Humour'. I felt that trying to look deliberately stupid was demeaning the memory of those four boys and the pain of their families. Although the publicity would have been useful, it was no longer the agenda I wanted, but had got hijacked by the photo editor's agenda; I refused to carry on and so they did not run the story. Conversely, just on the right side of the thin line between publicity and parody, between sticking to my message and selling out to someone else's, you may remember the very successful children's TV programme featuring cardboard characters Zig and Zag. One day I was asked to appear on the programme to explain what it was like being a rabbi and what the job involves. I cannot tell you how silly it felt bending down and talking to two pieces of painted cardboard one metre high, but as I found out afterwards from the countless parents who had watched with their children, it reached a surprisingly large audience and got across the essence of Judaism in a simple but effective way. It is not always easy to tell where boundaries lie.

Dilemma number three is: Energy and the extent to which it is invested. If you are doing a project you think worthwhile, how much energy do you expend promoting it? It is very time-consuming sending out press releases, trying to persuade editors it is a new issue that has not been covered before, that it is a human interest story, that it is substantial enough for them to include; so often it is tempting to say 'this is all wasting time I could better use in the project itself'. But then that means you fail to share the good news, abandon the airwaves and newspaper columns to items that you consider of comparatively little value. People inside the media often do not appreciate how difficult it is for those outside to make their voices heard.

A fourth dilemma is: Hard calls and whether to go public in the first place. As media spokesman for the Movement for Reform Judaism, I come across issues where we ought to speak out, but which I know will be misinterpreted or give offence. For instance, homosexuality: we are clear that being gay is not a sin or a perversion, but a natural state for those concerned; they were created homosexual by God, should not be subject to any discrimination, and their sexuality should not be a public issue at all. But saying that does upset some people, including more conservative members within our own ranks, and it would be much safer to stay quiet and concentrate on more acceptable issues – but would it be religious? Do we have a duty not to shy away from the media when it will lead to unpopularity? My answer is a resounding 'yes', but I am aware that being right does not stop one being vilified, while it may sometimes set one's cause back to go public too soon or too frequently.

The same applies with the fifth dilemma: Hurting others, especially friends. I have great respect for the commitment of former Cardinal Cormac Murphy O'Connor to inter-faith relations. But that meant it was hard being asked to go on ITN News to criticise him for something he said on an entirely different subject which many Jews found disturbing, when he compared the level of abortions that occurred being akin to the Holocaust. Do you say to yourself, 'look, he is a friend, turn a blind eye and in a few days the news will have moved on to something else'. Or do you think: 'if someone else had said that, there would be no question of a robust public response, so why give the Cardinal special favours?' In the end I did go into the studios, and although I was careful to criticise his policy, not him personally, of course the announcer slid them together with 'meanwhile the Cardinal has been attacked by Rabbi Jonathan Romain' ... and the message I gave got distorted.

This is connected with dilemma six: the Voice of conscience. What do you do when you feel that you disagree with something to which the rest of your faith group adheres? Because you are in the media, where you have the know-how and access to intervene, do you speak up and risk opprobrium, or toe the party line but feel deeply dishonest? I have had that struggle on two particular issues that many other rabbis support but I do not – one was the government proposal to introduce Holocaust Memorial Day, which I thought was the wrong name and should be broadened beyond a specifically Jewish experience to include all who suffer from prejudice and persecution – and be called instead Victims Day or Tolerance Day, but not Holocaust Day. I am also against the current rush to build faith-based schools – be they Jewish, Muslim or others – because however good their intentions, they result in children being segregated and that breeds ignorance, suspicion and hostility – which I feel is bad for the faith groups and disastrous for society as a whole. Both of these viewpoints are minority positions among rabbis – but I have access to the media – and balancing conscience and consensus is an awesome responsibility.

The seventh media challenge – personal Exposure – arises from the fact that, when working with religious programmes, you very often meet fascinating people from other faiths. It gets you thinking: 'well, they are so strong in their faith and it makes a lot of sense in many ways ... maybe my version is not the only path, or even the best of many, just one of many'. It makes you less absolute, more relative, and while you can be genuinely enriched by the interfaith contact, it can also undermine some of the certainties you once had (which you might think is for the good anyway), nevertheless, it can be a scary experience when you first encounter it. It can also mean that when you then go back to your own faith community you are not quite so at home as before with the other people there and the more limited horizons they have. It can be very painful encountering what previously was familiar to you but now appears as prejudice. One result is that there is a middle group evolving in this country in-between those of faith and those of no faith: an interfaith community in which a remarkable cross-fertilisation of ideas and experiences is occurring, and those in the religious media are often in the very midst of it.

In conclusion, amid all of the various challenges and dilemmas I have listed, my one Golden Rule for media survival is 'remember your roots'. A religious image which illustrates that best is Jacob's ladder, the one that appeared in a dream he had, where a ladder stretches from earth to heaven (Genesis 28.12). Religious figures may achieve dizzying heights through the media, and reach out to mass audiences, but their ladder has to be resting solidly on personal integrity and core beliefs, otherwise it will lack firm foundations and will eventually topple over. So, from this side of the microphone, it means aiming high but never forgetting the religious values that sustain us.

Chapter 12
Respect, Religion and the News

Indarjit Singh

Summary

The idea of news as a commodity is the focus of this chapter. Singh points out that the nature of a commodity is to meet 'the tastes and prejudices of targeted audiences'. What does it say about the appetite of consumers of news that negative stories predominate, particularly in the coverage of religion? Singh offers the answer that such negativity gives us 'reassurance that our behaviour is no worse than some of the things religious people get up to'.

Singh illustrates the focus on negative reporting by contrasting the lack of coverage of a high profile Sikh celebration against the coverage of the protest against the performance of the play Behzti. *Did the protest attempt to 'destroy theatres' or was it, for the most part, peaceful? Only a bystander's letter in* The Times *gave much indication that the protest was not bent on destruction.*

Singh differentiates his concerns about the play and about negative reporting from an objection to 'free speech'. Free speech is emphasised as a value embraced in Sikhism, along with equality and toleration. The difficulty, for Singh, is not freedom of speech but the selective focus and labelling involved in constructing the news.

News is generally understood to be objective information about life around us. In reality it is processed information and, like processed food, it is often presented in an attractive way that sometimes has little regard for the purity of what we get. News is a commodity, a commodity that sells, particularly if it is presented in a way that meets the tastes and prejudices of targeted audiences. Before going on to develop this theme, let me tell you an interesting story about such prejudice.

A few years ago, on reaching home after doing a broadcast on *Thought for the Day*, I received a phone call from the editor of a popular tabloid asking if I would like to write a regular column for their paper. It sounded interesting. I knew that the fees paid by tabloids are far higher than those paid by papers like *The Times* or the *Guardian*. The voice at the other end of the phone then went on to say that 'Asians are OK; they're making a positive contribution to British society; it's the blacks that are the problem!' My dream of a nice ready earner was immediately shattered and I said I wasn't really interested. A bit taken aback, the editor, who had just been listening to a Sikh talking on *Thought for the Day* added 'you are a Muslim, aren't you?'. This was before 9/11.

The media – newspapers, radio, TV and the internet – all quite understandably look to ratings, sales and earnings. Stories must appeal to emotion and sentiments of prejudice. Sadly, truth, balance and objectivity are often the casualties, as are the lives of innocent citizens as shown in the 2011 phone-hacking scandal. This particularly applies to news about religion. Religion makes good news, not for its ethical teachings, but because of our appetite for negative stories that give us reassurance that our behaviour is no worse than some of the things religious people get up to. We love negative stories about politicians and others in public life for much the same reasons. We Sikhs often complain that we are generally ignored by the media, but when we look at the content of so-called religious stories, perhaps we should be grateful.

The teachings of Sikhism, like emphasis on gender equality and respect for other faiths and other ways of life – the key to tackling extremism – do not excite passion or prejudice. Such teachings, though very relevant to the world of today, do not make catchy headlines and are therefore generally ignored. Statistics show that that between 2000 and 2008, the BBC carried more than 40 TV programmes on Islam, three on Hinduism and one very bad one on Sikhs called *Sikhs and the City*. Negative and derogatory stories about Muslims, however, have increased dramatically since 9/11. *Guardian* online comment statistics show 157 stories on the controversy over the Mohammed cartoons. The same statistics refer to 2,000 pieces on Christianity and a total of 2,000 on Islam. Nothing on Sikhism – we must have behaved!

In September 2004, the Network of Sikh Organisations (NSO) organised a national celebration of the 400th anniversary of the first reading of the Guru Granth Sahib in a packed Royal Albert Hall. It was a huge and highly significant occasion. HRH the Prince of Wales, Prime Minister Tony Blair, Michael Howard (the Leader of the Opposition) and Simon Hughes for the Liberal Democrats, joined the Bishop of London and the Chief Rabbi in the celebrations. We asked the newspapers, radio and TV to cover the event. The media, however, felt that there was no religious controversy in the celebration and therefore it was not newsworthy.

But Sikhs became national news a few months later, following Sikh concerns about a fictional play called *Behzti* in which paedophilia, rape, wife beating, drug abuse and murder accompanied by foul and obscene language was set in a Sikh place of worship.[1]

The play was staged over Christmas (the Christian season of goodwill to all). The backdrop showed Sikh holy artefacts, and the screams of the rape victim were accompanied by Sikh religious music. The play, defended by the theatre establishment as a serious work, was advertised with a poster showing a pair of lady's panties and was clearly designed to attract the lowest denominator of taste and appeal to those wanting to have a cheap laugh and leave with BNP-type prejudices reinforced, as hate mail received by myself and others demonstrated.

---

[1] For a different perspective on this play, see Jonathan Heawood's discussion of 'Taking Offence: Free Speech, Blasphemy and the Media' in chapter 16 of this book.

A Christian bystander at an overwhelmingly peaceful demonstration against the play pointed out in a letter to *The Times* that the demonstrators, demonised by the media, included parents, children and grandparents of both Sikhs and non-Sikhs. Sadly, on the Saturday evening, after a week of peaceful protest, a handful of demonstrators threw some stones. A couple of windows were broken and three people were taken into custody. But hype helps in the selling of news. The demonstration was described as a riot and Sikhs were accused on BBC2's *Newsnight* of 'destroying theatres'.

This opportunity for negative portrayal immediately made Sikhs newsworthy. The press went into overdrive with banner headlines, in an unsympathetic diatribe against the entire Sikh community with the mantra 'freedom of speech' being used to defend the right to slur and insult a small and visible minority. Incidentally, the demonstrators here were rightly referred to as Sikhs. But when Muslims demonstrated against British soldiers coming back from Iraq and Afghanistan, they are referred to as 'Asians'. Why? Why the use of the camouflage word 'Asian'? Was it to dilute public anger against the more powerful Muslim community by spreading it to unfairly include Hindus and Sikhs?

Coming back to 'freedom of speech', most people will agree that the concept of free speech, like that of human rights, is a good thing. But rights are limited by responsibilities. None of us have the right to say what we like, when we like and wherever we like in ways designed to threaten or harm. It is rightly against the law of the land. Language, the power to communicate our emotions and hopes and fears, is important to civilised society, but words can also manipulate public perceptions and, as history shows again and again, can become instrumental in generating prejudice and act as incitements to wound and kill.

The one area where Sikhs believe that the right to freedom of speech is absolute is the right to criticise those in authority who misuse their power for their own ends; particularly political and religious leaders who over the centuries have done so by torturing or killing those who disagree with them. The need, and indeed the responsibility, to criticise such behaviour, and stand up for those being oppressed, is central to Sikh teaching.

Our 9th Guru, Guru Teg Bahadhur, gave his life defending the rights of non-Sikhs to freedom of worship, taking defence of freedom of expression to a higher plane. Sikhs believe, however, that freedom of expression carries with it an attached responsibility to respect the rights and sensitivities of others. Sadly, a wide range of media frequently use, or misuse, the term 'free speech' simply to suit their own political agenda. Perhaps it should reflect on Kipling's words: 'give us the strength that can never seek, by thought or deed to hurt the weak'.

Alongside freedom of speech we should also consider selective media and government silence over evil behaviour in so-called friendly countries. Most of us here today will know that the year 2009 marked the twentieth anniversary of tanks and killings in China's Tiananmen Square. But how many are aware that it was also the twenty-fifth anniversary of the organised mass killing of more than 5,000 Sikhs throughout India. Why the disproportionate media coverage? Can it be that there is a tacit political and media understanding that for friendly countries, trade and political understanding become more important than the gross abuse of human rights? In 1984, I spoke to a senior UK cabinet minister about the government-inspired killing of Sikhs in India. He responded: 'We know what is going on. We are walking on a tightrope and have already lost one important contract with the Indian government' (The Westland helicopter contract).

For many of us, it is often difficult to know who is the 'goody or baddy' in the complex world of today and, unfortunately, we are often content to have our thinking done for us. The media plays on our reluctance to think for ourselves by helpfully labelling groups as 'terrorists', 'extremists', 'fundamentalists' and 'fanatics', to arouse sentiments of dislike or hate. Governments throughout the world, aided and abetted by the media do this all the time. Mahatma Gandhi and Nelson Mandela were both universally described as terrorists in their time. Following the government attack on the Golden Temple in 1984, Sikhs on the receiving end of state terror were labelled terrorists and extremists and these terms were readily picked up by the media in this country.

A true story illustrates the absurdity of the use of such terms to induce prejudice or hate. Soon after the attack on the Golden Temple, I was visited early one Sunday morning by two Scotland Yard officers who said they were talking to prominent Sikhs about possible repercussions here, of events in India. I liked the word 'prominent' and invited them in. They asked me if I was an extremist or a moderate. I replied that I was extremely moderate. Confused, they said they were concerned about fundamentalists. I said a fundamentalist Sikh was one who believed in the fundamentals of Sikhism like belief in the equality of all human beings, full gender equality, respect for the beliefs of others, as shown by the inclusion of Hindu and Muslim verses in our holy book, the Guru Granth Sahib, and a belief in looking after the wellbeing of the less fortunate. Yes, I continued, I tried to follow Sikh fundamentals.

Today the news media are full of these shorthand prompts to arouse fear or hate. There are also absurd, meaningless terms like 'war on terror' – as if we can really go to war against an abstract noun. Words used to justify questionable incursions in other lands. At a meeting of the International Commission of Jurists in Warsaw in September 2009, I argued that in talking about supposed terrorist activity, we should bear in mind that governments in many countries are not always benign, and not infrequently inflict terror on their own people for political ends, smearing those that resist as antinational, extremist or terrorist to justify repressive action.

Let me summarise. The news we read or listen to, particularly news about religion is often highly slanted or adulterated. What do we need to do to improve things? At a conference I attended in Windsor on 'News and the Media' we were reminded again and again about the importance of media training for faith communities to get their message across. Yes, it is important, but perhaps it is even more important for the media to learn more about newer faith communities. Much more needs to be done by all of us to remove damaging ignorance on which prejudice thrives. My request to the media is: go easy on smear words. Let us make our own minds up on key issues. On the mantra of 'free speech', consumer programmes tell us to be wary of things that are described as free. This should include the use of terms like free speech to justify the use of language designed to play on prejudice. The media should make clear that free speech is not an absolute right, but that one that carries attached responsibilities.

For me as a Sikh, free speech and its attached responsibilities are inextricably linked to religious teaching. It is right to discuss and hold different views on such teachings. Using the right of free speech to portray a negative view of religion clearly may help to sell papers or boost TV ratings, but it also harms society as a whole. Today the important ethical teachings of religion are largely ignored because religious leadership tends to focus on peripheral issues and these failings are compounded by a hostile media which sees religion as fair game for popular ridicule.

This negative view of religion has increased since 9/11 as seen in government initiatives like 'Prevent', which sees religion as a problem that needs to be contained, rather than important advice on balanced and ethical living. Today, we need the teachings of religion more than ever before to move us away from greed and selfishness, which seems to be on the increase in both public and private life, to concern for others and more balanced and responsible living

What commonly passes for religion today is an overlay of ritual, superstition, culture and bigotry that often buries underlying ethical teachings. We all have a responsibility to bring the ethical values to the fore, values that are the key to tackling many social concerns. The media are not exempt from this responsibility and can play an important role in robustly questioning intolerant practices that have grafted themselves on to our different religions and have little to do with ethical teachings. A sea-change in attitudes to reporting on religion is required but the gain to society would be enormous.

Chapter 13
Popular Media, News and Religion

Roger Royle

Summary

Roger Royle draws on over twenty years of broadcasting experience to offer reflections on the challenges of presenting religion in the news and other popular media. His chapter offers a range of stories that illustrate the complexities of 'broad-casting' news about religion, without distorting or patronising the audience. Recognising the difficulty of maintaining the integrity of both religion and the news story, Royle argues that treating 'religion in a lighter way' is essential if the values of religion are to be communicated to an audience 'for whom "talking heads" would have been a turn off'. This approach robustly refutes 'intellectual snobbery'. Along with a discussion of capturing and engaging audiences by embracing the media's desire for the outlandish, Royle offers a series of insights into the difficulties raised by 'compliance', political correctness, and dealing with complaints from pressure groups even from within one's own faith tradition. Referring to the 'Jonathan Ross/Russell Brand debacle', Royle reflects on the cautious media culture that has emerged from it. Offending people is of course unacceptable, but it must also be recognised that there are times when taking a broadcasting risk encourages people to 'rethink their attitude to life and certainly to religion'.

Is there an inevitable clash of values – even vocabularies – between religious representatives and journalists? Royle discusses this too, pointing out the difficulty of conveying the 'divine mystery in Sun-speak', and also the disparity between the media's love of celebrity and religion's emphasis on the equality of humankind before God. These differences may exist, but Royle concludes by insisting that religious representatives must not shy away from the challenge: 'religion has to be answerable for its beliefs and its actions in a way that is intelligible'.

The path down which I am about to take you may well be different from those travelled by many of the other contributors to this book. For those of you whose experience of 'religion and the news' comes from what used to be called the 'broadsheets' or BBC Radio 4 will have little knowledge of the world I have inhabited for the past thirty years.

This will be a very personal journey and will reflect my thoughts as a freelance broadcaster and journalist. Those involved in the administration or production of religious programmes and articles may disagree strongly. However, I believe that what I have to say needs to be heard.

My life, my ministry, has been to serve the 'popular' end of the media market. My world has been that of BBC1's *Songs of Praise*, BBC Radio 2's *Good Morning Sunday*, *Sunday Half Hour* and *Pause for Thought*. In years long gone I was involved with ITV1's Sunday evening religious output and the long departed *Epilogues* which came at the close of the evening's viewing. In print I contributed weekly articles to *Woman's Realm* and then *Woman's Weekly*.

None of these programmes or articles would come under the category of news but they were all religious and, as many of them were 'live', they needed to comment on current affairs. Some of the programmes could well be categorised as 'entertainment'. This, however, did not stop them from being newsworthy and in many cases they attracted a large audience.

It was within the world of the popular media that I felt at home. Not for me the protected world of the religious press or even a religious radio station, which, to me, can be seen as ghetto media. So as to experience the same demands and insecurities as other professional broadcasters and journalists I chose, in the main, to earn my living by being a religious broadcaster in a secular world.

In neither my journalism nor my broadcasting was I analysing in depth the breaking news stories of the day but was trying, in some way, to capture the essence of the story while maintaining a popular appeal. It is not easy to treat religion in a lighter way while keeping the integrity of both religion and the news story, unlike when you are broadcasting to a focused audience in a more serious way.

There was one problem I came up against: intellectual snobbery. It is certainly rife in the Church of England and holds large sway in the BBC's Department of Religion and Ethics. A culture seems to have grown up in the department that, consciously or unconsciously, seems to believe that anything second best will do for Radio 2. This can result in the audience being patronised and not always challenged in the way it should be.

Some of the broadcasting I did, especially on ITV's Sunday evening religious programme, *Royle Progress*, could be described as 'sugaring the pill'. News stories were presented in an entertaining way. *Royle Progress* was the first religious programme to have an audience. Many had had a congregation, but this was different. Not once were they asked to sing a hymn but they were encouraged to laugh and applaud. One of the stories we tackled was about a church on the Isle of Wight that was due to be turned into a snooker hall. The director, Bryan Izzard, who had great experience with light entertainment but was at one time also responsible for ITV's arts programmes, decided that rather than a straightforward interview with the church authorities the item should start with me playing snooker with Terry Griffiths and beating him. Having captured the attention of the audience, it was hoped they would stay with us when we discussed the serious matter of whether churches should be used in this way.

Once, before discussing the sensitive subject of hospices, I did an item about some parachuting nuns. They were raising money for a hospice. The novelty element of nuns descending from the sky hopefully encouraged viewers to stay tuned as we discussed the care of the dying. Again, for the sort of audience we were hoping, and in the main succeeding, to attract was an audience for whom 'talking heads' would have been a turn off.

Sadly, Southern Television lost the franchise, so I found a new home with Ulster Television, presenting a programme which went out locally after the *News at Ten* on a Monday evening. Both the day and the time of this programme, *The Royle Line*, attracted me. Here was a religious programme being transmitted outside the proscribed Sunday 'God slot'. However, in the early eighties, with the Northern Ireland 'troubles' at their height, the word 'eggshells' came immediately to mind. The need to be sensitive was imperative. But there were ways of discussing the 'troubles' without making matters worse. On one occasion I found myself on a sponsored charity run with both Catholics and Protestants. Asking three Catholic priests what they were doing mixing with a crowd like this may not have been seen as the most sensitive of opening questions but it did lead to a worthwhile conversation as to how wounds should be healed. There is no doubt that such a question would be vetoed today, when 'compliance' is more important than content.

A degree of sensitivity was also needed when questioning the interviewees on *Songs of Praise*. Again, this was in no way a 'news' programme but, because I was talking to people about their everyday lives, topics were bound to arise that questioned the state of the world in which we lived. Once it nearly went very badly wrong. I was in Northern Ireland. During my five years with *Songs of Praise*, I did most of the programmes from that part of the United Kingdom. The director was a very talented easy to work with Roman Catholic priest. My interviewee, according to my notes, was a former paramilitary member. Although the questioning was gentle, no Paxman/Humphries interrogation here, I naturally got onto the question of violence and how he could justify it. At which moment he asked for the recording to be stopped. 'Why are you asking me all these questions about violence?', he enquired. 'Because you are an ex-paramilitary member', I replied. 'I'm not, I'm an ex-alcoholic'. We restarted the interview!

Good Morning Sunday, which is now presented by Aled Jones, goes out on Radio 2, while Radio 4 listeners are tuned into *Sunday*. *Sunday* is very much a current affairs programme covering matters of faith and religious news. *Good Morning Sunday* is a mixture of music, interviews and dedications. The listeners, on the whole, knew I was an Anglican priest and what I said reflected my thoughts and my faith. I greatly appreciated the freedom I was given, which I hope I used responsibly. Today the programme is mainly scripted and so a tighter eye is kept on what is being said.

Amongst my regular guests were Rabbi Hugo Gryn and the then Bishop of Stepney, Jim Thompson. Although they did what we referred to as the 'prayer slot', both of them believed that your faith should affect your way of life and so neither shied away from what could be seen as sensitive subjects. Some of the other guests, such as Tony Benn and Edward Heath, were not exactly 'non-political'.

One Christmas morning I presented a programme that celebrated Christmas around the world. South Africa was represented by Archbishop Desmond Tutu. In a pre-recorded interview I asked him first how he would be spending Christmas and then what he thought South Africa wanted for Christmas. Bearing in mind apartheid was still the order of the day, he replied, 'Hope, because without hope we are lost'. On that note I wished the Archbishop a happy Christmas and played the next carol. The very fact Archbishop Tutu was chosen to represent South Africa greatly annoyed a right-wing Tory MP, who lost no time in making his opinion heard by the powers that be. The matter was resolved when he and I had coffee together in the Palace of Westminster!

The live Christmas day programme came, on several occasions, from Bethlehem. Once again, 'eggshells' were on my mind. Even the way that part of the world is referred to is complicated. Once, when I was recording a piece from the Herodian, I mentioned the 'Judaean wilderness'. A phone call was made to the BBC's Department of Religion and Ethics in Manchester to check whether this was acceptable.

The BBC produced a CD guideline as to what could and could not be said when talking about Israel and Palestine. Some Israeli as well as some Christian pressure groups are powerful. They keep a keen ear and eye open to what is being said, and the moment they disagree they are not backward in coming forward, as I know to my own cost. Pressure groups can have great influence and can make life uncomfortable for broadcasters.

However, pressure groups pale into insignificance compared with 'compliance'. Since the Jonathan Ross/Russell Brand debacle during which the much-loved actor Andrew Sachs was verbally abused, the BBC has been forced to watch its tongue. A ninety-second script for *Pause for Thought* on Radio 2 Chris Evans' *Breakfast Show* has to be checked by a producer and then rechecked by a senior producer. Anything that is thought not to 'comply' is seized upon. 'Political Correctness', 'Compliance's' comrade in arms, is often taken to greater lengths than I think it needs to be. But, naturally, the producer has the last say. Like its Radio 4 equivalent *Thought for the Day*, Radio 2's *Pause for Thought* is often topical. This is both a privilege and a responsibility and getting it right so it sits easily in a fast-moving morning breakfast show, as well as saying something meaningful, is not easy. While the editor and producer want something with an edge, when it is submitted it is often not accepted. Although they might encourage something controversial, they are very fearful it might be offensive. Then, controversy is often offensive to some.

Within the BBC's Department of Religion and Ethics there appears to me to be a fear of offending. In my view, this can constrict the boundaries to an extent that the freedom of taking a risk is no longer an option. Fortunately, Christ did not have a similar fear, even though it cost him his life. Offending people for the sake of offending has little point and can be just downright rude and unacceptable. However, there are times when people need to rethink their attitude to life and certainly to religion.

When presenting Radio 2's 70-year-old programme, *Sunday Half Hour*, I offended some listeners by remembering the departed in the final blessing. Most weeks I would ask for God's blessing on those we love both 'in this world and the next'. My reason for this was twofold. First of all, many of the listeners had been bereaved. Time and again they told me in their letters and e-mails that they used to listen to the programme with either their husband or wife, mother or father, brother or sister, but since they had died they now listened alone. So it became a special time for remembrance for them. Secondly, my father had died when I was a one-year-old. Remembering him has always been an important part of my prayer life. This was something on which I was not prepared to give in and for which I fortunately had my producer's backing. This was despite complaints to top brass in the BBC from influential Christians. I thought it only fair that sometimes I did not mention the departed out of respect to those who did not agree with me.

Although *Sunday Half Hour* is recorded, there were times when, because of particular events, the programme had to be re-recorded. On the death of the Princess of Wales I had to make my way through torrential storms in the Cheddar Gorge to re-record the programme in Bristol. When the Queen Mother died I was in Dominica, so someone else had to record fresh links to reflect the sadness the nation felt.

At the end of the first Gulf War I had to record a special programme from a church in Farnham in Surrey. We finished the recording half an hour before the programme was transmitted. Had it gone out live I wouldn't have been able to present it because at that time I was banned by the BBC from doing live broadcasts. During the war I had been to visit the Navy in the Gulf along with a delightful and very amusing comedian, Stan Taylor. When we visited the ships I gave a short 'uplift' talk before Stan went into his routine. In talking with the men afterwards, one of the things I discovered was that they resented having to pay for the phone calls home. The Americans got free phone calls. They were also none too pleased that most of their calls were spent correcting the misinformation their loved ones had received through the British media.

During my visit I made several broadcasts back to Britain from the ships, and on my return I did *Pause for Thought* with Derek Jameson on Radio 2. After I had done my set piece, Derek asked how it was for 'our boys' in the Gulf. I told him of their frustrations, adding that earlier that morning I had heard a BBC broadcasting on Radio 4 of what they said was a confidential document about the war, to which I objected. 'Confidential documents are meant to be kept confidential', I maintained in my naivety. This was brought to the attention of Jenny Abramsky, the then head of BBC Radio, and she had me banned. When I consulted David Hatch who, in his time, was a performer, a producer and a controller at the BBC and incidentally was also a child of the vicarage, he advised me 'to apologise and plead insanity'!

Religion and the media, let alone the news, are not easy bedfellows. Whereas the news wants soundbites, religion prefers to offer detailed, thought-through explanations. Apart from being a cartoonist's delight, the present Archbishop of Canterbury, The Most Reverend Rowan Williams, is a headline writer's nightmare. He does not do soundbites. His voice is a delight to listen to but what he has to say demands concentration, something not readily available in today's world. However, I do not think he has always been given the right advice. You only have to think of his lecture to lawyers, which involved some comment about Sharia law, discussed in earlier chapters, to realise that he needed guidance as to how the media might react. The popular media is certainly not his metier. So once, when I went to interview him on the meaning and value of the parables, I suggested that he illustrate with a story any point he wished to make and resist the urge to take off into the theological stratosphere. He was brilliant; like the Lord he serves, the Archbishop is an excellent storyteller.

The world of religion does not see things in the same way as the media. Yes, religion certainly has its standards and its beliefs, but for thinking believers it does not dwell in the black and white world that certain parts of the media delight in. Fundamentalists, of all faiths or none, are a godsend to the media. They know what they believe. They know what is right and what is wrong, and furthermore they are not afraid to say so. This then naturally leads to confrontation, one of the media's greatest delights.

Whereas religion may look for reconciliation, it is recrimination that's on the media's agenda. Religion, certainly in the form of Christianity, claims to spread the 'Good News'. That is the last thing a news editor wants. Good news does not sell, whereas bad news does.

Stories that show those who practise religion in a bad light or as hypocrites are always good news fodder. This is certainly true when it comes to sex or quarrels within what are meant to be loving communities.

The language of religion differs greatly from the language of most journalists. This can cause confusion. How do you convey a divine mystery in *Sun*-speak? The titles and organisational structures used by religion are also confusing. Making them understandable to the person on the Clapham omnibus is not easy, and religion does not go out of its way to make it any easier. So misunderstandings can and do easily arise.

Assuming a common understanding of the biblical stories is no longer wise. Whereas at one time you could refer to the 'patience of Job' or the 'wisdom of Solomon' you no longer can. You may get away with anything relating to Noah because of his ark and the animals, and the story of Joseph has been saved for posterity thanks to the skills of Tim Rice and Andrew Lloyd Webber. But calling someone 'a Judas' may have little or no meaning. So the communication gap between religion and the news media continues.

Ignorance rears its head in other ways as well. Earlier this year, I was listening to the Chief Rabbi giving a short broadcast on Radio 2 on the meaning and value of the Ten Commandments. As far as I was concerned, it was a superb broadcast. It was to the point, well-illustrated, very accessible and well delivered. However, the piece of music that followed was 'The Light of the World'. I am certain that this was in no way meant to be offensive, but it could easily have been.

One of the ways in which religion has benefited in the current secular climate is the growth of atheism. With people like Richard Dawkins, atheists now have a voice which is heard. Nor are they backwards in coming forwards when such subjects as medical ethics or the teaching of creation are being discussed. However, because of the BBC's insistence on balance, it means that when an atheist is interviewed so must be a believer. This sort of discussion may not always shed light because whereas the atheist knows exactly what he does or does not believe, the believer may not be quite so certain or even dogmatic in what he or she believes. Obviously, most interviewers will do their utmost to create confrontation but sadly for them not all believers will play the game. Religion has been given a great airing thanks to atheists and not just through the news media. When Philip Pullman's two-part play, *His Dark Materials*, was in repertoire at the National Theatre, time was found for a platform presentation with the Archbishop of Canterbury and Pullman in conversation.

There is another area in which religion and the news media find themselves poles apart, and that is as regards the cult of the 'celebrity'. Apart from some of the well-known Pentecostal preachers, the Christian Church prefers to see its ministers in the role of John the Baptist rather than taking centre stage. The Gospel text, 'Sir, we would see Jesus' is often given as a guide to Christian ministers; they are to remember that they are only the messenger. It is Christ people need to see through their teaching, their behaviour, their whole lives.

However, the late Pope John Paul II certainly became a 'celebrity' because of his devotion to Our Lady and his determination to spread the word, encouraging the faithful; he became an international megastar. Kissing the tarmac, his signature sign on arrival in a new country, was a news photographer's dream shot. Touring in his 'Popemobile' made him the centre of attention at any open-air gathering. The fact that he was Polish and could speak a multitude of languages made him marketable across the globe. Leaders of other nations visited him regularly in the full glare of publicity. Although he preached Christ, he was not ashamed to use his particular personality gifts to further his cause, and the news media loved him.

For his successor, Pope Benedict, things have not been so easy. Here is an intellectual, a German, someone associated in times past with the Hitler Youth, and a leader faced with the daunting task of bringing healing to those who have suffered sexual abuse at the hands of the Roman Catholic clergy. Here, again, is a person who has attracted the attention of the news media, but this time in what has often been a hostile manner: so hostile that it was thought by some to be an organised campaign to bring him down.

The press love personalities. When the former MP Anne Widdecombe was received into the Roman Catholic Church there was no shortage of reporters to cover the occasion. The Archbishop of York, the Most Reverend John Sentamu, cutting up his clerical collar or camping in his cathedral, York Minster, provided precious pictures for the press. Here was a minister who was a character doing something unusual. But then, York Minster is no stranger to publicity. It was struck by lightning when the controversial priest, David Jenkins, was about to be consecrated Bishop of Durham. This story brought joy to news editors and soothsayers alike.

The controversy over the appointment of the first outwardly gay bishop in New Hampshire in the USA, The Right Reverend Gene Robinson, gave the press two bites of the cherry. Here was a personality and a controversy, who could ask for more?

Divisions within the Church of England are grist to the media mill. The consecration of women bishops and the ordination of gay men or women as priests, subjects that divide the church, can always find space in the pages of our papers. What is even better is if a paper can engage a bishop or former archbishop to take up the cudgels for the side that sees itself as oppressed. Once again, controversy and celebrity are brought together in a common cause and the cause of religion generally suffers.

The wearing of religious symbols or dress, the acceptance of gay couples as boarders in bed and breakfast accommodation and attitudes towards medical ethics are but a few of the causes about which religious people have views which they are prepared to defend. Here again the news media is only too ready to highlight the divisions, either between differing religious groups or the rest of the world and religious groups.

The chance of religion reconciling itself to the personality and controversy demands of the news media is extremely slender. Somehow religion will have to learn to live with it. The thought of the world of religion employing specialised spin doctors to present its case would be abhorrent to the vast majority of believers. However, organised religion needs to work hard to make sure that it puts forward its case in a way that is understandable to the modern media. This will involve understanding how the news media now operates. People are no longer gathered round their cat's whisker radio waiting to be addressed at 6pm. The aggressive nature of today's 24-hour news gathering has to be understood and coped with. It is not a comfortable world to be part of, possibly it never was, but it can never have been so instant, so global and so cut-throat as it is today.

Religion cannot expect to live in a private bubble protected from the rest of the world. Nor can it demand respect it has not earned. Associated as it is with many of the world's troubles, religion has to be answerable for its beliefs and its actions in a way that is intelligible. Gobbledegook and religious clichés do not encourage greater understanding and so are sensibly ignored. Hopefully, in turn, the news media, while not bowing the knee or touching their forelock to religion, will take the trouble to try to understand where religion is coming from so as to produce clarity rather than confusion when reporting religious matters.

Reconciling Religion in Worlds of Violence

Ruth Scott

Summary

In Chapter 14, Ruth Scott draws on her personal experience of peace-building work in Northern Ireland to discuss the concept of balance in reporting religion. In situations of violent conflict, balanced and nuanced reporting is crucial. Twenty-four-hour news cycles and the pressure to produce a 'story' mean that media reporting on religion often lacks balance, and there is little appreciation of the diversity and complexity of different religious viewpoints: 'We cannot speak of the Christian/Muslim/Hindu/Atheist position', Scott writes, 'but only a Christian/ Muslim/Hindu/Atheist position.' Yet, as well as calling for greater balance and nuance in reporting religion, Scott's experience in broadcasting and peace-building also leads her to question the notion of 'balance' itself. What constitutes a balanced picture?

Addressing the coverage of the Truth and Reconciliation Commission, for example, Scott points out that Archbishop Desmond Tutu's encouragement to forgive was not universally welcomed: 'For some the idea of forgiveness was an anathema; a religious imposition'. Why, she asks, did the dissenting voices receive such little coverage? 'Did journalists feel that the extraordinary changes in South Africa, the ending of apartheid, and the creativity of the TRC had such a profoundly positive effect in the world that certain dissenting voices should not be heard?' Ultimately Scott's argument is that finding the 'right balance' may, after all, be impossible. Better then, would be to require an acknowledgement that reporting is always from a perspective: 'everyone stands in a particular place'.

'Reconciliation' is a word much abused by people who have little experience of violent conflict. Such is its complexity that reconciliation may not be possible in the lifetime of those who call for it. While individuals and communities may descend rapidly into violent conflict, peace-building is a slow, fragile process that is easily destabilised. From the outside, for example, Northern Ireland in 2012 may appear to be a province that has moved beyond its inadequately termed 'Troubles'. Those living in the working class communities from which many paramilitaries were recruited and those who are ex-paramilitaries or who work with them, will know the tensions and potential for violence in new generations that exists beyond the awareness of people who look on from a distance and perceive reconciliation as something done and dusted.

Reconciliation does not always look like we expect. While members of the UVF (Loyalist paramilitaries) and IRA (Republican paramilitaries) were bombing and shooting one another on the streets of Northern Ireland in the 1970s their leaders were, out of necessity, starting to talk to one another in the 'cages' of Long Kesh prison and, later, the 'H' blocks of the Maze prison. While the violence between their organisations carried on, they slowly built lines of communication in and beyond prison life that, over time, helped pave the way to the peace process unfolding today. Such conversations needed to be held secretly. Talking to the enemy while conflict persists puts the lives of those negotiating as much at risk from dissenting voices in their own community as from the enemy. In situations of violent conflict nothing is black and white, and sensitivity and subtlety of thought and action are crucial.

Such qualities, albeit for different reasons, might often seem to be lacking in the worlds of journalism and religion. The pressure is immense for journalists to come up with sensational stories in a competitive world of immediate and 24-hour news. For centuries, whatever the 'golden rule' of love at their core, religions have been guilty of defining themselves as 'chosen' communities whose identity is perceived in a superior way to differ from that of other religions, rather than to affirm their shared humanity. In these examples I am making generalisations, and here is my starting point as I explore the issues confronting those who seek to bring understanding between the worlds of journalism and religion, particularly in contexts of violent conflict.

Even as I write I can think of individuals and communities whose example contradicts my assertions: Journalists who try to report the complexities of any story and avoid sensationalising the facts, who take time to understand the context of the 'happenings' they record; people of faith who reach beyond the labels we claim for ourselves to understand the humanity of the other and who do not see life in black and white terms.

To tease this out further I want to say something about my own experience. As a priest with a degree and MA in Theology and Religious Studies, who has been a practising Christian for well over forty years, and who has worked for the last fifteen years with Jewish and Muslim colleagues on a variety of faith-based issues, I am all too conscious that if I have any expertise at all it relates to a limited aspect of Christian tradition and present practice, and to even less when it comes to other religions. At this stage in my life the religious labels we apply to each other do not convey clear pictures to me, but indicate only the immensity, complexity and diversity of religious belief and practice that come under umbrella terms such as 'Christian' or 'Hindu' or 'Atheist' etc. The more I learn, the more I realise how little I know. On the other hand, I know a good deal more about religion than many journalists who in the course of their work are called upon to report news stories containing a religious dimension. The lack of specialist knowledge found among some journalists who attempt to cover religion results in far from balanced accounts of stories about religion. The question of balance is particularly worthy of exploration. In this chapter, I consider whether seeking balance in the context of stories about religion, violence and reconciliation is a valuable approach.

The vastness and complexity of religion as a subject, and the limited understanding of those reporting it, including myself, would suggest from the start that though we might aim to achieve the 'right balance', that is a tall order, even before we consider the wider context of reporting about peace-time or violent conflict. Achieving balance in both news reports and programmes about religion relies upon a degree of expertise, even more so in conflict or post-conflict situations. It therefore seems sensible to use journalists or presenters who have some understanding of the complexity of religious expression. That is why I have reservations about celebrities, or people whose expertise lies in another field, being asked to present programmes or reports on religious matters. Without necessary expertise they are less likely to find the right balance of perspectives.

Not that the experts will necessarily get the balance right. They, like others, for example, can be seduced into having interviewees with polar opposite opinions about a particular issue. After all, that makes for attention-grabbing news items. On two occasions I have been asked to participate in a debate on Sunday morning television on BBC1. The first discussion was about women priests and the second on human sexuality, and gay clergy in particular. On both occasions the producer encouraged me to speak polemically, and was disconcerted when I refused to become argumentative with the person presenting a different view from my own. Polemical debate does not necessarily facilitate understanding. It may simply encourage people to take sides. To state one's own position and to say why one does not share the assertions of an opposing voice without moving from dialogue into diatribe is not easy but is essential, particularly within the context of violent conflict.

My friend, teacher and colleague, ex-Loyalist paramilitary, Alistair tells of his first encounters with Republican paramilitaries in groups set up to bring the two communities together. He began by wanting to put the enemy right on the facts as he saw them. His purpose wasn't so much conversation as conversion: getting others to see things his way. These encounters were often angry exchanges. He had to get beyond the political rhetoric to the real human stories of trauma, grief and fear that lay behind them, stories that bore similarities to his own. This kind of storytelling is a significant element in helping people move away from conflict to peace-building. It breaks down the psychological distance between enemies, helping them to re-humanise the other. Today, Alistair and I work together using a carefully structured process that brings together people from different sides of a violent conflict to share their personal stories in a safe, non-judgemental environment. It is not a miracle cure, but part of a long process of change that can be easily damaged by the insensitivity of anyone who does not understand how carefully one must tread in places of trauma. For journalists this can create problems. There is a conflict of interests between discovering a good story and recognising that in telling it one may damage, or even destroy a fragile journey of change.

I was greatly moved by the way in which playwright Guy Hibbert wrote his docu-drama, *Five Minutes of Heaven* (2009, directed by Oliver Hirschbiegel). The film tells the stories of Alistair (played by Liam Neeson) and Joe (played by James Nesbitt), the brother of the man he shot dead. Guy consulted both Alistair and Joe throughout the writing of the play. He did not put anything in that was not acceptable to both men. He was deeply sensitive to their stories, and was not exploitative. He wanted to understand their differing experiences and enable others through the film to do the same. Like screenwriters, journalists can open windows onto worlds that are far from balanced. I read newspapers and listen to, or watch, the news because I want to know what's happening in the world. I'm not looking for a sensational story but information engagingly shared that deepens my understanding.

One question journalists might want to ask in the context of violent conflict is whether their way of reporting events fosters understanding or fuels the conflict further. Religionists who apply adjectives like 'love', 'peace', 'compassion', 'mercy', justice' and 'understanding' to their pictures of God might want to consider whether their words and actions flesh out these ideals. This brings me to the issue of the use of language as we consider the notion of reporting religion in a balanced way.

Religion is not a science, even an inexact one. It is a different human language altogether, much more in line with the languages and purposes of the arts. Religion is far more subjective than many of us might want to acknowledge, theists and atheists alike. This subjectivity adds to the difficulty of reporting religion in a balanced way. Balanced from whose perspective? The academics' viewpoint (and they are a minority group in any religion), the men or women of diverse faith in the street, the general journalist who is looking for a good story, the atheist who sees religion only as a destructive force in today's world, the producers working in the few remaining religious departments of broadcasting companies, or religious correspondents on national newspapers? What is regarded as balanced may vary according to where you stand in relation to a particular story.

Balanced reporting of religion partly depends upon us understanding that religions are not monochrome, clear-cut entities. Their edges are blurred. Each faith tradition is made up of diverse, complex and sometimes diametrically opposed communities under the one umbrella. We cannot speak of the Christian/Muslim/ Hindu/Atheist position, but only a Christian/Muslim/Hindu/Atheist position. The major TV and radio networks and national newspapers recognise at least some degree of diversity of Christian position, but many reporters still have not come to grips with the immense diversity within Islam, for example.

I am confronted again by the question of whether 'balance' should be our guiding principle. Precisely because human life and the religious dimension of that are by nature chaotic, messy, and impossible to pin down neatly, is the word 'balance' redundant or at the very least, inadequate?

At the time of writing the BBC is somewhat sensitive about any broadcast relating to what is happening in Israel, the West Bank and Gaza: the unholy Holy Land. Three times recently when I have broadcast on that subject the producers have emphasised the importance of 'balance'. In one instance, when referring to the invasion of Gaza in January, I was asked to indicate that both Israelis and Palestinians had experienced destruction and suffering. The implication was that these experiences were equal in nature. To present such a view seemed highly unbalanced to me. In 2009 I spent six weeks working in Israel and the West Bank. Talking with Israelis in Sderot where the majority of Qassam rockets from Gaza fell, I gained a sense of the constant fear with which those Israelis lived day to day as the rockets exploded around them. Speaking to, and living with Palestinians in the West Bank I recognised how the inability to move freely in one's own territory and to access resources without constraint – to be in what feels like an open prison – can lead to despair. I understand too that the grief of an Israeli woman whose husband is killed by a rocket as he drives to work is not dissimilar to the grief of a Palestinian woman whose husband is killed by Israeli soldiers at a checkpoint. Grief is grief. What I cannot accept is that the deaths of 16 Israelis killed by Qassam rockets, and the damage to Israeli property caused by those rockets can be spoken of in equal terms to the deaths of over 1,400 Palestinians during the Gaza invasion and the damage to property there which, according to the UN, left more than 50,000 homes, 800 industrial properties and 200 schools damaged or destroyed, as well as 39 mosques and two churches, few of which have been reconstructed because of the blockade imposed by the Israeli government. This raises a number of related questions: What is the right balance when telling stories from this conflict? In focusing on the invasion, how much, if any, of the previous history of the region needs to be told in order to avoid presenting a distorted picture? Was the request for balance to do with trying to get at the truth, or to avoid any controversy the truth might spark?

To answer such questions it is useful to ask another set of questions relating to how the situation in South Africa was reported internationally during the apartheid years. Was equal airtime or newspaper print given to those who supported apartheid as well as those who opposed it, religious or otherwise? How far did reporters make judgements about the stories they covered, or did they simply convey the facts of a situation? Reporting facts about a single aspect of a complicated story may not be enough. One must hear the experience of a wide range of individuals and communities in order to develop a balanced picture. At what point was the unequal treatment of the majority of that country's population called 'apartheid', and then determined to be unjust and unacceptable by those reporting South Africa's story? Post-apartheid, does our view of what was considered 'balanced' reporting at the time challenge or confirm that judgement?

Within South Africa, journalism considered detrimental to apartheid was censored. In his book, *A Culture of Censorship: Secrecy and Intellectual Repression in South Africa*, Christopher Edmond Merrett writes about the Union of Black Journalists (UBJ) being targeted by the state. Black journalists, he says, 'were frequently assaulted, arrested and detained … At least 15 journalists were detained in the aftermath of Soweto, and a high proportion were linked to the UBJ'. Merrett states that, 'The decade of the 1980s was characterised by the rise of the "alternative", or anti-apartheid, press which, for the first time since the early 1960s, effectively competed for control of communication with the government'.

Clearly there is room for a great deal of research here that is beyond the scope of this chapter. What I want to note is that in conflict situations it is not always easy to access first-hand experience of crucial events due to political repression. Reporting becomes far more risky and emotive. When I experienced first-hand in Hebron the harassment and violence that Palestinians endure at the hands of some Israeli settlers and soldiers there, and learnt of the restrictions imposed upon them by the Wall, checkpoints and Israeli law regarding land and housing, I felt deeply angry about the injustice. I began to see all Israelis in a negative light. I wanted to tell the stories of the people I was with so that others might be alerted to what was going on and protest against it. I was conscious of taking steps along the process of dehumanising the perpetrators of the violence. I realised how in a short space of time I had moved away from objectively trying to research transformative relationships across a conflict divide to taking a clear stand for one community and against another. When I became aware of what was happening to my thoughts and feelings I was disturbed by how quickly I had lost sight of vital values like recognising that no community is monochrome – either all good or all bad. I was grateful to those Israelis I was privileged to meet who were speaking out against the Occupation and seeking a non-violent means to end it. Some of these people had lost one or more relatives in the conflict at the hands of Palestinians, and they were working with Palestinians who had lost relatives at the hands of Israelis, or been imprisoned and tortured by them (Families Forum/Parents Circle). Some were ex-fighters from both sides now working together through Combatants for Peace. It was a sobering experience to find that as a self-aware priest committed to conflict transformation and peace-building I was as capable as the next person of those reactions that in times of crisis can so easily lead us into violent conflict. I had to work hard to make sure I gathered all perspectives in this situation, not just those which supported the experience of the Palestinians I had lived with, otherwise my own reporting would have little integrity or power to change understanding. Why take note of an article or book that only reflects one community's perspective? That goes against everything I know about effective conflict transformation. It also goes against one strand of teaching in the Christian tradition. For example, in his letter to the Galatians St Paul writes that in Christ Jesus we are all children of God (Gal 3:26). The distinctions of race, religion, gender and social status disappear. No one matters more than anyone else. In the kingdom of God every person's story is to be taken seriously. Balancing and listening to other peoples' stories is a radical practice. If Paul's other letters and ongoing Christian history are anything to go by, this belief is hard to sustain and practice.

Selectiveness, conscious or unconscious, can mar peace-building processes as much as it can be a symptom of conflict. To many outsiders the Truth and Reconciliation Commission (TRC) in South Africa after the end of apartheid seemed like an extraordinary process; but when I and colleagues working in conflict transformation have been in South Africa subsequently, we have heard the anger and distress of South Africans in the townships who feel that their own stories of discrimination, repression and violent death among family members as a result of apartheid have gone unheard. For many left outside the news this process lacked balance. The forgiveness Archbishop Desmond Tutu encouraged through the TRC came too soon for those whose stories were not told. For some the idea of forgiveness was anathema; a religious imposition. The South African Truth and Reconciliation Commission also raises significant questions about balanced reporting. Where were their voices reported in the initial international news coverage? How far did journalists believe that the extraordinary changes in South Africa, the ending of apartheid, and the creativity of the TRC meant that certain dissenting voices should not be heard? To what extent was the notion of forgiveness as a positive practice generally unquestioned? How far was the world-wide regard in which Archbishop Desmond Tutu was held a factor that limited criticism of his encouragements to forgive?

More generally, it is not enough to understand the internal workings of religions in order to report them appropriately. Our sense of what is or is not balanced will also be affected by how we see the religious aspect of human expression in relation to any other dimension of human experience. For example, an extremist religious perspective may grow when the basic human need for security is not met. The focus of our attention in this case might not primarily be religion, but the causes of insecurity.

My friend and colleague, Alistair, born and brought up in Northern Ireland during the height of the Troubles, experienced his town being blown up by IRA bombs and knew people being shot on the estate where he lived. As a 12-year-old, he defined his town as Protestant, and God was on his side. He fought Catholics on the riot lines and, as a 17-year-old member of the UVF, shot dead a Catholic in a revenge attack. It was not until his time in prison that he began to understand that the religious dimension of the conflict was at the very least a convenient peg on which to hang all kinds of other issues that had more to do with social deprivation, political dissent, a deep sense of disempowerment and the failure of the normal forces of law to maintain peace. Those reporting the murders of 'Protestants' or 'Catholics' denied the complexity, fostering the view that the violence was religiously motivated when in fact so many other non-religious factors lay behind it.

After hearing me question the wisdom of defining those who had died as 'Protestant' or 'Catholic', a well-known BBC journalist said that it made sense to say the religious affiliation of those who had died because the readers wanted to know. Of course, it would be easy enough for any reader in Northern Ireland to know just from the name of the deceased or the place where they lived whether they were Catholic or Protestant, but those labels emphasise perceived differences while revealing very little about the attitude of the person to the conflict. For Alistair and other young lads caught up in the violence, knowing what side a dead person came from fuelled their own desire for revenge against the enemy. 'They've killed one of ours. We'll kill two of theirs.' It did not give them any insight into their shared humanity or common ongoing experiences of violence and grief.

Up to this point, we have considered questions related to 'balanced' reporting of stories in Israel, South Africa and Northern Ireland. There are interesting parallels in relation to recent coverage of the violence carried out by groups claiming Muslim allegiance. For example, in September 2009 there was a report in the *Observer* headlined, 'How Islamists track and kill Iraq's gays'. The article outlined how a group of 'hardline extremists' tracked down gay Iraqi men through internet chat-rooms on gay websites, kidnapped them, gave them 'the chance to ask God's forgiveness before they are killed', and then murdered them, often after using torture. Apart from wondering why this piece of news was selected in preference to so many other potential stories on the 'World' pages of the *Observer*, I moved between two responses. On the one hand, my immediate reaction was that the story challenged my own tentative thoughts about destructive religious practice being a symptom rather than a root cause of prejudice, bigotry and violence. On the other hand, I then considered how homophobia is not confined to those with a religious affiliation, even though religion is used by some as the peg on which to hang their prejudice. What did become clear is that I'm uncomfortable with the idea that 'millions of people' can have their understanding influenced by one very human hack in a way that may fuel ignorance and prejudice.

This story from Iraq raises another couple of questions. How can journalists discern whether religion is the critical factor underlying such action? Or are the drives behind such violence more to do with characteristics common to all human beings, religious and non-religious alike? If it is the latter, then journalists have a responsibility to reflect that reality, and not to emphasise religious labels or beliefs uncritically. If the roots of violence are not clear, then a balanced approach should highlight this ambiguity, rather than imply that a religious explanation lies behind the violence. Admitting to uncertainty about the roots of violence is rarely to be found in news reports, especially when at first glance religion appears to be the obvious primary cause.

No complex story can be accurately conveyed in a soundbite, or inch of print. We have already seen this through earlier discussions in this book. Several considered the coverage of an in interview and lecture given on 7 February 2008 by the Archbishop of Canterbury. My own perspective is different from what has already been observed about how this story was covered. A reminder: this was to be the first of six lectures to be given in Temple Church on the subject of 'Islam in English Law'. The Archbishop's offering was entitled, 'Civil and Religious Law in England: A religious perspective'. According to the publicity before the event, 'The aim of the series is to provide an opportunity to discuss, honestly, openly and courteously, some of the most difficult questions to which the systems of English Law and Shari'a Law give rise'. The lecture was preceded earlier in the day by an interview on BBC Radio 4's *World at One* programme, during which Dr Williams suggested that the adoption of elements of Islamic Shari'a law in the UK 'seems unavoidable'. According to the *Independent*'s website the same day, his comment proved very inflammatory: 'Archbishop ignites Sharia law row' ran the headline. (Because of advances in IT, news travels faster than ever today, provoking potentially destructive knee-jerk reactions that with more careful reflection might have been avoided.) The Archbishop's comment was ill-chosen, and obviously provoked a reaction, but without news reporters fanning the flames of controversy, I suspect the matter would simply have sparked and died.

As it was, on 9 February, the *Mail Online* announced, 'Sharia law row: Archbishop is in shock as he faces demands to quit and criticism from Lord Carey'. From my perspective, it was a storm in a teacup, fuelled by parts of the news media wanting a story and playing on the fears and prejudices of our present society. How far does rolling, 24-hour news put pressure on journalists to come up with stories where no story of note exists?

Rowan Williams should have known better than to say what he did, was a comment I heard often at the time. Why? In some communities Shari'a law is being used with regard to particular issues, and the sky has not fallen. I read the Archbishop's lecture, wondering if it warranted the headlines it received. There was nothing controversial in it at all. It was typically one of the Archbishop's carefully argued and thoughtful offerings, aimed at and delivered to an audience literate in the law and/or religion. I for one do not want to belong to a society that stifles intelligent debate for fear that the media will blow up out of proportion the words of those participating. I was grateful when after a few days of this kind of unacceptable journalism one or two commentators in the broadsheets began to 'voice' my own criticisms. Much of the reporting was irresponsible and destructive. Which brings me back to the notion of balance.

My sense from all this is that I do not think balance is a good objective when it comes to reporting religion, or any other subject for that matter. Balance and truth are not necessarily the same thing. Rather than seeking balance, I want the reporting of religion to enable understanding. This requires accurate reporting of what has happened from the perspectives of all parties involved, knowledge of the wider context and a degree of self-awareness that helps any reporter to know the limits of their knowledge and to prevent their own ignorance from clouding the issues.

If the task is to open up understanding, it is not only those reporting the news that bear responsibility in this endeavour. Their audience must also play a part in the process. Knowing the fallibility of all human beings, and the complexity of human life, we cannot assume that because something is in print or on a screen of one kind or other, it is necessarily accurate. I am stating the obvious, yet time and again people, including journalists, react as if what they read in newspapers, see on TV or find on the internet is the truth, the whole truth and nothing but the truth. We have more information technology at our finger-tips than ever before, but the truth eludes us as much as ever, not only because it is elusive, but also because such technology can be used as much to communicate our ignorance, as it can to open up our understanding. Both parties need to be aware that the news reported can never completely convey reality and there will always be more questions waiting to be asked and explored. In short, I suggest, balance is neither

an obtainable nor a helpful objective. Enabling understanding is what we should
be about, and that is always unfinished business. In situations of violence it is also
extremely difficult to do.

In the UK certain daily papers are known to support one political perspective
over and against another. The *Guardian*, for example, is associated with left-wing
politics, and the *Sun* with Tory perspectives. In Belfast particular daily papers
were regarded as sympathetic to the Loyalist cause and others to the Republican
viewpoint. No reporting can ever be entirely objective. Everyone stands in a
particular place. By recognising where we stand and by being open to the stories
of others whose position is different we may be able to offer a more accurate
picture of reality but we can never be wholly objective. In times of violent conflict
maintaining a degree of objectivity is harder.

Reporting the news is only one aspect of the work of the news media. Comment,
opinion, support for one view over and against another and economic viability all
influence the stories covered, what gets left out and the way in which the story is
shaped. News as propaganda becomes much more evident in situations of conflict.
The news is not always about conveying truth. Likewise, religion claims to be
about Truth, but there is plenty of evidence to suggest that what motivates many
people of faith is the desire for security, and that can be very different from truth.
Both the news media and religious groups wrestle with questions of truth and
living with integrity in the face of violent conflict.

SECTION 4
Contesting Religion and the News

Figure 12   Jerusalem's Dome of the Rock and the Western Wall (also known as
              the 'Wailing Wall' or 'Kotel'), seen through barbed wire. The Holy
              Sepulchre church is outside the frame. Courtesy of Ryan Rodrick
              Belier / Shutterstock.com

Introduction to Section 4: Contesting Religion and the News

This section picks up on two of the themes that have emerged strongly in several of the earlier contributions – the changing place of religion in British society, and the changing nature of media and broadcast journalism. The writers in this section reflect on the tensions caused by these changes: the challenges and opportunities posed to traditional broadcast media by the development of blogging and Twitter, the tension between religious freedom and freedom of speech, and the tension between making complex legal rulings on religion simple to understand and distorting their significance. Richard Harries closes the section with some theological reflections on how people can engage with this changed media environment as part of the world created, loved and redeemed by God.

Chapter 15
Religion and New Media: Changing the Story

Simon Barrow

Summary

In this chapter Simon Barrow examines the relationships between institutional, inherited religions and the rise of the internet-based new media. While the media has adapted to fast-changing technologies, religious institutions have not necessarily made the best available use of the platforms available to them. What once used to happen in private, such as debates, synods or assemblies, is now public knowledge. Barrow argues that religious institutions must respond to a globalised world, which is driven by communication and market imperatives.

The rise of social networking and participant-orientated media necessitate good public relations, and there is a need to rephrase, explain, revise, reposition and recapitulate 'traditional' ways of thinking and speaking. Religious bodies need to contradict the extremes, which are so often posited in the media, as well as rejecting the labels and stereotypes, which the media force upon them. Barrow suggests that it is only through engagement with the media that a different style and fresh content will change the way in which religion is reported in the news.

It is no coincidence that the decline and mutation of institutional, inherited religious beliefs and organisations over the past fifty years (particularly in northern and western Europe)[1] has occurred at the same time as a massive revolution in the media – and especially the rise of the internet-based, digitally conveyed 'new media' as part of the growth of the 'network society'.[2]

Print publications and newsgathering organisations have had to adapt or die in a 24/7 online environment where the boundary between producer and consumer is being continually eroded. Blogs and 'citizen journalists' have often been getting

---

[1]   See, for example, H. McLeod, and W. Usdorf (eds), *The Decline of Christendom in Western Europe, 1750–2000* (Cambridge: Cambridge University Press, 2003).

[2]   M. Castells, *Communication Power* (Oxford and New York: Oxford University Press, 2009).

to the story before traditional reporters.[3] Competition for attention, let alone advertising, has become ever more intense.

Similarly, faith bodies working with self-understandings rooted in slow-moving religious traditions and inherited institutional models can find themselves dislocated by the pace with which belief mutates as part of the broader process of cultural change in a globalised world – that is, one driven both by communications and by market imperatives.

News and the knowledge democracy

This democratization of knowledge economies and of belief systems has occurred simultaneously and interactively.[4] Authority and veracity as the monopoly of the few is no longer credible in an environment framed by the online world. The culture of instant publishing, rapid response and hyperlinked connectivity makes the maintenance of collective memory and accumulated wisdom uneven, and challenges traditional hierarchies of knowledge management – such as the priesthood or the *magisterium*. Yet these are the very resources which have been among the chief strengths of historic religions, alongside strong local networks.

At the same time, the levelling trend within the news and comment media (with the latter increasingly encroaching on the former) has substantially changed the agenda regarding the way religion is perceived, reported, described and analysed. What were once self-contained language systems are now probed and dissected by a general audience. Deference has given way to suspicion, and granted authority to sceptical investigation. Specialist understandings of religion, and the interpretative abilities that go with it, should be more important in an environment where 'religious factors' are more widely granted. But in practice, like other specialisms (scientific ones, for example), they are not always easy to locate effectively, either within the religions themselves or in terms of the demands of media.

Interior space for reflection and deliberation within and between religious bodies has also been diminished. For example, thirty years ago most of the business of bodies like the General Synod of the Church of England or the General Assembly of the Church of Scotland was conducted beyond the gaze of the onlooking world. Now it has become what feels like public media property. While this has produced a gain in transparency within structures that have too often been reluctant to divulge their inner powers and procedures, this has come at the expense of politicising almost every aspect of discussion, consultation and

---

[3]   P. Grabowicz, 'The Transition to Digital Journalism', Knight Digital Media Centre, Berkley Graduate School of Journalism, California, USA. http://multimedia.journalism. berkeley.edu/tutorials/digital-transform/web-20/ (accessed 12 August 2011).

[4]   M.N. Smith, 'Democratizing Knowledge', *Humanities*, September/October 2005, Vol. 26, No.5; N.O. Hatch, *The Democratization of American Christianity* (New Haven, CT: Yale University Press, 1991).

decision-making. The result has been an erosion of trust and potential for risk-taking, many would claim – just at a time when those qualities are arguably more important than ever before.

We now live in what Professor John Naughton has dubbed a 'WikiLeakable world',[5] where private diplomacy cannot be guaranteed and where the stark options are either to find a way of living with this or to switch off the internet – which, short of a vastly damaging cyber-war (of the kind to which current 'hacktivism' is but a prelude), is about as viable as seeking to repeal the law of gravity. There are simply no fences upon which to sit on the never-ending information superhighway. Yet many in current leadership positions within faith bodies have still not adequately grasped what is happening, or are still trying to hold on to a past where their voices were heard more prominently, with less questioning and with more inherent regard than is ever going to be the case now, or in the foreseeable future.

Barriers and bridges

As part of the resistance to the breaking down and revision of walls between media and mediated, there are strong attempts by some church bodies to retain 'God slot' style footholds in the established news and entertainment broadcast environment. The refusal of a-theistic and minority religious voices on BBC Radio 4's *Thought for the Day* feature, which focuses on spiritual and ethical reflection, might be seen as one instance of this, reinforced by territorial concerns within the Corporation itself. Interestingly, local media has been less restrictive towards 'alternative' and non-religious voices.[6]

There is a corresponding failure on the part of many Christian and other faith groups to generate creative, innovative and responsive news-based content within the mainstream media. A truly engaging religious or spiritual perspective cannot go it alone any more. It has to recognise and interact with other, often challenging, agendas. Lack of adaptation to the media environment also equates with displaced energy and resources: too much time and money is spent on complaining or on material aimed at a dwindling 'in crowd'.

The 'walled' approach to an irreversibly plural news and features culture across all media streams inevitably proves inhibiting rather than freeing for religious organisations with a message and an identity to convey. On the one hand, great effort is spent trying to defend 'quarantined' segments of media space for something called 'religion', which in turn has smaller general or crossover audiences. On the other hand, opportunities to generate and engineer new spaces for reporting and reflecting concerns and ideas which emerge from religion, but are not restricted by that, are

---

5   J. Naughton, 'Live with the WikiLeakable world or shut down the net. It's your choice', the *Guardian*, 6 December 2010.

6   L. Clifford, *'Thought for the Day': Beyond the god-of-the-slots* (London: Ekklesia, July 2010).

missed or sidelined. The prominence of Christian motifs ('What would Jesus do?') and news agendas generated by the recent presence of the Occupy economic justice movement's tents outside St Paul's Cathedral in London is but one example of the way in which religion can fruitfully benefit from the changing media landscape – if it is prepared to be more open and less prescriptive. (See also chapter 1.)

Changing the agenda

Thankfully, some of the more media-savvy religious bodies, notably the non-governmental organisations and para-church agencies that already operate in a broader environment, recognise this. As a result, they are striking out in fresh directions. Christian Aid, the UK-based churches' international development and advocacy organisation, is one example.[7] In 2010, the NGO began recruiting and allying in order to extend its message into the blogosphere and to capitalise on the rise of social networking sites. It recognised that 'news', which remains the core currency of its attempts to influence major global and national policy on poverty reduction, aid, tax, debt, environment, trade, conflict and a plethora of other issues, is not a simple supply and demand industry mediated only by traditional actors (newspapers, TV and radio). Rather, it revolves around the ability of those seeking to 'make the news' to shape the agenda and mobilise more people on an expanding digital terrain, instead of expecting an external media industry to do the job for you.

'Social media' (blogging, Facebook, Twitter, LinkedIn and a host of other niche tools, as well as cross-linking sites like Posterous) is evidently central to this alternative approach.[8] This will remain the case generically, irrespective of the waxing and waning of particular platforms, the shifts in affiliation or interest among the young,[9] or the issues of regulation that arise with the implication of such media in events such as the summer 2011 urban disturbances.

The rise of participant-oriented media has major public relations implications, evidently. PR has become the obverse of journalism. There is no place to hide in the continuous and contiguous online world. What might once have been 'internal religious debates', such as vituperative arguments about sexuality within the churches, have now become public political property, and have exposed what –

[7]   Christian Aid (http://www.christianaid.org.uk/) is an international development charity. It works with people of all faiths and none in around 50 countries, to eradicate poverty. The initial move was a financial one, but has transitioned towards the public policy and media arena. See: Ashcroft, D., 'Christian Aid embraces Social Media to help Fund Raising', KMP Digitata, 20 August 2010.

[8]   M. Tommasi, '50 Definitions of Social Media', *The Social Media Guide*, n.d., http://thesocialmediaguide.com/social_media/50-definitions-of-social-media (accessed 12 August 2011).

[9]   M. Warman, 'Young people "bored" with social media', *Daily Telegraph*, 15 August 2011.

to many people looking into the religious world from the outside – can seem a narrow, introspective, unattractive landscape.

Un-processed and un-exposed theological language likewise finds far less traction in a wider cultural environment in which the assumptions and beliefs of religion are correspondingly less generally accepted, more diverse and much more contested. The need to rephrase, explain, revise, reposition and recapitulate 'traditional' ways of thinking and speaking becomes both important and problematic in this new situation, philosophically as well as practically.

There is a real danger of being 'lost in translation' here, of course. But equally, it could be said, there is an opportunity to recover elements of the tradition obscured or obliterated by a top-down 'Christendom' approach to receiving, formulating and transmitting faith. Non-conformity and liminality become virtues rather than liabilities in the changed media environment. Moreover, rightly understood, 'tradition' – the wisdom accumulated and built up down the ages – is not static, but a dynamic force.

In this context, it is worth noting that it is now over 65 years since the German theologian Dietrich Bonhoeffer, writing from a prison cell in the darkest period of his nation's history, spoke of the need to address biblical ideas of life and hope to people living well outside the church's universe. [10] His quest was to discover for (and with) them a new, 'non-religious' language for so doing. In the 1960s, **when Bonhoeffer was first 'in vogue'**, this was too easily seen as ditching traditional faith. On the contrary, many subsequent interpreters aver, Bonhoeffer was seeking to recognise its continually fresh face. Biblical language, he recognised, gained its power from pointing to constancy in immediacy, and to 'the transcendent in the midst'. [11]

Shifting boundaries

The democratisation of media – its passing into the hands of many non-specialists – has also meant a shifting boundary between 'professional' journalists and a growing phalanx of reporters and commentators from civil society. [12] So, religion writers on national newspapers must now produce supplementary blogs that will attract informed and critical response to news and features. A good example is Ruth Gledhill's *Articles of Faith* in *The Times* (London), which has been (hopefully temporarily) imprisoned by Rupert Murdoch's paywall as part of a corporate

---

[10] See 'Dietrich Bonhoeffer (1906–1945)', Boston Collaborative Encyclopedia of Western Theology, http://people.bu.edu/wwildman/bce/bonhoeffer.htm (accessed 12 August 2011).

[11] J.C. Pugh, *Religionless Christianity: Dietrich Bonhoeffer in Troubled Times* (London: T&T Clark / Continuum, 2009).

[12] J.V. Pavlik, and S. McIntosh, *Converging Media* (Oxford: Oxford University Press, 2010).

attempt to reclaim big beast ownership within a predominantly free-content media jungle.[13] (See chapter 5.)

Far from undermining their role, this has positively 'upped the game' of the professionals. The *Guardian*'s online *Belief* section, like the *Washington Post*'s religion debates, has similarly opened up thoughtful discussion about religion well beyond the coterie of specialist correspondents. On the other hand, as a quick survey of reader comments on the *Guardian*'s Comment-is-Free web section will indicate, it has also enabled a stream of uninformed invective and over-confident assertion, while sometimes marginalising more circumspect expertise. How to value genuine depth of knowledge without succumbing to elitism is a continuing challenge in the new media space.

There is a *faux* democracy to be contended, too. This is one that grants privilege to the loud and lazy under the superficial rubric that 'anyone's opinion is as valuable as anyone else's'. From a knowledge and content viewpoint, it clearly isn't. But the preferred ecology for addressing this problem is surely participant regulation rather than institutional restriction. It is encouraging, therefore, that bodies with religious specialisms, including academic ones like the University of Chicago Divinity School (with its regular *Sightings*) and the University of Stirling (with the multi-disciplinary blog *Critical Religion*) are increasingly seeking to become content commentators and providers themselves.[14] *Religion Dispatches* and *Killing the Buddha* are two other web-based initiatives that have succeeded in capturing diverse audiences with high quality writing about religion.[15]

Bypassing the mediators

Through the electronic media religious bodies now also have the chance to present themselves directly, rather than just being 'reported' by a second- or third-hand news disseminator. But being 'automatic to the people' can produce startlingly mixed results. Sometimes faith groups seem to have little idea about how eccentric or repellent they are being in their behaviour and disposition. Internal wrangling overcomes any sense of proportion. Yet a more open media environment with

---

[13]   Ruth Gledhill maintains an archive of 'Articles of Faith' at: http://ruthgledhill. blogspot.com/ (accessed 12 August 2011).

[14]   'Sightings', University of Chicago Divinity School, http://divinity.uchicago.edu/ martycenter/publications/sightings/. 'Critical Religion', University of Stirling, http://www. criticalreligion.stir.ac.uk/, and in collaboration with Ekklesia, http://www.criticalreligion. stir.ac.uk/blog/ekklesia/ (all accessed 12 August 2011).

[15]   *Religion Dispatches* is 'a daily online magazine dedicated to the analysis and understanding of religious forces in the world today, highlighting a diversity of perspectives': http://www.religiondispatches.org/. *Killing the Buddha* is 'A religion magazine for people made anxious by churches': http://killingthebuddha.com/ (both accessed 12 August 2011).

porous news boundaries provides ample scope for highlighting everything from the peculiar, in its earlier meaning, right through to the plainly odd.

Bartholomew's *Notes On Religion*[16] is one notable website that has for several years provided detailed, informed analysis of the genesis, architecture, archaeology and spread of weird and wonderful beliefs in today's world. In so doing, it often points out that what may appear exotic or offensive to the general observer can still be profoundly influential: Christian Zionism in Israel, and racially or nationally exclusive religious ideologies in less-known corners of Europe, for instance. Alterity becomes ubiquitous, but no less 'other' now that the scope for discovering more and more about more and more is the norm.

Both tech-savvy aggressive religious conservatives and proselytising 'New Atheists' have been undeniably adept at using the new media environment, especially social networking, to spread their message. However, they seem less aware that they are appealing far more to 'their own' than to those of different outlooks. When media-aided tribalism breaks out like this, the circle of persuasive discourse tends to become vicious rather than virtuous. In turn, the more enthusiastically argumentative types of belief and non-belief have shaped the corporate news agenda in directions that do not necessarily generate the amount of light that would normally correspond with a healthy degree of heat.

In theory, the electronic and digital media, by feeding wider involvement and challenging the previous monopoly of major news and content providers, offer the possibility of variegation, subtlety and nuance in more dedicated 'communities of discourse', too. In practice, the dominant values of polarisation and simplification all too often rule. This is partly because of 'what cuts through' and 'what sells', and because image and entertainment shapes narrative in a world of spectacle.[17] It is also, crucially, because the non-linear nature of digital media makes deep learning and the long-lasting corrective mechanisms difficult. Errors and simplifications multiply as quickly as their opposite, and perhaps more so because they demand less of those they capture. Again, the best response is persistence rather than abdication. 'Evangelists' and 'evangelicals' are still assumed by many reporters to be the same thing, but equally, print and online periodicals are increasingly noting their important differentiation.

Stereotypes: What is shaping whom?

One question posed to those who report about faith issues is: 'What stories about religion provoke debate, and what does this say about the subject of religion?' For me, a more important question might be, 'What *lenses* are most frequently used to

---

[16] *Bartholomew's Notes on Religion*, edited by Richard Bartholomew: http://barthsnotes.wordpress.com/ (accessed 12 August 2011).

[17] G. Debord, *The Society of the Spectacle* (New York: Zone Books, 1995).

report religion, and what does this say about the way religion and the media feed off one another?'

For example, a clear numerical majority of religious people on our planet seem relatively peaceable and accommodating – other than where nationalism, conflict over resources, perceived threat and strong ideology raise their heads in a context where demagogues gain sway. Where that is the case and where countervailing educative resources or traditions are thin, the exception can become the rule. But it is still, statistically, an exception. Al Qaeda, the terror network, does not represent Islam, any more than Anders Breivik, the Norway killer, stands for Christianity. Yet it is sex, violence, exoticism, personalities, power plays, extremism and menacing commitment that sells website space as well as newspapers. This tells you as much about certain styles of media and reporting regimes as it does about different types of religion or belief.

Two other strongly ingrained, and in my view unhelpful, narratives currently inform much religion reporting in the West. The first is the idea that most disputes within faith communities arise from a root conflict between the past and the present; between 'conservatism' (traditional adherence to the basic tenets of the belief system) and 'liberalism' (a postmodern abandonment of these same convictions). This has an element of truth within it, of course. But its distorting capacity is considerable and usually overlooked, especially when it suits the most vociferous protagonists within struggles for religious authority.

For instance, it is the over-simplified 'conservative versus liberal' mentality that often portrays fundamentalism in Christianity and Islam – comparatively recent outlooks based on contorted forms of post-nineteenth century rationalism – as normative for what it means, and has always meant, to be a 'proper believer'.[18] Oddly, both atheist advocate Richard Dawkins and a hard-line Southern Baptist pastor are likely to share this view, with one opposing and one supporting its outcomes.

But in many cases what is happening inside a religious community is not like this at all, as those with deeper involvement will often recognise. The reality is that adherence to 'tradition' involves constant adaptation to change – as the diverse, evolving perspectives of the Hebrew and Christian biblical narratives illustrate. Refusal of change is not inherent to religion. Rather, it is what happens when what has been passed on becomes captive to narrow, particularist viewpoints. Liberality is a key, though not uncontested, element of what is transmitted from the religious past, as the radicalism of Jesus suggests. Similarly, appropriate conserving (from which we get the conservative impulse) is very much a present-day preoccupation, as well as a biblical one.

---

[18]   S. Barrow, 'Facing up to Fundamentalism', Ekklesia, http://www.ekklesia.co.uk/research/070201 (accessed 12 August 2011).

Labels, filters and commitments

It is also frequently taken for granted in much contemporary reporting and comment about beliefs that there is an unassailable conflict between two finally contradictory filters labelled 'religion' and 'secularity'. But 'religion' understood as a set of discrete propositions and rituals set apart from the rest of life is a fairly modern conception, as philosophical and historical theologian Nicholas Lash, among others, has pointed out. In fact the 'secular' was historically understood to be the whole fabric of worldly existence – as distinct from an eternal perspective, rather than some arbitrary definition of life as being naturally separate from 'religion'.[19]

Similarly, in today's world, the observable reality is that there are many forms of religion adapted to the relational (but not necessarily value) pluralism secularity assumes, and there are equally many forms of religion resistant to it. There are also forms of secularism that welcome the religious alongside the non-religious in the public sphere (without privileging one over the other), and others that reject it by defining 'the religious' as a necessarily private sphere. This is something adherents are usually unable to do, because their beliefs are inextricably linked to public performance, institutions and goods.

What is less frequently understood and reported is that people of faith and people of good faith (but not religious belief) can and do find ways of living and cooperating together without resorting either to imposed state religion, or to the wholesale exclusion of religion from the public square. The zone in which this peaceable interchange, instructive argument and helpful cooperation happens is civil society, and in this arena the tension is not usually between religion and non-religion *per se*, but between authoritarian versus open or inclusive convictions – whether they are grounded in a conception and experience of the transcendent, or whether they explicitly reject such categories.

The religion and society think-tank that I jointly head up, *Ekklesia*, which bases its research and advocacy work on a national and international news briefing service, is specifically committed to illustrating how the currently dominant narratives of liberal versus conservative, religious versus secular, and faith fundamentalism versus angry atheism are neither representative nor necessary to the way religion and belief takes shape in particular locales.[20]

Bringing people together across the divides to discover how different belief traditions can inform common commitments to peace-making, restorative justice, social solidarity, environmental sustainability and economic sharing is both

---

[19] N. Lash, *The Beginning and the End of 'Religion'* (Cambridge: Cambridge University Press, 1996).

[20] Ekklesia 'is an independent, not-for-profit think-tank which examines the role of religion in public life and advocates transformative ideas and solutions rooted in theological thinking and dialogue with others': http://www.ekklesia.co.uk/content/about/about.shtml (accessed 12 August 2011).

practical and possible – if under-reported. Investing in conversation rather than confrontation needs to be the future of both religion and media – and not just in the interactions between the two. Otherwise the possibilities opened up by the radically changing digital media environment will be in danger of being swamped by cacophony.

Journalists have an inbuilt professional tendency to prefer speech (however noisy) to silence (however profound), as well as venerating headline-worthy bad news over worthy but un-dramatic good news. Only engagement and subversion will challenge this. A new generation of religious dramatists, producing mystery plays for a new generation, is needed. That is why the willingness and capacity of 'ordinary people' (religious and otherwise) not just to join the new media circus, but to improve it by offering a different style and fresh content, is so important. The revolution is on, but it is in its very early stages, and it is not being televised. That was yesterday's medium. Today's and tomorrow's is multiplatform.

Chapter 16

Taking Offence: Free Speech, Blasphemy and the Media

Jonathan Heawood

Summary

In this chapter Heawood considers the conflict between freedom of religion and freedom of expression. Citing the protests against the play Behzti, *Heawood makes the case for considering this to be a pivotal moment in the redefining of the relationship between freedoms of religion and of expression. It was followed by the media storms surrounding* Jerry Springer, The Opera, *a production of Marlowe's* Tamburlaine, *and Monica Ali's novel,* Brick Lane. *Media coverage of these, and other controversies involving the right to free expression, encouraged the perception that 'religion and free speech had become implacably opposed'. Heawood examines this media polarisation in the context of repeated criticisms of newspapers and broadcasters that, due to economic pressures, complex news stories are simplified and under-researched.*

Heawood nonetheless acknowledges that there may be an underlying tension between religion and free speech. He illustrates this tension by giving an analysis of blasphemy law, culminating in its repeal in 2008. The 2006 Racial and Religious Hatred Act, however, replaced much of the work of the law of blasphemy but with the emphasis now 'on people who have been offended by a particular speech act'. This shift in emphasis, Heawood argues, reinforces the media narrative that believers and advocates of free speech are at loggerheads. He concludes by arguing that this conflict between two fundamental rights is not as great as it is made to seem. Their commonality lies in the protection they both give from state interference.

Recent controversies in Britain have highlighted the potential for conflict between the values of religion and freedom of expression. These conflicts have played out prominently in the print media, where they have been represented as a function of the so-called 'clash of civilisations'. Alongside these controversies, the British government has attempted to legislate against 'religious hatred', leading to fears that legitimate forms of artistic expression and public debate might be criminalised. This chapter considers the media coverage of such controversies and the intertwined history of the rights to freedom of religion and freedom of expression, before concluding that both religious believers and free speech advocates benefit more from a liberal regime than they do from a return to censorship.

One

From 1737 to 1968, the Lord Chamberlain's office sought to protect the feelings of British theatregoers. Playwrights from Aristophanes to George Bernard Shaw, Henrik Ibsen and Samuel Beckett were censored by the Lord Chamberlain's office on grounds including indecency and blasphemy. By the late 1950s – when they recommended that Harold Pinter should cut 'the pointless pieces of blasphemy' in his masterpiece *The Birthday Party* – the censors' blue pencil was wearing thin.[1] It was finally discarded at the end of the liberal 1960s, when British society declared that its morals no longer needed protecting by the state. However, more than 30 years later, censorship returned to the theatre. The blue pencil was no longer in the hands of an officer of the crown, but wielded by a group of protestors who gathered outside a British theatre on a winter afternoon in December 2004.

The protesters objected to the production of *Behzti*, a play by the British Sikh author Gurpreet Kaur Bhatti, which was two weeks into a successful, if controversial, run at the Birmingham Repertory Theatre.[2] The play deals with the rape of a devout young Sikh woman in a Gurdwara (temple), by the head of the Gurdwara renovation committee. In a remarkable plot twist, it transpires that the rapist has previously been in a sexual relationship with the victim's father. These circles of corruption and secrecy are linked to the way in which the temple authorities conspire to silence the rape victim in order to protect their temple's reputation.

The play – which the author described as provocative but sincere – had been shown to members of the Sikh community whilst it was still in rehearsal in an attempt, perhaps inspired by Arts Council of England's funding conditions, to initiate dialogue. Unfortunately for the playwright and the theatre, the dialogue soon became extremely heated. Sewa Singh Manda of the Council of Sikh Gurdwaras in Birmingham announced that '[i]n a Sikh temple, sexual abuse does not take place, kissing and dancing don't take place, rape doesn't take place, homosexual activity doesn't take place, murders do not take place'.[3] On these normative grounds – which recalled the attitude of the Lord Chamberlain's office towards the plays they scrutinised – Singh Manda and other local religious leaders lobbied the theatre to have the play rewritten. Vincent Nichols, then Roman Catholic Archbishop of Birmingham, agreed with his Sikh colleagues that locating the rape in a Gurdwara was offensive: 'Such a deliberate, even if fictional, violation of the sacred place of the Sikh religion demeans the sacred places of every religion'.[4] However, the theatre refused to edit the play, and the negotiations turned into protests during which three people were arrested for public order offences and three police officers

---

[1]   See Dominic Shellard, Steve Nicholson and Miriam Handley, *The Lord Chamberlain Regrets: A History of British Theatre Censorship* (London: British Library, 2004), plate 19.

[2]   For a different perspective on the play and its reception, see Indarjit Singh's earlier chapter (12) in this book on 'Respect, Religion and the News'.

[3]   The *Independent*, 21 December 2004.

[4]   http://news.bbc.co.uk/1/hi/england/west_midlands/4107437.stm (accessed 1 May 2011).

were injured. Performances were suspended when windows were smashed at the theatre on 18 December. Two days later, the theatre management took the decision to cancel the production.

The closure of *Behzti* seemed to define the relationship between religion and freedom of expression in the United Kingdom in the early-twenty-first century. For artists and free speech advocates, the fracas outside the Birmingham Rep epitomised a disturbing trend towards religious censorship. Lisa Appignanesi described the events as 'a clear signal of the intolerance of religious groups to artistic expression'.[5] She argued that, since the abolition of the Lord Chamberlain's office in 1968, the censorship of drama had not disappeared, but had merely migrated from the state to the streets. Shami Chakrabarti described the closure of the play in similar terms as 'censorship through intimidation' and 'mob rule'.[6] In stark contrast, the Home Office minister Fiona Mactaggart said that the 'free speech of the protesters' was 'as important as the free speech of the artist'.[7] Yet the speech of the protesters – backed up with violent actions – had forced the playwright into hiding, whilst the author's speech – identifying the scope for abuse and corruption within a religious community – was silenced. Gurpreet Kaur Bhatti subsequently described the play as an attempt 'to explore how human frailties can lead people into a prison of hypocrisy'.[8] In the foreword to the play she wrote that 'only by challenging fixed ideas of correct and incorrect behaviour can institutionalised hypocrisy be broken down'.[9] In the United States, the playwright's free speech would be afforded the highest protection under the First Amendment of the Constitution. In the UK, nobody seemed to know what to do about *Behzti*.

The mainstream press and specialist religious papers waded into the controversy, hosting divided opinions on the subject. The *Guardian* described the *Behzti* affair as 'a classic conflict between the artist's right to freedom of expression and a community's wish to have their faith treated with dignity'.[10] Whilst religious leaders deplored the violence of some protestors, they seemed to endorse their message that playwrights and other artists should steer clear of religious symbols. According to the *Church Times*, John Sentamu – then Bishop of Birmingham – said that the author was 'right to explore [sexual abuse and power manipulation], but not in the context of a sacred place'.[11] Sentamu was part of the group which attempted to persuade the Birmingham Rep to amend the play before it opened. The *Independent* quoted Mohan Singh of the Guru Nanak Gurdwara in Birmingham as

---

[5]   *Free Expression is No Offence*, Lisa Appignanesi (ed.) (London: Penguin, 2005), Introduction, p. 6.

[6]   The *Independent*, 21 December 2004.

[7]   *Daily Telegraph*, 22 December 2004.

[8]   *Free Expression is No Offence*, p. 28.

[9]   Ibid., p. 31.

[10]   'Tale of Rape at the Temple Sparks Riot at Theatre', www.guardian.co.uk, 20 December 2004 (accessed 1 May 2011).

[11]   *Church Times*, 24 December 2004.

saying after the play's closure: 'We were in negotiations with the Rep a week ago and they didn't budge. That's when they should have budged'.[12] These comments seemed to imply that authors and theatre companies should be obliged to respond to the concerns of religious groups, at the expense of artistic expression.

In the wake of the *Behzti* affair, other plays and books were affected by protests on the grounds of religious offence. Performances of *Jerry Springer, the Opera* were cancelled in regional British theatres after demonstrations by Christian groups; a production of Christopher Marlowe's *Tamburlaine* at the Barbican in London was edited to remove derogatory references to Mohamed; Monica Ali's novel *Brick Lane* was burned and the production of a film version was prevented in the area where the novel is set; and the publisher of *The Jewel of Medina* by Sherry Jones was firebombed by extremists who objected to the novel's depiction of Mohamed's relationship with his first wife, Aisha.

The media followed these real and attempted acts of censorship with interest, leading to a widespread sense that religion and free speech had become implacably opposed. However, this may have been a function of the media coverage as much as any underlying clash of civilisations. Monica Ali has described the 'marketplace of outrage' in which emotions that run (or are seen to run) high enough will fetch 'a good price' in the media.[13] The controversy over the film production of her novel *Brick Lane* began with an article in the *Guardian* which reported the views of a couple of self-appointed 'community leaders' in the London borough of Tower Hamlets. Ali questions the legitimacy of such 'leaders', and notes the discrepancy between the extent of the coverage and the tiny scale of the protests against the film, which included no more than 70 men and as few as two women. One observer subsequently told Ali that the protesters were actually outnumbered by representatives of the press.[14] In Ali's view, the media's desire to record community 'outrage' creates a market for such public expressions of emotion. She concluded that this kind of journalism, hungry to chart an apparent clash of civilisations within a few miles of Fleet Street, may have had the perverse effect of heightening or even provoking such confrontation. She notes that more Bangladeshis in Tower Hamlets auditioned to appear in the film than protested against it.

Ali's concern about the media coverage of this affair echoes a wider critique of the traditional British media, which is currently faced with falling advertising revenue and the migration of content and readers to the internet. Some newspapers and broadcasters have been accused of responding to this highly competitive climate by simplifying complex news stories and failing to research or report the nuances of religious events.[15] This does not mean that there is no difference of opinion between the free speech of artists and writers and the views of religious believers in early twenty-first-century Britain. There is a very real debate, and one

---

12   The *Independent*, 21 December 2004.
13   'The Outrage Economy', in the *Guardian*, 13 October 2007, Review, p. 4.
14   Ibid., p. 5.
15   See other chapters in this volume, for example chapters 10–13.

with important implications for the relationship between religion and the state. However, as the primary conduit for information and ideas, the traditional media still holds great power to shape this public debate. The tendency of the media coverage to highlight extreme views may create an incentive for precisely these views to be expressed. The consequent perception that free speech and religion are at odds with one another – whether based on fact or media fiction – has profound consequences for the human rights framework, not only in this country but also around the world. It risks undermining the very values which provide tolerance to religious believers and allow a diversity of religions within a single state. Those who argue that their religious rights are separate from, or opposed to, the rights of artists and writers, contribute to an onslaught on the same legal framework which protects them from state oppression and civil strife.

Two

The word 'blasphemy' derives from the Greek *blasphemos*, or 'evil speaking'. It suggests that there can be evil in speech itself, that blasphemy is a kind of living language that not only describes evil, but also does evil. This religious emphasis on the performative quality of language is hardly surprising. Religions depend upon words to do things. From animist shamans to Anglican priests, language is used in religions to bless, to invoke and to intercede. If gods can respond to our prayers then presumably they also take note of our blasphemies. Religions have long sought to protect the feelings of their gods by preventing the expression of extreme views about sacred matters. However, this protective attitude also allows religious authorities to silence dissenting voices, not only on questions of faith, but also on the conduct of church leaders. The objections to *Behzti* may have been motivated by religious concerns, but they also served to protect the interests of religious authorities and, potentially, to dissuade real abuse victims from coming forwards.

In England, blasphemy was the province of the Church courts until 1676, when John Taylor was convicted of blasphemy for saying that Jesus Christ was a 'bastard' and a 'whoremaker' and that religion was a 'cheat'. His judge, Sir Matthew Hale, described these 'wicked and blasphemous words' as 'not only an offence against God and religion, but a crime against the laws, States and Government; and therefore punishable in this court'.[16] Hale's ruling set a precedent for three centuries of blasphemy cases, in which the courts considered the impact of blasphemous words not only upon god and religion but also upon civil order. In the words of Kenan Malik, 'blasphemy was less about defending the dignity of the divine than of protecting the sanctity of the state'.[17]

---

[16]   Cited in Kenan Malik, *From Fatwa to Jihad: The Rushdie Affair and its Legacy* (London: Atlantic, 2009), p. 157.

[17]   Ibid., p. 157.

By the turn of the twentieth century, blasphemy was essentially a public order offence: the courts considered blasphemous speech acts in terms of 'their tendency to endanger the peace [...], to deprave public morality generally, to shake the fabric of society and to be a cause of civil strife'.[18] Yet, even with this emphasis on the social implications of blasphemy, it sits awkwardly in the secular legal system: it requires courts to hear theological arguments; and it treats gods as potential litigants. In 1985, the Law Commission recommended the repeal of blasphemy, arguing that 'one person's incisive comment (and indeed seemingly innocuous comment) may be another's "blasphemy"'.[19]

Such arguments against blasphemy were nothing new. As far back as 1644, the poet John Milton urged Parliament not to respond to the religiously charged instability of the time by introducing new forms of censorship on religious or political grounds. He argued vehemently against measures which required publishers to submit their books for scrutiny before being published. Instead, he suggested that all ideas, good and bad, should take their place in the marketplace of ideas. '[W]ho ever knew Truth put to the worse, in a free and open encounter?' he asks.[20] In the context of a society at war with itself, Milton showed a remarkable trust in the capacity of the intellectual free market to regulate itself without government interference: 'Give me the liberty to know, to utter, and to argue freely according to conscience, above all liberties'.[21] He rejected the fears of those who claimed that blasphemies would unduly influence those who heard them, noting that even the Bible 'describes the carnal sense of wicked men not unelegantly' and 'brings in holiest men passionately murmuring against Providence', without infecting its readers.[22]

Two centuries later, John Stuart Mill argued equally forcefully against state interference in religious belief and observance. In his seminal essay *On Liberty* (1859), he states that 'the peculiar evil of silencing the expression of an opinion is that it is robbing the human race, posterity as well as the existing generation – those who dissent from the opinion still more than those who hold it'.[23] In this essay, Mill articulates the so-called 'harm principle', which has since become a cornerstone of liberal thought and the human rights framework: 'the only purpose for which power can be rightfully exercised over any member of a civilised

---

[18] *Bowman* v *Secular Society* [1917] AC 406, cited in *Media Law & Human Rights*, 2nd edition, Andrew Nicol, Gavin Millar and Andrew Sharland (eds) (Oxford: Oxford University Press, 2009), p. 42.

[19] Law Commission, *Offences against Religion and Public Worship* (London, 1985), p. 57.

[20] John Milton, *Complete English Poems, Of Education, Areopagitica*, fourth edn (London: Everyman, 1993), p. 613.

[21] Ibid., p. 613.

[22] Ibid., p. 590.

[23] John Stuart Mill, *On Liberty*, Gertrude Himmelfarb (ed.) (London: Penguin, 1974), p. 76.

community, against his will, is to prevent harm to others'.[24] As an illustration of this principle, Mill cited Christ's execution. He notes that Christ – 'who left on the memory of those who witnessed his life and conversation such an impression of his moral grandeur that eighteen subsequent centuries have done homage to him as the Almighty in person' – was sentenced to death for blasphemy.[25] Like Milton, Mill argues that blasphemy laws always run the risk of silencing voices which may subsequently be recognised as extremely valuable.

Such arguments led to the development within today's human rights framework of the twin rights to freedom of expression and freedom of religion. In the wake of the Second World War, the United Nations recognised the importance of these individual rights if global citizens were to have the capacity to resist tyranny. The preamble to the Universal Declaration of Human Rights (1948) describes 'freedom of speech and belief' in the same breath as among 'the highest aspiration[s] of the common people'.

Article 9 of the European Convention on Human Rights (ECHR), incorporated in British law as the Human Rights Act, thus protects the right to 'freedom of thought, conscience and religion' and recognises the citizen's freedom 'to change his religion and belief'. This right is limited only by those restrictions which are deemed 'necessary in a democratic society in the interests of public safety, for the protection of public order, health or morals, or for the protection of the rights and freedoms of others'. Article 10 of the ECHR protects the right to hold, receive and impart information and ideas (freedom of expression). It is similarly balanced against the rights of others. This mutual balancing act ensures that neither right can be used at the expense of the other. The European Court of Human Rights has heard many free speech cases over the years, and has established a principle – which would have pleased Milton and Mill – that Article 10 is applicable 'not only to "information and ideas" that are favourably received or regarded as inoffensive but also to those that offend, shock or disturb the state or any sector of the population'.[26] This latitude also applies to religious belief, which can be held or manifested in a number of ways, so long as these do not cause direct harm to others. Within these broad principles, the European Court grants individual member states a considerable flexibility, or 'margin of appreciation', to set a socially acceptable balance between these rights and others. This has sometimes meant that the European Court can appear inconsistent in its attitude towards free speech.

For instance, in 1976 Mary Whitehouse successfully sought leave to bring a private prosecution against the publishers of the magazine *Gay News*, which had earlier that year published a poem, 'The Love that Dare Not Speak its Name', by James Kirkup. The poem featured explicit sexual imagery relating to Christ's death and resurrection, describing his penis ('that great cock') as 'the instrument

---

[24] Ibid., p. 68.

[25] Ibid., p. 85.

[26] *Media Law & Human Rights*, 2nd edition, Andrew Nicol, Gavin Millar and Andrew Sharland (eds) (Oxford: Oxford University Press, 2009), p. 14.

| of our salvation, our eternal joy.'[27] The publishers were convicted of blasphemy, and Denis Lemon, the editor of *Gay News*, was fined £500 and sentenced to nine months suspended imprisonment. On appeal, the prison sentence was retracted but the conviction was upheld. The House of Lords agreed that the poem was blasphemous and when the case eventually came before the European Court of Human Rights the judges controversially concluded that 'the protection of the rights of citizens not to be offended in their religious feelings by publication was a legitimate aim'.[28] In other words, the law of blasphemy was upheld as a function of Article 9, despite its considerable impact on freedom of expression.

However, the law came under increasing pressure as the British population became more diverse, and the law of blasphemy – which protected only adherents of the Church of England – was shown to be discriminatory. An attempt to charge Salman Rushdie with blasphemy failed on these grounds. In 2008, blasphemy was finally repealed. In its place, the balance in English law between free speech and religion is now governed by the Racial and Religious Hatred Act 2006. This law distinguishes between the criticism of religious beliefs and practices and the criticism of religious believers. It protects believers, but not beliefs – people, not gods – from so-called hate speech, on the grounds of religious belief. At the time that the Bill was passing through Parliament, the government affirmed that Rushdie – whose novel *The Satanic Verses* had caused uproar after its publication in 1988 – would not have been charged under this new law.

Nonetheless, the new approach, which seemingly embodies Mill's harm principle, still causes concerns to artists and free speech advocates. The Religious Hatred Act does not require the police to oversee religious speech; instead, it relies on people who have been offended by a particular speech act to report this. In the words of Nicholas Hytner, Artistic Director of the National Theatre, these new measures appear to create 'a climate where the taking of offence is thought to be sufficient excuse for violence and intimidation'.[29] However, the Act includes a clause (the so-called PEN amendment), which exempts artistic and religious expression from these provisions, no matter how much they convey 'antipathy, dislike, ridicule, insult or abuse of particular religions or the beliefs or practices of their adherents'.[30] No successful prosecutions have yet been brought under the Act.

Writers like Gurpreet Kaur Bhatti should now have the law on their side. Why, then, does *Behzti* remain unperformed in the UK, whereas a French-language version of the play has been produced in Brussels? Is it a mark of British respect towards religious believers – or a symptom of censorship that has migrated from state institutions into the fraught arena of community relations? Is it appropriate to allow religious communities, or those who claim to speak on their behalf, to

---

[27] The poem is published in full at http://www.pinknews.co.uk/news/articles/2005-6519.html (accessed 1 May 2011).

[28] Ibid, pp. 147–8.

[29] The *Independent*, 21 December 2004.

[30] Racial and Religious Hatred Act (2006), section 29J.

determine what may or may not be said about religion? These arguments have been played out not only in British public life; they have also been rehearsed at the United Nations Human Rights Council, the political body responsible for setting the UN's human rights policy. Every year since 1999, a resolution has been laid before the Council urging the UN to combat the 'defamation of religions'. These resolutions have been proposed by members of the Organisation of the Islamic Conference (OIC), and claim to be motivated by concerns about the growth in 'Islamophobia'. They would allow states to penalise anyone who spoke out against religious beliefs or practices. The heated debates over these resolutions take place against a backdrop of great danger for writers who touch on matters of religion, such as the Afghan journalist, Sayed Parvez Kambakhsh, who in 2008 was sentenced to death for blasphemy, having raised concerns about the status of women in Islamist Afghanistan. After a global outcry, President Hamid Karzai granted Kambakhsh an amnesty in 2009 and he left the country. Other writers, such as the Bangladeshi poet Taslima Nasrin, have been imprisoned or forced into exile for the publication of so-called 'blasphemies' which threaten the power structures of religious conservatism.[31]

As Sejal Parmar has noted, the OIC resolutions 'undermine directly international guarantees on freedom of expression by protecting religions and potentially lending support to the state suppression of religious or dissenting voices'.[32] In other words, the apparent protection of religion in international human rights law can lead to threats to individual religious believers.

These resolutions, with their references to 'dignity' and 'equality', draw on the notion that religion and free speech are implacably opposed. Yet they reveal the dangerous trends that lie behind this apparent opposition, which reinforces a divide between free speech advocates and religious believers. For in fact, the right to freedom of expression and the right to freedom of religion have something very important in common: freedom from state interference. So long as we live in a world with multiple religions, and large numbers of non-religious people, the freedom of religion must involve an acceptance of other beliefs and traditions – and of mutual criticism. This is a crucial aspect of the social contract that religious believers sign with the state: respect our freedom and we will respect the freedom of others. This does not mean that religious leaders should necessarily hold back on their rhetoric against other religions. In fact, it was the anti-religious threat posed by the Religious Hatred Bill that led to a backlash against it from religious groups themselves. In their points of dissent, difference and divergence, most religions contain the seeds of blasphemy against other religions. In protecting religious freedoms, society is also protecting the right to speak out against religious beliefs

---

[31]   See *Another Sky: Voices of Conscience from Around the World*, Lucy Popescu and Carole Seymour-Jones (eds) (London: Profile and English PEN, 2007), pp. 206–7.

[32]   Sejal Parmar, 'The Challenge of "Defamation of Religions" to Freedom of Expression and the International Human Rights System', *European Human Rights Law Review*, issue 3 (2009), 353–75, p. 374.

and practices: and in protecting the right to speak out, society is also protecting religious believers. If freedom of speech is diluted, so is freedom of religion, and all citizens suffer.

Chapter 17
Law, Religion and the Media: More Spinned Against than Spinning?

Mark Hill

Summary

In Chapter 17, Hill offers a legal analysis of cases involving landowning, homosexuality, 'pastoral breakdown', the status of Sharia law, and defamation. In each case, Hill draws out the sometimes vast discrepancy between the legal ruling and the manner in which the ruling is reported in the press. In all cases it is religion that receives the worst hearing in news reports, even if it had the best in the courts. Having offered his case studies, Hill offers a series of explanatory remarks as to why religion comes off worse in the press. Echoing Romain's earlier concern (chapter 11), Hill begins by noting that religion has long been the subject of comedy in the media, latterly with the television series Rev. *This is reflected, he argues, in the news reporting of religion. But in asking further why religion is a source of humour, Hill is unsatisfied with the answer that it is in order to maintain circulation.*

Is news reporting inherently inaccurate? Several contributors have raised concerns on this matter, and Hill makes them explicit by noticing that the press reports on legal rulings involving religion are no more inaccurate than news coverage of other legal matters. But why should this be? Again Hill offers an explanation: the law is complex, as is religion, and therefore journalistic inaccuracies abound in these fields. Nonetheless, drawing a different contrast with science reporting than Beckett in chapter 7, Hill points out a disparity with the accuracy demanded of science reporting and the inaccuracy tolerated in religious coverage. Hill urges that a solution be found to remedy misreporting: 'A more accurate (and less partisan) understanding of the judicial determination of religious litigation is a worthy constitutional goal in a multi-faith society benignly governed by the rule of law'.

The media love to report on religion and on the pronouncements of the English judiciary. For the journalist, therefore, high profile litigation involving faith communities can be pitched twice over to receptive editors. This contribution considers several recent decisions of the courts and how those legal determinations have been reported in the media. It concludes with some speculation as to why religious litigation is consistently misreported in the press.

Some recent cases

Aston Cantlow

Let me start with a sleepy village in Warwickshire, the church where Shakespeare's parents were married, and whose chancel was in need of repair. The parochial church council brought a claim in Coventry County Court under the (then) little-known Chancel Repairs Act 1932. The claim was disputed and it eventually found its way to the House of Lords, where the highest court in the land made important judicial pronouncements concerning the legal status and personality of the Church of England. Lord Nicholls of Birkenhead observed:

> Historically the Church of England has discharged an important and influential role in the life of this country. As the established church it still has special links with central government. But the Church of England remains essentially a religious organisation. This is so even though some of the emanations of the church discharge functions which may qualify as governmental. Church schools and the conduct of marriage services are two instances. The legislative powers of the General Synod of the Church of England are another. This should not be regarded as infecting the Church of England as a whole, or its emanations in general, with the character of a governmental organisation.

Lord Rodger of Earlsferry, in a concurring speech, observed that 'the juridical nature of the Church [of England] is, notoriously, somewhat amorphous'. These assertions may seem both obvious and self-evident, but the Court of Appeal had previously reached the opposite conclusion on the specific question of whether a parochial church council is a public authority for the purposes of the Human Rights Act 1998. The Court of Appeal regarded the established nature of the Church of England as imbuing its component institutions with a governmental function sufficient to render them public authorities. However, this analysis – rendering the Church of England a 'public authority'– would have had the effect of preventing the Church of England being a 'victim' under the Human Rights Act and exercising certain rights, including that of freedom of religion.

None of these significant legal and constitutional points made an appearance in the copious press coverage which the case engendered. Instead, the sympathy of the writers was reserved for the two individuals with the legal responsibility for the repair of the chancel. They were portrayed as being poor, hard-done-by individuals on the verge of being thrown out of their home by a wicked, insensitive and over-reaching parish church. Few in the media reported the truth of the matter which is that the 'lay rectors' (as they are properly styled) had acquired the property at an undervalue in consequence of the obligation to repair the chancel. They knew from the very outset that they had that liability. Indeed, they extracted a legal indemnity from a family member in respect of their prospective obligation. They tried, ultimately without success, to engage the provisions of the Human Rights Act 1998 and they succeeded only in increasing the amount they had to pay. However, the notable thing is that the lay rectors had by far the best run of the media coverage. The real headline should have been 'Church of England Secures Right to Freedom of Religion' but it never appeared. Instead, the press offered misguided sympathy to a substantial landowner whom the parish reluctantly had to take to court in order to enforce its legal rights and the landowner's corresponding liability.

Diocesan youth officer

More controversial, perhaps, is the case of Reaney v Hereford Diocesan Board of Finance. This matter was brought in the Employment Tribunal in Cardiff and the Claimant was a young man who had worked for several charities and had applied for the post of youth officer in the Diocese of Hereford. He went through the process of selection, and he was the favoured candidate of the panel which interviewed him; but ultimately he was not appointed because the Bishop formed the view that, being a practising homosexual it was not appropriate that he should take the post of youth officer. The argument advanced in the Employment Tribunal was that the post of youth officer did not come within the narrow band of exemptions pursuant to which one could impose a requirement concerning sexual orientation, namely where 'being of a particular sexual orientation is a genuine and determining occupational requirement'. The case put by the applicant and his legal team was that the statutory exemption had to be read down so narrowly that it applied solely to ministers of religion. He had the backing of lobbying organisation Stonewall, which paid his legal costs and ran his publicity machine.

On this point of law they lost. It went against them because the tribunal was of the view that the statutory exemption was not to be narrowly construed, solely to cover ministers of religion, but it was to be more widely interpreted so as to include those leaders within the Church, lay or ordained, who had positions of appropriate leadership. So the legal bulldozer, which they had hoped would obliterate the exemption, stalled somewhat. The case, in fact, succeeded, but on a very different basis: the job had not been advertised on the basis of 'genuine occupational requirement' and this only arose at the last minute when the Bishop's approval was sought. If one merely read the press coverage, one got an incredibly one-sided and erroneous view of the case. Indeed, the reader might very well be excused for thinking that the law had in fact changed as the applicant had contended for. That is not the case at all. Mr Reaney won on the very particular facts of that case, but the exemption survived unscathed. Aided by briefings from the campaigning organisation Stonewall, the media promoted a partial and erroneous interpretation of the Tribunal's findings. The Church seemingly did nothing to promote an accurate understanding of the case.

Trumpington

Next is the case of Trumpington, once a tiny village on the outskirts of Cambridge but now swallowed up into the ever-expanding town. The issue before a statutory Tribunal of the Church of England was pastoral breakdown – the nature of the relationship between priest and the parish. There were all sorts of allegations regarding the way the priest behaved and an equally lengthy counterclaim by him as to their behaviour. This matter took many years to be resolved and eventually it was dealt with by means of a Tribunal, held in public and lasting five days. Insensitive to the tragedy of pastoral breakdown, the media portrayed this case as the 'Spitting Vicar of Trumpington', such headline appearing prominently throughout an entire series of BBC's *Have I Got News for You* over the right shoulder of Paul Merton. The case was caricatured for public consumption despite the innate distress for the individuals concerned.

Sharia

The 'Sharia Law debate' triggered by the Archbishop of Canterbury in February 2008 has been discussed in greater detail in other contributions to this publication. I considered it a rather anodyne lecture, certainly not deserving of the headlines which it attracted. Indeed, I was present in the Great Hall of the Royal Courts of Justice in the evening and heard every word of the moderate and balanced piece. I thought that the lecture summarised and reflected the law of England as it currently is and as it has been for quite a while, there being nothing remarkable nor exceptional in his text. The catalyst for the media frenzy, as is now generally acknowledged, was not the text of the lecture, but a mildly ambiguous answer giving in a recorded interview on BBC Radio Four earlier in the day (see Christopher Landau's chapter). The Press ran (and ran) with an erroneous (or highly exaggerated) version of the true story. In the following days, there was some correctional material: Lord Phillips of Worth Matravers (then Lord Chief Justice) delivered a public lecture entitled 'Equality Before the Law', and correspondents sought to redress the balance in the broadsheets. Senior politicians were equally ill-informed in their commentary. Simplistic statements suggest a clear dichotomy either to recognise all aspects of Islamic law or to give no accommodation at all. For instance, Downing Street was said to be clear that 'British laws based on British values applied' while the Culture Secretary Andy Burnham commented, on BBC1's *Question Time*, that 'You cannot run two systems of law alongside each other. That would be a recipe for chaos'.[1] Such comments were not limited to the Government: a few months before the Archbishop's lecture David Cameron (then Leader of the Opposition) commented that, 'Those who seek a Sharia state,

---

[1]   BBC1 *Question Time* broadcast on 7 February 2008.

or special treatment and a separate law for British Muslims are, in many ways, the mirror image of the BNP'.[2]

Judicial intervention in religious disputes

More recently, a defamation case fell to be determined by Mr Justice Eady. The matter concerned an article published in the *Sikh Times* concerning division in a Sikh congregation in England which had its origins in the legitimacy (or otherwise) of the leader of a strand of Sikhism in India whose authority was questioned; intimating that he was an impostor. The claimant, a reclusive Indian who spoke no English and had never visited England, sought damages based upon alleged defamatory meanings of the article. The defendant journalist took the preliminary issue at trial that the claim was non-justiciable. Having reviewed a number of authorities, Mr Justice Eady was able to identify and describe:

> ... the well-known principle of English law to the effect that the courts will not attempt to rule upon doctrinal issues or intervene in the regulation or governance of religious groups. That is partly because the courts are secular and stand back from religious issues while according respect to the rights of those who are adherents or worshippers in any such grouping. It is also partly because such disputes as arise between the followers of any given religious faith are often likely to involve doctrines or beliefs which do not readily lend themselves to the sort of resolution which is the normal function of a judicial tribunal. They may involve questions of faith or doctrinal opinion which cannot be finally determined by the methodology regularly brought to bear on conflicts of factual and expert evidence. Thus it can be seen to be partly a matter of a self-denying ordinance, applied as a matter of public policy, and partly a question of simply recognising the natural and inevitable limitations upon the judicial function.

This principled application of the law became somewhat distorted in the press, perhaps unsurprisingly, as the press portrayed the decision not so much as demonstrating deference to religious sensibilities, but as a pivotal decision in establishing journalistic freedom, and the concern that the United Kingdom was becoming the libel capital of the world. Similarly, in the more recent case of Macfarlane v Relate Avon Limited, an application for permission to appeal a decision of the Employment Appeal Tribunal was refused. Lord Justice Laws rejected the contentious written evidence of Lord Carey of Clifton (a former Archbishop of Canterbury), and emphasised the independence of the judiciary and the inappropriateness of convening Christian judges to adjudicate upon matters where religious faith is engaged. He said:

---

[2]   From a keynote address made at a conference in Birmingham in late January 2007. Extract widely reported, for example by *The Politics Show*, BBC West Midlands: http://news.bbc.co.uk/1/hi/programmes/politics_show/6316161.stm (accessed 1 May 2011).

... the conferment of any legal protection or preference upon a particular
substantive moral position on the ground only that it is espoused by the adherents
of a particular faith, however long its tradition, however rich its culture, is deeply
unprincipled.

It is long-established that the secular courts will not venture into matters
concerning the doctrine or internal regulation of faith communities, but it is
noteworthy that this principle received scant attention in the newspaper coverage
of the Singh case, which promoted instead the rights of investigative journalists to
publish legitimate stories of public concern without threat of oppressive litigation.

So, what conclusions (if any) can be drawn from these and other examples?
Why does the press adopt such a curious stance in its reporting of religion in
general, and religious litigation in particular?

Figures of fun?

Religion is and always has been a source of humour rather than of information
in the broadcast media. The tele-visual image of the clergy is, not infrequently,
the single dimension caricature of *All Gas and Gaiters*, *Father Ted*, *The Vicar of
Dibley* and, latterly, *Rev*. Few can forget the seasonal merriment derived from the
newspaper reports of the former Bishop of Southwark's discomfiture a couple of
years ago as he made his way home from a diplomatic reception. The headline,
'Bishop Leaves Irish Embassy Party Drunk' is not particularly newsworthy.
Surely a more revealing (and distinctly less likely) headline would have been
'Journalist Leaves Irish Embassy Party Sober'. But we are unlikely ever to get
away from the 'Randy Rector' and the 'Vicars in Knickers' stories in the red-
tops and elsewhere. Like the poor, they are with us always. But why is it that the
press will consistently run titillating stories such as these and seem reluctant to run
serious stories with a religious content, or when they do so, they are either cavalier
as to their accuracy or are actively partisan in their reportage? Is 'circulation' an
adequate or a responsible answer?

Inherent inaccuracy?

Perhaps news reporting, by its very nature, is inherently inaccurate. Why should
religion, for example, be treated any differently from any other form of news? It
is a well-known, and rather trite, truism that journalism is the first draft of history.
But the press do not consistently report legal proceedings accurately. Take, for
example, the widespread coverage in the media of the case of Debbie Purdy, the
last case to be determined by the Judicial Committee of the House of Lords prior
to their re-composition as the Supreme Court and relocation to the other side of
Parliament Square. It was widely asserted in the media that the decision of the Law

Lords had led to a change in the law on assisted suicide. Quite the contrary: there is no change in the law. The law was the same following the decision as it had been before. The Law Lords expressly said it was not for them to change the law: only Parliament could do that. All the Law Lords did was to enjoin the Director of Public Prosecutions to revisit and to make more public the already existing guidelines articulating the manner in which the discretion to prosecute would be exercised in cases such as these, and the factors which will be taken into account. Speaking at the York Session of General Synod on 10 July 2010, as a prelude to the controversial debate on the Episcopal ordination of women priests, the Archbishop of York appealed for an end to 'spin and propaganda' in the media against the Archbishop of Canterbury. Dr John Sentamu warned that enough is enough. He told the Synod:

> It deeply saddens me that there is not only a general disregard for the truth, but a rapacious appetite for 'carelessness'compounded by spin, propaganda and the resort to misleading opinions paraded as fact, regarding a remarkable, gifted and much-maligned Christian leader I call a dear friend and trusted colleague – one Rowan Williams.

Complexity of the law?

The reason for the inaccuracies in the reporting of legal cases may be more to do with the law itself. English jurisprudence may well be complex; it may well also be perceived to be irrelevant. Practising lawyers, it is suggested, conspire to obfuscate and confuse because it is only in the dark underworld of grey areas of questionable meanings that they can make a living. Maybe the misreporting is not through malice but through ignorance. Maybe there is substance in the remark of Harriet Harman that the courts of the land are becoming redundant and that everything will now be dealt with in the court of public opinion. But home affairs are complex, and so are foreign affairs. Why should there be a lower threshold of accuracy for the reporting of litigation concerning religious matters than there is, for example, for scientific journalism?

Insufficient regulation of the press?

There is a variety of ways to safeguard an accurate and a more truthful press. The role of the Press Complaints Commission, applying its Editors' Code of Practice, is well known, but additionally there are private law remedies in defamation as well as the emergent torts concerning invasion of privacy. But there are those who feel that the self-regulation of the PCC is insufficiently robust and, by its nature, it is a reviewing rather than a preventative body. And civil litigation is costly, time consuming and speculative. The libel courts tend to be the preserve of the rich and super rich: few have the resources of Max Mosley, the head of the governing body of world motorsport, the International Automobile Federation (FIA), for example.

Cost of litigation?

Religious leaders will rarely sue for libel, as generally they cannot afford to nor would it be appropriate to use charitable funds in the pursuit of defamation actions. The press know very well that they can write with relative equanimity whatever they choose, safe from legal redress. The case of His Holiness Sant Baba Singh Ji Maharaj v Eastern Media Group Limited and Singh (above) is exceptional: the Claimant was indeed extremely wealthy (in part, it was suggested, by a misuse of religious offerings) but he instructed his legal team (solicitors, junior barrister and QC) on a 'no win, no fee' basis. A former Church of England priest by the name of Jonathan Blake (now the bishop of Greater London and presiding archbishop of the Open Episcopal Church) appeared on *Richard and Judy* on Valentine's Day in 2001, presiding at what was called a 'gay wedding'. The following day he was described in the *Daily Mail* as a self-styled bishop, in consequence of which he issued proceedings for defamation. Mr Justice Gray determined that doctrinal issues concerning Episcopal consecration and the Petrine succession were non-justiciable and stayed the proceedings. Bishop Blake, however, represented himself and did not incur the costs of instructing solicitors or counsel. The media can be forgiven for considering religious leaders as fair game since they generally lack both the inclination and the funds to sue for defamation.

Effectiveness of religious press officers?

The reason why churches are not achieving uniformly accurate press reporting may not be so much due to the inadequacy of legal constraints at all but simply because they are not expressing themselves, their positions, their arguments and their justifications as well as they might. The Church Militant is perhaps not quite as militant as it ought to be: Christian apologists may be too apologetic. In the case of Reaney (above) two powerful organisations lay behind the parties: Stonewall in the case of the applicant youth officer, and the Church of England on the part of the Bishop and the Diocese of Hereford. The publicity war was won hands-down by Stonewall, which managed to spin perceived popular victory out of legal defeat, and all credit to their audacity and ingenuity in doing so. Likewise, the landowners in the Aston Cantlow case (above), who were rumoured to have hired professional publicists, got the better of the parish, the diocese, and the Church of England generally in the playing out of the story in the press. I venture, with apologies for the ghastly pun in the sub-title for this paper, that in the ongoing battle between religious organisations and the media, it would appear that Churches find themselves 'more spinned against than spinning'.

Postscript

Religious organisations generally do not get a good press: ridicule and titillation in the pursuit of improved sales figures seem to take precedence over neutral, accurate and balanced reporting. The solution is in their own hands. A more systematic, coherent and robust press office might help redress the balance, particularly in the case of the Church of England which, by its nature, is dispersed. As Lord Hope of Craighead observed in the Aston Cantlow litigation, 'the Church of England as a whole has no legal status or personality'. Symptomatic of this, Lambeth Palace, the Archbishops' Council and each individual diocese have separate press offices: a more unified approach would reduce (though not eliminate) the prospect of inaccurate or mischievous reporting.

However, there may well be a straw in the wind suggestive that future court decisions (in the higher courts at least) might stand a better chance of being more accurately reported. As already mentioned, Pretty was the last case determined by the Law Lords in the House of Lords. The first case before the Supreme Court (admittedly on a procedural matter concerning public funding) arose from a dispute concerning admission to a Jewish school. The substantive hearing lasted a few months with an unusually large bank of nine Supreme Court Justices allocated to hear the case. The issues raised were complex, and there was a lack of unanimity amongst the justices, but the lengthy decision running to ninety-two pages was accompanied by a five-page Press Summary setting out the background, the judgement and the minority or dissenting judgements. The Summary includes a clear caveat as to its status, but nonetheless provides the interested reader with a full and measured overview of the legal points at issue and the manner in which they have been determined by the court. This innovative procedure means that the press will be less reliant upon partial versions being disseminated by the parties, and it is hoped that gradually the lower courts (the Court of Appeal and High Court in turn) will adopt a similar methodology. A more accurate (and less partisan) understanding of the judicial determination of religious litigation is a worthy constitutional goal in a multi-faith society benignly governed by the rule of law.

Chapter 18
Towards a Theology of News

Richard Harries

Summary

In Chapter 18, Richard Harries offers some reflections 'towards a theology of news'. Christian theologians should pay attention to the news, he argues, because media 'is part of the world which God creates and redeems'. According to Christian theology, Harries argues, human beings are both made in the image of God, and crucifiers of the God who came amongst us: we have the capacity for altruism and self-transcendence, and also the capacity for great evil and selfishness. The line between 'goodie' and 'baddie' runs through each of us. This leads Harries to emphasise the importance of the free press, and he draws on Niebuhr's theological defence of liberal democracy to argue that 'Our capacity for truth makes a free press possible: but our inclination to untruth makes a free press necessary'. Harries then draws out practical lessons for the UK context: Christians should oppose press monopolies, support a strong legal framework to maintain the balance between privacy and public interest. Church and media share the vocation to truth-telling, Harries concludes: 'In a highly corrupt world dominated by the collusion of political power and money, often allied to the management of what is reported and what is left out, this vocation can be both crucial and dangerous'.

For the purpose of this chapter it is important to distinguish between the media generally and news. Religion has a concern with the media as a whole, first of all because all life is included in the embrace of God, and secondly because, if a religion is concerned to share its message as widely as possible, any suitable opportunities must be taken. As Roger Royle reminded us in an earlier chapter, this must include the realm of popular entertainment, as well as Radio 4. We might add that it should also include Radio 3 and *The Times Literary Supplement*. For our society now consists, more than ever before, of a series of sub-cultures and very few people have the ability and temperament to communicate in more than one or two of them.

The news, or what might be called the news milieu or environment, is what comes to us via a range of media as being of wide interest and importance. The word interest immediately suggests, rightly, that there is an overlap between the wider media and news, as for example when it is reported on the news that England have retained the Ashes, or a particular author has won the Booker Prize or Ann Widdecome has been eliminated from *Strictly Come Dancing*. But what matters about news is that it has been decided by someone or a group of people that certain facts are important and should be known to a wider public, not just a specialist sub-group. Obviously this requires both selection and presentation, and this will depend on a particular perspective, which itself will be rooted in a set of political, moral and commercial beliefs. These may be judged by others to be either admirable or distorted. But nothing in this life is neutral or value free, certainly not the news. If some things are selected as important, then it means many more will go unreported. To give just one example, Andrew Brown once pointed out in what is always a highly perceptive analysis of the press in the *Church Times*, that there were reports in the previous week of sharks attacking people but nothing about 250 Eritrean refugees being held in shipping containers in the desert, with the women being raped and the men tortured for ransom, whilst their families listened down mobile phones.

Many of the chapters in this book have stressed how religious communities of all kinds, Roman Catholic, the Church of England, Muslim, Jewish and Sikh, feel misreported, sometimes in a way which is highly damaging both to the communities themselves and the social fabric of society. Template journalism formed by a hostile stereotype shapes far too many stories. Some of the chapters also suggest steps that might be taken, by both the media and those religious communities to remedy this. I will not repeat what has been said elsewhere. Clearly it is of great concern that religious matters should be reported with proper professional standards.

Why a free press matters

My major concern is different. It is with a theology of the news environment, of which the reporting of religion is only one aspect, even though one that raises certain issues in a sharp form, as I indicate towards the end. The whole news environment is of concern to Christian theology, and I write here only from that perspective, because it is part of the world which God creates and redeems. But in addition to this there is a special concern, because the reporting of news is in the end about power, and this raises the question of how power is to be viewed and managed. This power is both financial and political, the two being so often interlinked in the modern world. It is not just Mr Putin in Russia or Mr Berlusconi in Italy, but also in the United Kingdom and the United States where business and political interests can be intertwined.

Christians try to hold together a double vision. On the one hand there is eternity with its great reversal of worldly values in which we are told the first will be last and the last first. There all human power will be put in its proper place. Media moguls, reporters and Bishops alike will be deeply grateful if allowed to eat the crumbs off the table of the heavenly banquet. But Christians are concerned with the penultimate as well as the ultimate, and this involves managing power as best we can in a fallen world; managing it in the interests of society as a whole, and for the sake of that true justice whose fruit is peace.

A sober estimate of human beings indicates that there is a great deal of common decency around, occasional flashes of altruism, a universal drive to pursue one's own self-interest, and all too often occasions when that pursuit becomes inordinate and harmful to the interests of other people. To put this in terms of Christian theology, we are at once made in the image of God, with some capacity for moral discernment and even self-transcendence, and crucifiers of the God who came amongst us. The great American theologian Reinhold Niebuhr reflected this understanding of human beings in his important defence of liberal democracy as summed up in his aphorism,

> Man's capacity for justice makes democracy possible: but man's inclination to injustice makes democracy necessary.[1]

A free press is an integral feature of a proper democracy, and the justification of a free press from the perspective of Christian theology is the same as that for democracy as a whole. So if Niebuhr's aphorism is transposed into terms relevant to the press, it might go like this:

Our capacity for truth makes a free press possible: but our inclination to untruth makes a free press necessary.

This position can be stated in secular terms, such as Thomas Hobbes's view that liberty is power cut up into little pieces, or Ralph Dahrendorf's, that it is conflict and conflict alone that safeguards the diversity and difference of human choices. The point is that liberty, respect for the choices of an individual human, is fundamental to a proper understanding of what is to be a human being in society. A free press is fundamental to safeguarding that.

No high moral ground

As this book has brought out strongly, religious communities feel they receive unsympathetic and sometimes hostile treatment by the press. But perhaps this is an especial reason why we should look first to ourselves. Jesus told a vivid parable which contrasted someone who thanked God that they were not as others and someone who simply said 'God have mercy on me, a sinner' (Luke 18: 9–14). He commended the latter attitude. Then there is the telling statement:

> Why do you look at the speck in your brother's eye, with never a thought for the plank in your own? (Luke 6:41)

---

[1]   Reinhold Niebuhr, *The Children of Light and the Children of Darkness* (London: Nisbet, 1945), p. vi.

When we reflect on the kind of utterance we hear, or perhaps even deliver from the pulpit ourselves, can we be so sure that it is exempt from the kind of criticisms we make of the press? Would it, for example, show even the basic professionalism of a leader in one of the broadsheets?

The fact is that Christians do not form a particular elite of 'The good' and never have done. The present situation in which the attack dogs of the new atheism have seized the high moral ground accusing religion not just of being untrue but immoral, may do a service in forcing us to examine just what it is we stand for. This is, quite simply, the gospel of grace. The gospel is not about telling us that we are better than other people. We are not. We are the same as everyone else. The difference is that we believe we are held, as everyone is in principle held, by a divine love that will not let us go, despite everything. Of course, we should expect and hope that this makes a difference to the way we behave, and unless we had some evidence of this in the people we most admire, no doubt we would give up the faith altogether. But what we have failed to get across to a wider public is that those of us who are preachers and teachers of the faith are in principle no better or worse than the average reporter. Andrew Brown put it with characteristic sharpness, when discussing the WikiLeaks story:

> All of the information in it will find its way to the people in whose hands it will do the most harm. There is a well-known half-truth that information wants to be free. But if information wants anything at all, it wants to be malicious, just like us.

All human behaviour is deeply ambiguous, as the best novelist bring out. All motives are mixed. If, as Shakespeare suggested, 'There is some soul of goodness in things evil', there is no less some seed of evil in things good. The world cannot be divided up into 'goodies' and 'baddies'. The line goes through each one of us.

Working on the four kinds of behaviour to be found in all sectors of human society, whether amongst church people or reporters, we can affirm that there is a fair amount of common decency around in the media. Even religion can sometimes be treated in a sympathetic manner. In 2010 there were at least two very good stories that bear this out: the remarkable rescue of the Chilean miners, with its very strong religious overtones, and the Pope's visit to the UK. The Pope arrived highly defensive to face an extremely hostile press, but within a day or so the whole mood had changed so that by the end the visit was regarded as a success both by the press and the Vatican. On the other hand, in Egypt after there had been an attack on the Coptic Cathedral at Christmas, and later, in February 2011, when the political revolution was happening, Muslims surrounded Christian churches to prevent them being harmed. This was reported, but it did not receive the same level of publicity as an attack on a church would have done.

Then, there are occasional flashes of altruism, and here we ought to recognise and celebrate the good number of reporters who put their lives at risk, not just by going to dangerous places, but because they try to expose corruption in high places. Anna Politkovskaya, the journalist who exposed corruption in the highest circles, is an obvious example, but she is only one of dozens, perhaps hundreds, of reporters killed in Russia in the course of their work.

Then there is the fact that all of us pursue our own interests. There is nothing wrong with this in its proper place, and when kept in bounds. Indeed, it is essential both for human survival and the functioning of society. However, this can too easily develop into an inordinate self-interest which sometimes goes beyond the wire of what is legal, and often goes as close to it as it can.

Power cut up into little pieces

'Our capacity for truth makes a free press possible, but our inclination to untruth makes a free press necessary'. The implications of this in relation to the press are: Our capacity for truth, expressed in the presence of common decency amongst many reporters and occasional heroic altruism by the few, make a free press possible. Our inclination to untruth, as shown in the universality of self-interest with its tendency to become inordinate, means that a free press is necessary. The implication of this in practice is that:

1. There must be no monopolies. The avoidance of monopolies has been a guiding principle in the operation of a proper free market ever since the time of Adam Smith. This has been of particular concern in the UK when there was a fear Rupert Murdoch's News Corporation, which prints one in three of Britain's paying newspapers, would acquire more than the 40 per cent stake it already owns in BskyB, which has a bigger UK budget than the BBC.

2. There must be a strong legal framework, not only to ensure that there are no monopolies, but to maintain a proper balance between freedom to expose what is in the public interest, and safeguarding privacy when it is not. Allied to this there must be proper means of redress if people feel that they have had their private life violated or had lies told about them.

Where there is a clear and robust legal framework in place to ensure that these principles are in operation, then we can rely on a combination of the desire for truth and ordinary self-interest to keep a wide range of views in the public realm. An investigative reporter onto some corruption scandal will, like all of us, be a mixture of motives: a desire to expose the truth and a desire to enhance his or her own reputation for doing so. It is this combination that keeps a free press alive and working. If news is always in danger of becoming a processed commodity, at least a society which has a number of sources of news offers a variety of commodities processed in different ways.

Speaking truth to power

'Speak truth to power', a phrase which may go back to eighteenth century Quakers, and which came into prominence in the 1950s, sums up the highest and most serious aspect of those responsible for news. It is a great phrase, but the vocation is one which tests human integrity to the limit. The dangers of collusion and the wrong kind of compromise are all too obvious.

In Evelyn Waugh's novel *Helena*, Helena, the mother of the first Christian emperor, Constantine, locates the sites in the Holy Land associated with Jesus, and reflects on the three magi:

> You came at length to the final stage of your pilgrimage and the great star stood still above you. What did you do? You stopped to call on King Herod. Deadly exchange of compliments in which began that unended war of mobs and magistrates against the innocent.[2]

The press have the power to stir, incite, calm or educate the mob, that is, mass public opinion of which we are all a part. It will always do this against a background of power, both financial and political. A 'deadly exchange of compliments' with power can all too easily lead to innocent people being hurt.

One major feature of the present book is the way that the traditional media is losing ground to the new media, Google, Facebook, Twitter, blogging and so on. No doubt we are just at the beginning of this revolution and there is much more change to come. From the standpoint of Hobbes, for whom liberty is power cut up into little pieces, this makes for an enlargement of liberty, for power is being cut up into very small pieces indeed; for even a small piece, a photo on a mobile phone, can rapidly reach a worldwide audience, as it did in demonstrations in Teheran in 2009.

The church and conflict

In chapter two of this book on 'Religion in the Media Today' the authors assert that 'we may conclude that, in general, there is a conservative and pro-Christian emphasis in British newspapers'. As they point out, this result comes as a surprise because media professionals are less religious than the population as a whole, and there is a common complaint from religious people that the media is highly secular. So what are we to make of their finding about a conservative and pro-Christian emphasis?[3]

What we also need to take into account is that these conservative and pro-Christian papers do not make them any less critical of the church that actually exists, if anything it makes them more critical. Often what they want is a church that

---

[2]   Evelyn Waugh, *Helena* (London: Penguin, 1950), p. 239.

[3]   See also chapter 3 for a different perspective.

has passed, one which used the 1662 prayer book, or which stood four-square on solid middle class values, and which did not criticise the status quo. These papers do not want a prophetic church, one which speaks truth to power. Sometimes they call for more leadership, but in fact the Archbishop of Canterbury, to take just one example, often gives an example of leadership, but it is in a direction they do not wish to travel (see, for example, the criticism of him resulting from his editing an edition of the *New Statesman* in June 2011). What they want is Christianity as a cultural phenomenon, firm on mainstream values, valuing its church buildings and artistic heritage. In 2011, for example, there was a huge amount of celebration in connection with the 400th anniversary of the King James Version of the Bible, which began with a paean of praise from Richard Dawkins in the *New Statesman*, the only religious reference in their Christmas edition. Some sections of the press are at once pro-Christian and hostile to the church as it actually exists at the moment, because they do not like the message that some church leaders proclaim, as for example during the time of Margaret Thatcher's government when, the Labour Party in Parliament being weak, the Church of England became a kind of unofficial opposition, voicing the hurt of mining and other communities where the affects of her policies were being particularly felt.

Even more integral to the church than its prophetic voice, which is so hard to get right, there is its core message: for to believe in God is to believe in one who by definition makes a total difference to the way we view life. This is, of course, highly threatening. So, to put it unfairly, it is much easier to focus on the disunity, scandals and hypocrisy of the church – which do, of course, need to be exposed. It is telling that the research analysed in chapter two showed that the highest number of references to religion, 30 per cent, were in ITV advertising. Clearly, in such a context religious references must be anything but threatening; they must be trivial, funny or reassuring.

At the Cumberland Lodge Conference Ruth Gledhill, the religious correspondent for *The Times*, ended her presentation by saying that religious communities will be satisfied by the way they are reported when they themselves are harmonious and the press is interested in reporting harmony.[4] 'Neither will happen', she said. In short, the present uneasy situation will continue. There are a number of implications of this that need to be thought about.

First, despite all the evidence of disharmony most Church of England leaders do all they can to work for harmony and fear conflict. Do we actually need to have a more positive view of conflict – not violent or aggressive conflict of course – but the statement of strongly held views that might run counter to conventional opinion? The same point emerges from Ruth Scott's contribution to this book, in her discussion on balance in broadcasting. Does an attempt to get balance in fact mean overlooking some fundamental injustice? The press thrives on conflict, the church fears it, whilst at the same time it feeds the media's image of the church as disharmonious.

---

[4]   See also Ruth Gledhill's chapter on 'Mirrors to Power' (chapter 6) in this book.

Yet, there should be conflict of one kind: conflict between truth telling and all collusive relationships of power and money. The press and religious bodies ought at least on occasion to be able to collaborate in this task. But what about the press itself? If the press are in some sense the guardians of truth who, to draw on Plato, are the guardians of the guardians? On the whole, one section of the media does not like to criticise another. Dog does not eat dog. The exception is *Private Eye*, which in addition to its exposures in the areas of politics and business also has a page entitled 'Street of Shame'. But this is very little compared to the size and influence of the media as a whole.

The core task of the church is truth-telling. So, at its best, is journalism. In a highly corrupt world dominated by the collusion of political power and money, often allied to the management of what is reported and what is left out, this vocation can be both crucial and dangerous.

—

Chapter 19
Conclusion: The Futures of Religion and the News

Jolyon Mitchell and Owen Gower

Over the next few years the international news media's attention will almost inevitably turn to one country in South America. Why? Because Brazil is set to host the 2014 World Cup and Rio de Janeiro the 2016 Olympics. Like their predecessors, these rituals of international sport will be televised and watched by hundreds of millions of people around the world. For some, these are expressions of a new global religion, which has even gone so far as to replace traditional forms of worship. Instantaneous images, slow motion replays and high definition pictures will bring the vast arenas into homes, bars and cafes, anywhere with a connected small or large screen. One icon has already been used on many occasions to represent the location of these sporting events. Even better known than Rio's *Estádio do Maracanã* (Maracanã stadium), where the deciding game of the 1950 World Cup was played, this statue is inextricably connected with Rio, and looks down from Corcovado ('Hunchback') Mountain: it is known as *Christo Redentor* (*Christ the Redeemer*).

Some interpret the statue's out-stretched arms as representing the welcoming, open doors attitude of Rio's people. From fingertip to fingertip it measures about 98 feet (30 metres). Close up, the size of the figure is intimidating. It is 98.5 feet high, and stands on a substantial plinth, giving the monument a total height of 130 feet (39.6 metres). Pictures of this huge figure of Christ, completed in 1931 to mark over a century of Brazil's independence, are found on countless postcards, calendars and in many news reports. Photographs are taken from behind the figure, revealing the city, the coast and the hills. Many shots face eastwards and include both Guanabara Bay and *Pão de Açúcar* (Sugarloaf Mountain). The stunning vista undoubtedly contributed to the statue recently being voted one of the seven new wonders of the world. The figure has also appeared in popular films, including *2012* (2009, Roland Emmerich), which controversially depicted the statute's collapse (followed by the destruction of the Sistine Chapel and St Peter's in Rome) in the midst of a series of earthquakes and other global environmental catastrophes.

Stand beneath this soapstone-faced, art deco statue of Christ and look away from the coast, inland to the West. It is hard to miss on a nearby ridge, also in Tijuca Park, at least a dozen transmitters and aerials.[1] Unlike the transmitter for

---

[1] See Jose Drummond, 'The Garden in the Machine: An Environmental History of Brazil's Tijuca Forest', *Environmental History* (1996) 1 (1): 83–105.

the first TV station in Rio, at the top of the Sugar Loaf Mountain, they are plainly visible on what looks like a slightly flattened neighbouring peak. They can also be seen from parts of Rio. Compared to the sculpture of Christ, looking over the city, these edifices are rarely photographed, though they perform the vital functions of connection and communication. The juxtaposition of this famous religious statue and these less well-known aerials provides a metaphor for reflecting on the possible relations between religion and the news. The aerials stand on their own hill looking across at *Christo Redentor*. What is their relationship, their connection with each other? Through this book we have heard expressions of co-operation, criticism and creativity.

Figure 13   Rio de Janeiro. View of Christ the Redeemer Statue on Corcovado
              Mountain and Radio and Television aerials in Tijuca National Park.
              Courtesy of Celso Diniz / Shutterstock.com

First, *co-operation*: communicative tools have helped to turn this statue into an internationally recognised icon. Likewise, news broadcasts from Rio and Brazil have kept this 635-tonne statue of Christ in the public eye. Like many other religious symbols, buildings and events it has been put to various journalistic uses. Compare two recent news reports on the statue. The *Catholic News Service* ran a story related to its recent eightieth anniversary (2011), highlighting its catholic roots and the local Archbishop's (Orani João Tempesta) personal interpretation, who claimed that it 'as an icon of Rio de Janeiro' which 'represents the Brazilian citizen: as a person who follows Jesus Christ, and welcomes others, as the monument does with its open arms' (12 October 2011). While Julia Carneiro, covering the same story for the BBC, is far less explicitly theological, emphasising the history of its construction, its appeal to tourists and its visibility throughout Rio. Near the end of her 1 minute 48 second report she describes it as a 'symbol of the city regardless of religion' (7 October 2011). Both reports are co-operative rather than iconoclastic: as they mark an anniversary and thereby publicise the enduring popularity of an explicitly religious symbol. Nevertheless, the journalists interpret it in very different ways. Communicative co-operation between religion and journalists comes in many forms. It has evolved over the last three hundred years. It has a long history, which is commonly overlooked, but underlined by poignant events such as a memorial service held at St Bride's church in Fleet Street, entitled the 'Price of Freedom', for 'journalists, cameramen and support staff who have lost their lives while bringing us the news' (9 November 2011). As has become clear in several of the chapters in this book (especially in part 3 on 'Representing Religion'), many religious leaders remain keen to co-operate with journalists and editors.

Secondly, *criticism*: in Rio some of the antennas appear to spring up out of Tijuca Forest, like sharp spikes pointing upwards beyond the clouds. From certain viewpoints within the park the growing forest of aerials actually obscures most of the figure of Christ. This symbolises the competition, perhaps even conflict, between two powers vying for the attention of the city. In a similar fashion, the theme of conflict recurs frequently through the preceding pages of this book. There are different kinds of conflict, criticism and misunderstanding between religion and the news. It is a two-way process. Several contributors to this book are highly critical of what they perceive as a 'fortress mentality' where religious institutions or leaders hide from the press, behind closed doors (e.g. chapter 7). While others critically observe how journalists are drawn to conflict, scandals and internal divisions: what Catherine Pepinster describes as 'spats' (chapter 8). This is nothing new, but remains a recurring criticism among religious leaders who perceive that conflict is the dominant news frame (e.g. chapters 1, 2, 4 and 7). Questions have also been raised about both the quality and quantity of religious news coverage. Why are certain religious groups such as the Sikhs (chapter 12) given so little space in the news? Why are some religions effectively invisible? Who should control and censor remains a recurring question and has led to frequent conflicts. If journalists are, as Ruth Gledhill suggests, 'mirrors to the world' then do they have a responsibility to reflect accurately the discord that they encounter? As Richard Harries underlines in the previous chapter, conflict has many forms. It does not necessarily lead to violence. Peaceful forms of conflict can disrupt, challenge and undermine the status quo. Journalists covering religion can be both constructive and creative when uncovering injustice and 'speaking truth to power'.

Thirdly, *creativity*: both the transmitters and the statue reflect the extraordinary creativeness to be found within different communities. The statue of Christ constructed between 1922 and 1931. Designed by a Brazilian engineer Heitor da

Silva Costa, it was partly sculpted by Paul Landowski in Paris and shipped over to Brazil, where it was taken by the cog-train most of the way up the 2300 feet (700 metre) high mountain. The antennas on the neighbouring hill similarly reflect both inventiveness and persistence. Many of the modern ones look like miniature red and white Eiffel Towers, topped with single lightning rods. While the establishment of communication networks is now largely taken for granted, connecting a nation the size of Brazil is no mean feat, and one with a comparatively long history. Brazil's first radio transmitter was erected in 1922, 'on top of the Corcovado Mountain, overlooking Rio de Janeiro'.[2] The Catholic church now operates 181 radio stations in Brazil,[3] and several large Pentecostal churches have developed extensive multi-media empires which produce, along with many other programmes, their own news and current affairs reports.[4]

In the preceding chapters we have seen how both journalists and religious broadcasters can be not only critical but also highly creative in how they interact with news stories. Roger Royle's personal reflections on popular media, news and religion (chapter 13) illustrate some of the difficulties faced by representatives of religion seeking to communicate to a wide audience. In a very different cultural and religious setting from South America, we have seen how British journalists can draw upon a wide range of resources to cover a story about religion. These stories, such as the Archbishop's reflections on Sharia Law, take on a life of their own and attract multiple creative interpretations (see, for example, Christopher Landau's discussion of his interview with Rowan Williams in chapter 5). How often journalists actually draw upon all that is available to them is open to further scrutiny. The personal and spiritual autobiographies of journalists can unintentionally shape their accounts. For this reason it is refreshing to read how a journalist such as Ruth Gledhill (in chapter 6) reveals some of her own background and journey.

Following on from these observations it would be possible to reduce these three processes, of co-operation, criticism and creativity, into a crude historical description of the relations between religion and the news. In such a scheme, co-operation between journalists and religious leaders would primarily be in the past, while criticism and conflict would be in the present, and a desire for more creative interactions would be a hope for the future. This is obviously an oversimplification as it is clear from many of the accounts within this book that these processes of co-operation, criticism, and creativity have been at work throughout the long and complex history of religion and the news. They often work together.

---

[2]   See Elizabeth Fox, 'Latin American broadcasting', in Leslie Bethell (ed.), *Latin America since 1930: Ideas, Culture, and Society* (Cambridge: Cambridge University Press, 1995).

[3]   Keith A. Roberts and David Yamane, *Religion in Sociological Perspective*, Fifth Edition (Thousand Oaks, London and New Delhi: Sage, 2012), pp. 348–74, especially p. 356.

[4]   Dennis A. Smith and Leonildo Silveira Campos, 'Christianity and Television in Guatemala and Brazil: The Pentecostal Experience', *Studies in World Christianity*, Volume 11.1 (2005), pp. 49–64.

Consider, for example, the coverage of what became a major foreign news story with significant religious elements: the destruction of the Buddhas of Bamiyam in central Afghanistan (March, 2001) by the Taliban. In many parts of the world it was interpreted as a form of cultural vandalism and modern iconoclasm. Some writers spoke of 'them' and 'us'. The 'other' was not always those behind the acts of destruction, but rather those who self-identified more generally as Muslim. This approach became more common after 9/11.[5] In several papers and other news reports, 'we' were effectively White, Christian and European. Nevertheless, journalists co-operated with religious leaders, including several Muslims, as they analysed the decision to dynamite these sixth-century statues. Both creative and critical reports, including numerous photographs, are preserved on various Internet sites. Soon after the Buddhas' destruction, plans to build the Spring Temple Buddha in China were announced. It was recently completed at nearly 500 feet (c. 150 metres), making it the highest statue in the world, though up to this point it has received far less coverage than either Brazil's Christ or the destroyed Buddhas. Blow off a hand, however, and it would probably find its way alongside half-submerged cruise liners, shattered cityscapes and dynamited Buddhas. Whether religious or not, dramatic, destructive, images are hard to trump when it comes to competing for attention in the news.

The ever-increasing immediacy of news is a well-known fact. The digital revolution is transforming journalism. The use of satellites, mobile phones and other digital electronic media allows immediate, insistent and graphic transmission of news, which many politicians and increasingly religious leaders perceive they have to respond to on the day. Moreover, as John Witherow, the editor of *The Sunday Times* claimed at the Leveson enquiry: 'newspapers are caught up in an absolute revolution. We've never had a challenge like this in more than 200 years' (17 January 2012). As both Andrew Brown (chapter 9) and Simon Barrow (chapter 15) have suggested, this challenge is rooted in a combination of factors: the free public access of news online, the rise of citizen journalism and the convergence of communication technologies.

In the light of these observations the relationship between religion and the news is undergoing a series of transformations. These have implications for evolving stories, contested contexts, creative journalists, and expressive audiences (see chapter 1). It is, as Paul Woolley argues in chapter 4, a 'relationship worth getting right'. Woolley and several other authors in this book recommend increased media literacy, especially among religious leaders (see also chapter 7). Some religious leaders, from a range of traditions, are more than aware of the importance of this skill. The *Telegraph*'s former religious correspondent, George Pitcher, for example, outlined in the *Church Times* 'ten media tips for the Church', which included the appeal to 'stop being a victim', be 'clear on the core offer', 'integrate' within different media, speak in accessible terms, provide 'rabid rebuttal', 'allow access'

---

[5]   Stuart Allen, *News Culture*, Second Edition (Maidenhead: Open University Press, 2004), pp. 348–74.

and 'stand by the weak' (14 October 2011). This was published just before the St Paul's protest story hit the headlines (see chapter 1). Each point is open to debate, but they raise important issues and are translatable across religious traditions. They are, however, by no means the end of the story.[6] Such tips represent another step in an ongoing conversation between religion and the news.

As several authors in this collection argue, there is wisdom in developing a more profound understanding of the news (e.g. chapters 15–18). Why does the news matter? What distinctive stories, practices and beliefs does a religious tradition offer for reflecting on and engaging with the news media? There is much more to media literacy than simply media training on how to answer questions or cope with a crisis. These pass. Even the term 'media literacy' is open to question – as it suggests an emphasis upon a primarily literate or reading approach to texts, which are commonly highly visual. It also implies that once you become media literate, you can read the media. Media awareness is a more dynamic process. For this reason 'media education' may be a better term, as it also implies that an individual is never completely 'literate' when it comes to the media. Becoming media educated is an ongoing process, and is far more complex than is often perceived. Both religious leaders and journalists are themselves on a continuum: students always learning about an ever-evolving communicative environment. Developing further skills in co-operation with journalists, constructive criticism of news, and communicative creativity are all good starting points.

What then of journalists, editors and broadcasters? How necessary is the challenge, made by several authors in this book, that journalists become more religiously literate? In what is sometimes grandly described as a 'post-secular world', how important is it for journalists and their colleagues to develop a critical understanding of religious beliefs, traditions and practices? A journalist may personally perceive religion as a largely harmful or spent force, or, alternatively, as vital to human flourishing and to the wellbeing of the world, or, combining these two, as embodying the 'ambivalence of the sacred'.[7] At least some recognise that it is vital for journalists to deepen their religious understanding.

Many of the contributors to this book affirm that this is a vital development. In much the same way as the term 'media literacy' is debated, so the phrase 'religious literacy' is a contested one.[8] What emerges is that it is more than simply knowing 'facts' about religious traditions. If improved insight and accuracy in coverage is the aim, then increased knowledge is a useful foundation. This includes grasping

---

[6]   See Christopher Landau's article on 'How to stop being a media victim', *Church Times*, 11 November 2011. Landau argues that more important than improved tactics of media engagement is a theology of confident public engagement.

[7]   See R. Scott Appleby, *The Ambivalence of the Sacred: Religion, Violence, and Reconciliation* (London, Boulder, New York and Oxford: Rowman and Littlefield, 2000).

[8]   See Elaine Graham, 'Religious literacy and public service broadcasting: introducing a research agenda', in Gordon Lynch, Jolyon Mitchell, and Anna Strhan, *Religion, Media and Culture: A Reader* (London and New York: Routledge, 2012), pp. 228–35.

'the basic tenets' of different faiths, understanding 'religious practices and their meanings', and being able to distinguish 'the subtle' but important 'differences among confessions, traditions and denominations'.[9] Understanding the 'varieties of religious experience', as well as religious practices, doubts and beliefs is a lifelong challenge, though one worth embarking on for those working in a rapidly evolving 'stop-watch' communicative culture.

There are signs that some journalists and religious leaders are working towards building bridges between communities that may have much to learn from each other. As we write, there is a move to explore the feasibility of developing a religious media resource centre. This would aim to bring together other organisations already working in this area and the expertise of scholars and even religious leaders.[10] This is but one initiative amongst many future possibilities.

Another more concrete project is already in the public domain. The BBC's College of Journalism now provides an online guide on 'Religion' for journalists, which is also open to the public.[11] It contains lucid briefings and details about all the main religious traditions. They offer a 'journalist's guide' in the following order on: Christianity, Islam, Judaism, Hinduism, Buddhism, and Sikhism. There are also a number of short films outlining these traditions and related issues. On this site Roger Bolton, presenter of BBC Radio 4's *Sunday* programme [1998–2010], also presents a brief film on 'Journalists and Religion' and explores why religion is such an important topic for journalists to get right. He argues that 'religion matters as much as if not more than before', and that 'religion is likely to be at the centre of many people's lives', even if the journalists themselves view it with scepticism. Bolton concludes his report by arguing that: 'Journalists have to get in touch with what these religious minorities and majorities believe, and report them accurately, because if you can't be relied to report them fairly and accurately then why should they believe you when you report on anything else?'[12]

This persuasive short film resonates with many of the themes in this book. Both illustrate how it is possible to retain healthy scepticism, to ask critical questions, to face flawed religious or media representatives, to challenge injustice, deceit and an over-comfortable status quo, while at the same time retaining respect and empathy for those who live, believe and act differently from ourselves. Combining conversation and criticism can facilitate creativity. Moving between the two mountaintops, each with its own edifice, is a potentially difficult exercise, but the original perspectives from each can provide an enriching view of our fragile world.

---

[9] See *BBC Governors 2004 Report.*

[10] This initiative might follow in the footsteps of the highly successful Science Media Centre. It is another example of a future initiative that could contribute to the improvement of relations between religion and the news.

[11] http://www.bbc.co.uk/journalism/briefing/religion/ (accessed 2 January 2012).

[12] http://www.bbc.co.uk/journalism/briefing/religion/roger-boltons-challenge/ (accessed 2 January 2012).

Select Annotated Bibliography

Teemu Taira and Jolyon Mitchell

Appignanesi, L. (ed.), *Free Expression is No Offence* (London: Penguin, 2005).
This book examines the issue of free speech in a post-9/11 world. The authors argue that it is imperative that our freedom of speech is not curtailed if we are intent on allowing those of all faiths and those of none, as well as all different cultures, to live peacefully side-by-side.

Arthur, C. (ed.), *Religion and the Media: An Introductory Reader* (Cardiff: University of Wales Press, 1993).
This is a pre-internet collections of essays on religion and the media. It includes several useful articles on news, including essays on: the 'Theology of the Nine O'Clock News' and Islamic perspectives on News.

Badaracco, C.H. (ed.), *Quoting God: How Media Shape Ideas about Religion and Culture* (Waco: Baylor University Press, 2005).
This volume consists of essays by scholars and journalists. The geographical scope extends from North America to Asia, the Middle East and Latin America. In addition to Christianity and Islam, articles also deal with Falun Gong, Japanese traditions and challenges in reporting religion and science.

Barendt, E., *Freedom of Speech*, 2nd edn (Oxford: Oxford University Press, 2005).
Barendt examines the meaning and scope of freedom of speech by studying the varied approaches of different legal systems and constitutional traditions (including England, the United States, Canada and Germany) with regards to privacy, copyright and reputation. Case law is pitted against philosophical and political arguments for free speech.

Buddenbaum, J.M., *Reporting News about Religion: An Introduction for Journalists* (Ames: Iowa State University Press, 1998).
The first part of the book is an introduction to religion in the United States, but the second part examines religion news in print media, radio and television, their trends and audiences. The third part investigates the selection and use of sources in reporting religion and analyses written news stories about religion.

Buddenbaum, J.M., and Mason, D.L. (eds), *Readings on Religion as News* (Ames: Iowa State University Press, 2000).

This collection of over one hundred articles on religion and news takes the reader on a journey through three hundred years of American history. The anthology is divided into four parts. The first set of stories comes from the Puritan era, when journalism was regularly used as a persuasive tool to promote visions of a 'New Jerusalem'. The second (c.1800–1945) charts how news about religion helped to define American politics and culture. The third and fourth (post-1945 and 1990s) describe the move to more 'detached' forms of journalism.

Bunt, G.R., *Islam in the Digital Age* (London: Pluto Press, 2003).
The Internet and Al-Jazeera are the main news outlets and opinion makers in the Arab world. This study investigates the ways in which different groups of Muslims draw on the Internet for news, and for making sense of the events in the world.

Campbell, H.A., *When Religion Meets New Media* (London and New York: Routledge, 2010).
This book consists of a series of case-studies which examine the use of new media technology in the Abrahamic religions in different societies. It shows how processes of negotiation – including fears, hopes, rejection, engagement, innovation as well as doctrinal and pragmatic reasoning – take place when communities make decisions on the application of recent media. It also shows how new media technologies change the ways in which news travels to, and is selected by, religious communities.

Carey, J., *The Faber Book of Reportage* (London: Faber and Faber, 1987).
An extensive selection of eye-witness accounts that invites the reader to travel from Thucydides reporting on a plague in Athens nearly 2500 years ago via John Wesley preaching in Hull to a broad range of major stories in the twentieth century.

Casanova, J., *Public Religions in the Modern World* (Chicago: The University of Chicago Press, 1994).
Even though this widely debated sociological study on the 'deprivatisation' of religion does not investigate media or news, it is useful text for reflecting on the ways in which religious news coverage relates to the role(s) of religion in the public sphere. The main argument is that secularisation does not necessarily lead to privatisation of religion, and that religion is returning – and that it should return – into the public sphere.

Castells, M., *Communication Power* (Oxford/New York: Oxford University Press, 2009).
The rise of communication power in the new communications environment is studied from a psychological point of view, referencing neuroscience, cognitive psychology and case studies from around the world (ranging from media deregulation and the influence of media on politics in the United States to media control in Russia and China). Castells maintains that the new communication system of mass self-

communication (including instant messaging, social networking and blogging) has profoundly altered power relationships.

Clark, L.S. (ed.), *Religion, Media, and the Marketplace* (New Brunswick: Rutgers University Press, 2007).
Scholars in history, media studies and sociology explore widely the connections and mutual influence between media, religion and the commercial marketplace. Some contributors investigate representations of religious issues in the news.

Cohen, Y., *God, Jews and the Media: Religion and Israel's Media* (London and New York: Routledge, 2012).
In this book Cohen analyses the relationship between Judaism and a range of media, providing a comprehensive examination of modern Jewish identity in the information age. Covering Israel as well as the Diaspora populations of the UK and US, the author examines journalism, broadcasting, advertising and the internet to give a wide-ranging analysis of how the Jewish religion and Jewish people have been influenced by the media age.

Couldry, N., *Media Rituals: A Critical Approach* (London and New York: Routledge, 2003).
Draws on a range of scholars and examples to reflect on the place of media rituals in today's communicative environment.

Couldry, N., *Media, Society, World: Social Theory and Digital Media Practice* (Cambridge: Polity, 2012).
This theoretically driven text encourages readers to reflect on the significance of the evolution of traditional and new media on many aspects of everyday life, including: power, ritual, religion, ethics, politics, social order, and justice.

de Vries, H., and Weber, S. (eds), *Religion and Media* (Stanford: Stanford University Press, 2001).
The essays in this volume attempt to make sense of the conceptual, analytical and empirical difficulties involved in addressing the complex relationship between religion and media. It understands media widely and uses anthropological case studies covering areas including Indonesia, Poland, Japan, Venezuela, Australia and Turkey. Empirical analysis of news coverage of religion is not its primary focus, but one of the strengths of the volume is its theorising the 'return of religion' in relation to mass media, information technologies and changes in the structure of communication. Its theoretical standpoint is often located in continental philosophy and cultural theory.

Eickelman, D.F. and J.W. Anderson (eds), *New Media in the Muslim World: The Emerging Public Sphere* (Bloomington: Indiana University Press, 1999).
Underlying many of the essays in this book is the belief that new uses of media shape belief, authority and community in the Muslim world and transcend local

and state boundaries. This volume is an effort to analyse such developments and the redefinition of Muslim publics that result from them. It also points towards the question of the interaction of 'old' and 'new' media.

Ferguson, D., *Faith and Its Critics* (Oxford: Oxford University Press, 2009).
In this book David Ferguson analyses the arguments and public pronouncements of the 'new atheists'. He places their theories into a broader historical context.

Fortner, R., and M. Fackler (eds), *Ethics and Evil in the Public Sphere* (Cresskill, NJ: Hampton Press, 2010).
In this collection of essays in honour of one of the world's leading media ethicists, Clifford G. Christians, a wide range of scholars tackle media, values and global media. Many essays engage with news and several consider religious issues in relation to the news.

Gearon, L. (ed.), *Freedom of Expression and Human Rights: Historical, Literary and Political Contexts* (Brighton: Sussex University Press, 2006).
This is a critical and contentious overview of the relationship between writing and political dissent from early Greek democracy to modern universal human rights. Several writers suggest that freedom of expression is affected not only by law but also by ideological and theological factors.

Goethals, G.T., *The TV Ritual: Worship at the Video Altar* (Boston: Beacon Press, 1981).
Early examination by an art historian of how television and television news take the place of religion in satisfying human needs.

Haskell, D.M., *Through a Lens Darkly: How the News Media Perceive and Portray Evangelicals* (Toronto: Clements, 2009).
This is a study of media portrayal of Evangelicals in North American newspapers and television which also examines Evangelical lobbying and journalists' opinions on Evangelicals.

Hatch, N.O., *The Democratization of American Christianity* (New Haven, CT: Yale University Press, 1991).
In this book Hatch explores the changes in the Christian church shortly after the American Revolution and explains how democratisation, with common people becoming extremely influential in religious movements, influenced the development of Christianity in America.

Herbert, D., *Religion and Civil Society: Rethinking Public Religion in the Contemporary World* (Aldershot: Ashgate, 2003).
This book theorises the re-emergence of religion in the public sphere in the modern world and analyses aftermaths of four cases: the Satanic Verses affair and Muslims

in Britain, the Solidarity movement and Catholicism in Poland, the genocide in Bosnia and Nasser's Egypt. News media play a role in some of the cases, while the rest of the book provides a sociological framework for contextualising the news media within civil society.

Hirschkind, C., *The Ethical Soundscape: Cassette Sermons and Islamic Counterpublics* (New York: Columbia University Press, 2006).

This study demonstrates the importance and effectiveness of micro- or counterpublics that often bypass mainstream media news. The cassette sermon became one way in which Islamic revival developed and spread in Middle Eastern cities. Furthermore, the cassettes illustrate the difficulty with the category 'news': the content of the cassettes includes information about the world, combined with devotional, political and ethical messages.

Hoover, S.M., *Religion and the News: Faith and Journalism in American Public Discourse* (Thousand Oaks, London and New Delhi: Sage, 1998).

At the heart of this widely cited study is the question: 'Why is it that in the United States, the most religious of the Western industrial countries, the coverage of religion by the secular press continues to be so controversial? Hoover employs theoretical, empirical and historical tools both to answer this question and to investigate the relation between religion and the news. Interviews with journalists and audiences enrich this significant study.

Hoover, S.M., *Religion in the Media Age* (London and New York: Routledge, 2006).

This book is about the intermingling of media and religion in the experience of media audiences. It focuses on household media consumption and the ways in which media are engaged in people's meaning making practices, religion, values and identity. Whilst dealing explicitly with religion and the news in some chapters, its overall aim is to understand religion in the age of ubiquitous media.

Hoover, S.M. and Clark, L.S. (eds), *Practicing Religion in the Age of Media: Explorations in Media, Religion, and Culture* (New York: Columbia University Press, 2003).

A collection of essays on various topics related to media and religion. Some essays offer perspectives on religion in news coverage and religious controversies in American news journalism.

Hoover, S.M., and K. Lundby (eds), *Rethinking Religion, Media and Culture* (London: Sage, 1997).

The rationale of the volume is to triangulate religion, media and culture into a coherent theoretical framework. The articles do not concentrate on religious news as such, but they facilitate understanding of how religion and media converge and thus create frameworks for portrayals and discourses of religion in the news.

Hoover, S.M., and N. Kaneva (eds), *Fundamentalisms and the Media* (London: Continuum, 2009).
> Religion in the news media, especially when it is framed in terms of conflict, is often related to Islam or fundamentalism. Essays in this volume look at 'fundamentalisms' and 'the media' together and address the resulting relations and interactions from the perspectives of history, technology, geography, and practice.

Horsfield, P., Hess, M.E., and A.M. Medrano (eds), *Belief in Media: Cultural Perspectives on Media and Christianity* (Aldershot: Ashgate, 2004).
> The essays in the volume examine mediated Christianity, mediated meaning-making and the complex relationship between media and Christian institutions. The articles illuminate how communities interact with both Christianity and media in different international contexts, including Ethiopia, Ghana and Latin America.

Højsgaard, M. and Warburg, M. (eds), *Religion and Cyberspace*, London and New York: Routledge, 2005).
> This is an overview of religion on the Internet which addresses the opportunities and challenges cyberspace brings to its users. The question of net news – its theological dimensions and group-based usage – is addressed in a couple of articles.

Klausen, J., *The Cartoons that Shook the World* (New Haven: Yale University Press, 2009).
> This book is an investigation of the conflict that developed after the Danish newspaper Jyllands-Posten published twelve cartoons of the Prophet Muhammad in 2005. Klausen interviewed politicians in the Middle East, Muslim leaders in Europe, the Danish editors and cartoonists, and the Danish imam who started the controversy. Klausen concludes that the Muslim reaction to the cartoons was orchestrated by those with political interests and that the cartoon crisis was, therefore, ultimately a political conflict rather than a colossal cultural misunderstanding.

Knott, K., *Media Portrayals of Religion and their Reception: Final Report* (Leeds: University of Leeds, 1984).
> A summary of research conducted in 1982–3 on portrayals of religion and their reception in British daily newspapers and terrestrial television channels.

Knott, K., Poole, E. and T. Taira, *Media Portrayals of Religion and the Secular Sacred* (Ashgate: forthcoming).
> Comparative and longitudinal study of coverage of religion in British mainstream newspapers and television. By replicating the 1982–1983 study in 2008–2010, this project shows what has changed in almost 30 years in portrayals of religion in British media.

Knott K. and J. Mitchell, 'The Changing Faces of Media and Religion', in L. Woodhead and R. Catto (eds), *Religion and Change in Modern Britain* (London and New York: Routledge, 2012), pp. 243–64.
> This essay explores how media coverage of Christianity in Britain has grown less deferential and more irreverent, that representations of religion in the media have diversified rather than disappeared and that the BBC still plays a major role. Knott and Mitchell also examine the changing and growing importance of media for religion in the post-war period, and how the use of different media helps to shape various forms of religious organization, power, commitment and identity.

Larsson, G. (ed.), *Religious Communities on the Internet* (Uppsala: Swedish Science Press, 2006).
> Some articles in this edited volume show how news travels transnationally between religious communities with the help of communication technology, especially websites, satellite-TV and radio. The case studies are mainly related to Islam.

Lash, N., *The Beginning and the End of 'Religion'* (Cambridge: Cambridge University Press, 1996).
> Emerging from Lash's Teape lectures delivered in India, he argues in this collection of essays that religion is not a particular territory that may be ignored at whim. He does not directly deal with news but he reflects on how politics, art, science, law and economics are inextricably bound up in religions. Part I explores the dialogue between Christianity and Hinduism while Part II studies the relationship between theology and science, secularity and eschatology.

Layard, R., *Happiness: Lessons from the New Science* (London: Allen Lane, 2005).
> Despite the common belief that the richer people are the happier they will be, Layard claims that this is not true. This book studies the causes of happiness and shows by means of psychology, sociology and applied economics how these findings can be integrated into our lives so that everyone can live a better, happier life. He explores the spread of television and the rise of individualism.

Lehikoinen, T., *Religious Media Theory: Understanding Mediated Faith and Christian Applications of Modern Media* (Jyväskylä: Jyväskylä Studies in Humanities / University of Jyväskylä, 2003).
> This study suggests that the media has become the main way by which religious groups and institutions reach people. This means that religions have to improve their internal media outlets and also reach wider audiences through mainstream media whose views and values sometimes differ strongly from those of religious groups and institutions.

Lundby K., (ed.), *Mediatization, Concept, Changes, Consequences* (New York and Oxford: Peter Lang, 2009).

This collection of essays goes beyond considering production, texts and audiences to consider some of the broader processes through which media, including news, transforms the textures of the 'social world'.

Lynch, G., *The Sacred in the Modern World: A Cultural Sociological Approach* (Oxford: Oxford University Press, 2012).

Lynch's study of the sacred in the modern world draws on several examples pertinent to understanding the relation between religion and the news. For example, he analyses the neglect and abuse of children in Irish residential schools and the BBC's controversial decision not to air an appeal for aid for Gaza.

Lynch, G., Mitchell J., and Strhan, A., *Religion, Media and Culture: A Reader* (London and New York: Routledge, 2012).

This book brings together a selection of significant writings to explore the relationship between religion, media and cultures of everyday life. This Reader is structured around four major themes: i) religion, spirituality and consumer culture, ii) media and the transformation of religion, iii) the sacred senses: visual, material and audio culture, iv) religion and the ethics of media and culture. Several essays deal explicitly with news and religion.

Marsden, L., and Savigny, H. (eds), *Media, Religion and Conflict* (Aldershot: Ashgate, 2009).

This collection of essays reflects considerable interest in Islam-related news, but the volume also includes essays on the Vatican and US presidential elections. The book is a clear sign of renewed interest in religion and news among scholars of International Relations.

Marshall, P., Gilbert, L., and Ahmanson, R.G. (eds), *Blind Spot: When Journalists Don't Get Religion* (Oxford: Oxford University Press, 2009).

A collection of essays largely examining news stories reported by major media sources in which religion was ignored or misrepresented. The topics range from the Pope's media coverage, to Islam in Iran and Iraq, to underestimation of the importance of religion in reporting on US presidential elections. The media outlets examined are mostly based in the United States.

McLeod, H., and Usdorf, W. (eds), *The Decline of Christendom in Western Europe, 1750–2000* (Cambridge: Cambridge University Press, 2003).

This book is an attempt to explain why, for over two centuries, religion and the religious social order has been in decline in Europe. Historians, sociologists and theologians attempt to explain what the religious condition of Western Europe is at the start of the twenty-first century and why Christendom declined, by tracing a course of events in England, Ireland, France, Germany and the Netherlands. An essay on 'the impact of technology on Catholicism in France' provides useful insights on radio and television.

Melton, J.G., Lucas, P.C., and Stone, J.R., *Prime-Time Religion: An Encyclopedia of Religious Broadcasting* (Phoenix: Oryx Press, 1997).

> This encyclopaedia consists of 396 A-Z entries and appendices related to religious broadcasting in radio and television. It has a strong North American emphasis in the entries and it charts the history of its religious broadcasting from 1921 to the present.

Meyer, B., and Moors, A. (eds), *Religion, Media and the Public Sphere* (Indiana: Indiana University Press, 2006).

> Essays in this volume focus on areas outside Europe and North America. Only some of the articles deal explicitly with news, but the book is useful in trying to understand how media and news change the role of religion in national public spheres worldwide.

Mitchell, J., *Media Violence and Christian Ethics* (Cambridge: Cambridge University Press, 2007).

> This book includes detailed discussion of how and why audiences remember (and forget), reframe (and frame) and redescribe (and describe) news about violence, as well as interact with photojournalism, film, advertising and new media. Mitchell provides extensive analysis of the coverage and receptions of a wide range of international news stories. He investigates why some stories, such as the attacks on 9/11 and 7/7 or the War in Iraq dominate news frames, while others, such as civil war in the Democratic Republic of Congo are commonly overlooked.

Mitchell, J., *Promoting Peace, Inciting Violence: The Role of Religion and Media* (London and New York: Routledge, 2012).

> In this book Mitchell investigates how media and religion combine to promote peace and to incite violence. In the first half of the book, on inciting violence, a wide range of media are analysed, including news reports, stained glass, sermons, posters, radio broadcasts, magazines and cartoons. In part II, on promoting peace, Mitchell explores how documentary and feature films bear witness to past acts of violence, how film-makers reveal the search for truth, justice and reconciliation, and how new media become sites for non-violent responses to terrorism and government oppression. He covers a range of countries, including Iran, Ireland, Rwanda, South Africa and the UK.

Mitchell, J. and Marriage, S. (eds), *Mediating Religion: Conversations in Media, Religion and Culture* (London: T&T Clark, 2003).

> A collection of essays dealing with religion and media. Some articles focus on religious news, mainly Islam. The volume includes four annotated bibliographies on media ethics; film and religion; new media; and communication theology.

Moore, K., Mason, P. and Lewis, J., *Images of Islam in the UK: The Representation of British Muslims in the National Print News Media 2000–2008*, Cardiff: Cardiff School of Journalism, Media and Cultural Studies (commissioned by

Channel 4). http://www.cardiff.ac.uk/jomec/resources/08channel4-dispatches. pdf. 2008.

> The report consists of the content analysis of around a thousand newspaper articles about British Muslims in the British Press from 2000 to 2008, an analysis of the Muslim visuals/images from 2007 to 2008 and an examination of media coverage of selected cases about British Muslims in the British press. On the basis of this research the report suggests that over 65 per cent of newspaper articles about Muslims in the UK characterise them negatively either as a 'problem' or a 'threat'.

Morgan, D. (ed.), *Key Words in Religion, Media and Culture* (New York: Routledge, 2008).

> This volume includes fifteen essays defining the main areas of investigation in media and religion, from production to media contents to reception. Every chapter is named according to one key word, such as economy, technology, public, narrative, text, audiences, and circulation. There is no separate chapter on 'News', but many of the essays deal with different parts of the process of reporting religion.

Mutanen, A., *To Do or Not to Do God: Faith in British and Finnish Journalism*, Reuters Institute Fellowship Paper, Oxford University. 2009. http:// reutersinstitute.politics.ox.ac.uk/fileadmin/documents/Publications/fellows__ papers/2008-2009/Mutanen_-_To_do__or_not_do_God.pdf

> This report is based on interviews with Finnish and British journalists, editors and religious affairs correspondents. The author, who is a journalist herself, interviewed thirteen British and twelve Finnish key players who contribute to news coverage of religion in the daily press. The report reveals varying editorial policies of newspapers in two different countries. It also shows the ambivalent attitudes of the journalists who try to maintain quality while knowing that it is not easy to please everyone – from owners to customers to religious communities – when writing about religion.

Nicol, A., Millar, G., and Sharland, A. (eds), *Media Law & Human Rights*, 2nd edn (Oxford: Oxford University Press, 2009).

> This volume provides practical coverage of how human rights principles impact media law. There is comprehensive and up-to-date coverage of all the important English case law and decisions of the European Court of Human Rights.

Noonan, C., *The Production of Religious Broadcasting: The Case of the BBC*, unpublished PhD thesis. Department of Theatre, Film and Television. University of Glasgow. 2008. http://theses.gla.ac.uk/614/01/2008noonanphd.pdf

> An effort to understand how religion is – and has been – conceived in the BBC's television and radio production, and how recent trends are changing attitudes. The thesis is based on interviews with media professionals and on historical analysis, and argues that producers covering religion in the BBC are subject to the demands of a competitive broadcasting environment. Even though the findings do not relate

to hard news directly, the interviews reveal much about the culture in which media professionals do their work in contemporary Britain.

Nord, D.P., *Faith in Reading: Religious Publishing and the Birth of Mass Media in America, 1790–1860* (New York: Oxford University Press, 2004).
This historical analysis of the connections between reading, North American religious publishing and the origins of modern media culture show the important role Protestantism has played in the area both institutionally and theologically.

Pattie, C., Seyd, P., and Whiteley, P., *Citizenship in Britain: Values, Participation and Democracy* (Cambridge: Cambridge University Press, 2004).
This book presents an empirical study of citizenship in Britain, incorporating surveys of political participation and voluntary activities and exploring the beliefs and values which underpin them. It explores the difference between 'good' and 'bad' citizens and the consequences that a lack of civic engagement has on modern democracy.

Pavlik, J.V., and McIntosh, S., *Converging Media: a new introduction to mass communication* (Oxford: Oxford University Press, 2010).
This is a study of how the technologies we use every day influence our current media environment. Print, visual and audio media relate to and influence each other and this inextricable and dynamic relationship is explored in detail.

Philo, G., and Berry, M., *Bad News from Israel* (London: Pluto Press, 2004).
This is a study of the news coverage of the current conflict in the Middle East. The primary material is television news, its content and reception, especially in Britain and in the United States. The study shows the differences in how Palestine and Israel are reported and the high levels of ignorance about conflict in this region, particularly among young people. Religion is not the main focus of the study, but it connects well with thinking about how religion, ethnicity and political preferences impact on news coverage. One of a number of significant studies about news emerging from the Glasgow Media Group.

Poole, E., *Reporting Islam: Media Representations of British Muslims* (London: I.B. Tauris, 2002).
A systematic examination of the ways in which British Muslims are represented in the British national press. The book includes case studies of tabloid and broadsheet stories, analysed by quantitative and qualitative methods. It exposes the frameworks used in the construction and interpretation of Islam, and argues that Muslims are predominantly excluded from Britishness. It also compares newspapers and analyses reception of news stories.

Poole, E., and Richardson, J.E. (eds), *Muslims and the News Media* (London: I.B.Tauris, 2006).

Seventeen essays and an editors' introduction make this a significant study. It provides a critical overview of Islam in current news coverage, in both British and international contexts. Many contributions examine media representations of Islam in the context of the war on terror, in which Islam is seen as threat. The book also discusses the role of Muslims themselves in news production and consumption.

Rajagopal, A., *Politics after Television: Hindu Nationalism and the Reshaping of the Public in India* (Cambridge: Cambridge University Press, 2001).

The study demonstrates the ways in which religious programming in mainstream television facilitated the political campaigning of Hindu nationalists and brought them together. The book is not about religious news as such but it shows the power of media and particularly television in the mobilisation of religious groups.

Richardson, J.E. *(Mis)Representing Islam: The Racism and Rhetoric of the British Broadsheet Press* (Amsterdam: John Benjamins, 2004).

A critical discourse analysis of Islam in the British press. The framework extends to the questions of racism, xenophobia and anti-semitism in British society. The study investigates the ways in which newspapers reproduce anti-Muslim racism and the material is based on systematic collection of data instead of anecdotal evidence.

Richardson, J.E., *Analysing Newspapers: An Approach from Critical Discourse Analysis* (Basingstoke: Palgrave, 2007).

This textbook, although not having religion as its primary focus, offers methodological tools for critical analysis of media coverage of religion. By showing how newspaper journalism works, it provides many examples of the ways in which Islam, Muslims and Arabs are represented or misrepresented.

Said, E., *Covering Islam: How the Media and the Experts Determine How We See the Rest of the World* (Fully Revised Edition with a New Introduction, London: Vintage, 1997).

Of all Said's works this is most directly focused on the news media. The book argues that the news media has huge power in determining how people understand Islam and that the term Islam – as it is employed in the media – is in part fictional and in part an ideological category used in maintaining the power relations between the West and the rest. Even though much has happened since the publication of the first edition in 1981, its theoretical views – developed also in other publications by Said – are still important in critical studies of media representations of Islam.

Seaton, J., *Carnage and the Media: The Making and Breaking of News about Violence* (London: Allen Lane, 2005).

This book explores relationship between news-makers and news-watchers. Seaton analyses how images of war and tragedy are presented by the media and how they are consumed. It includes some discussions of the place of religion and martyrs.

Schultze, Q.J., *Christianity and the Mass Media: Toward a Democratic Accommodation* (Michigan: Michigan State University Press, 2003).

> In the United States the major disputes between religion and the media usually involve Christian churches and so-called secular media. Schultze attempts to demonstrate how both parties have borrowed each other's rhetoric, and points out respective weaknesses and pretensions. He argues that the tension between Christian groups and the media in America is ultimately a good thing that can serve the interest of democratic life.

Silk, M., *Unsecular Media: Making News of Religion in America* (Urbana: University of Illinois Press, 1998).

> An analysis of how American news media cover religion. Even though the media is seen as secular in many ways, and despite the tensions between religious views and the news media, the study illustrates that many of those who actually write about religion have a positive attitude towards the subject matter.

Silk, M. (ed.), *Religion on the International News Agenda*. The Pew Program on Religion and the News Media, The Leonard E. Greenberg Center for the Study of Religion in Public Life, Hartford: Trinity College. http://www.trincoll.edu/depts/csrpl/religint.pdf. (2000).

> The report consists of seven essays on religion in the news and the content covers different parts of the world. The primary purpose of the report is to help American journalists better grasp the religious dimension of international news stories, but its usefulness is not limited geographically.

Stout, D. (ed.), *Encyclopedia of Religion, Communication and Media* (New York: Routledge, 2006).

> This A-Z organised reference work analyses how and why religions in the world have used different means of communications. It includes material on religious communication in public life, from news coverage and political messages to media evangelism.

Stout, D.A., and Buddenbaum, J.M. (eds), *Religion and Mass Media: Audiences and Adaptations* (London: Sage, 1996).

> An audience-based examination of the ways a variety of Christian traditions experience media news in the context of institutional religious influences and expectations. A large part of the volume deals with the question of what major Christian denominations in the United States teach their members about appropriate media use.

Stout, D.A., and Buddenbaum, J.M. (eds), *Religion and Popular Culture: Studies on the Interaction of Worldviews* (Ames: Iowa State University Press, 2001).

> Many essays in the volume address the question of the relationship between religious traditions and mass media. It does not simply take news content as its focal point, but

asks what various religious leaders teach their members about media use and how religious groups differ in the ways they define 'media literacy'.

Suman, M., *Religion and Prime Time Television* (Westport: Greenwood Press, 1997).
An examination of the presence and absence of religion in US prime time television. It investigates primarily fiction, but also addresses the question of religion in factual programming.

Tumber, H. (ed.), *News: A Reader* (Oxford: Oxford University Press, 1999).
A comprehensive and useful reader on news with essays or extracts from seminal works on the definitions of news, production of news, economics of news, sources of news, objectivity and ideology of news.

Underwood, D., *From Yahweh to Yahoo! The Religious Roots of the Secular Press* (Urbana: University of Illinois Press, 2002).
An historical examination of the ways in which religion has shaped journalism in the United States. Underwood argues that religion and journalism have had a parallel development: religion has been entwined with the growth of the media and American journalists operate as personifications of the old religious virtues.

Warburton, N., *Free Speech: A Very Short Introduction* (Oxford: Oxford University Press, 2009).
Warburton explores a range of controversial free speech issues, including setting limits on freedom of speech, how to balance free speech with sensitivity for religious and minority groups, and how the Internet has influenced the debate.

Articles

Barrow, S., 'Facing up to Fundamentalism', Ekklesia, http://www.ekklesia.co.uk/research/070201 (accessed 12 August 2011).
A description, analysis and overview of Christian fundamentalism in particular and the 'fundamentalist mindset' more generally, including guidelines for response.

Casanova, J. (2008), 'Public Religions Revisited', in H. de Vries (ed.), *Religion: Beyond a Concept*, New York: Fordham University Press, 101–19.
The author reflects the argument of his influential 1994 book on *Public Relations* (see above). The idea that religion has re-entered the public sphere of European societies as a contentious issue provides one possible framework for thinking the role of news media, even though Casanova does not write about media.

Coffey, J. (2001), 'Secularisation: is it inevitable?' *Cambridge Papers* 10(1).
Coffey examines why sociologists of religion have become increasingly sceptical about traditional secularisation theory (which holds that secularisation is the

inevitable by-product of Modernisation). Coffey argues that Christians should not succumb to cultural pessimism.

Cohen, Y. (2005), 'Religion News in Israel', *Journal of Media and Religion* 4(3), 179–98.
> A case study of the ways in which Israeli newspapers, radio and television cover religion. The coverage was found to be limited to the Jewish faith and to the Orthodox streams of Judaism. Religion news in the secular media was mostly limited to religious political parties, public personalities and rabbis. The centrality of secular-religious relations in the Israeli public arena resulted in the subject often being addressed in the media.

Cottle, S. (1998), 'Making Ethnic Minority Programmes Inside the BBC: Professional Pragmatics and Cultural Containment', *Media, Culture and Society* 20(2), 295–317.
> This article examines the production context and professional aims informing the production of ethnic minority programmes (which often involve religious aspects) by ethnic minority producers inside the corporation. It offers critical insights into the relatively closed world of the BBC, its corporate ethos and programme-making environment in the 1990s.

Hackett, R.I.J. (2006), 'A New Axial Moment for the Study of Religion?', *Temenos: Nordic Journal of Comparative Religion* 42(2), 93–112.
> This essay makes a case for more analytical attention to media as a social field in which religious forms of expression and differentiation may feature prominently.

Hargreaves I., (2003), *Journalism: Truth or Dare* (Oxford: Oxford University Press, 2003).
> A lucid account of journalism in the UK from experienced editor and journalist turned academic. Covers wide range of subjects, including historical, political and ethics issues.

Hjarvard, S. (2008), 'The Mediatization of Religion: A Theory of the Media as Agents of Religious Change', *Northern Lights* 6(1), 9–26.
> In this article Hjarvard argues that the media has become a key player in religious change. The suggestion is applicable both to personal convictions and institutions. By using Danish material as an example, Hjarvard argues that the media controls the amount, content and direction of religious messages in society. The media also shapes religious representations and replaces the authority of religious institutions.

Hollander, B.A. (2010), 'Persistence in the Perception of Barack Obama as a Muslim in the 2008 Presidential Campaign', *Journal of Media and Religion* 9(2), 55–66.

This study explores the factors causing misperception of Barack Obama as Muslim and whether exposure to the news media, which often attempted to debunk the myth, influenced perceptions. While conservative political and religious beliefs were associated with belief in Obama as Muslim, exposure to the news media did little to moderate this effect.

Kerr, P.A. (2003), 'The Framing of Fundamentalist Christians: Network Television News, 1980–2000', *Journal of Media and Religion* 2(4), 203–35.
According to this article, Christian Fundamentalists are reported in a consistent, mildly negative manner in the United States. Politics is often the main focus of newscasts involving Fundamentalists, and conflict has been the most prevalent news value. Although often portrayed as being somewhat intolerant, racist, violent, and prone to impose their views on others, Fundamentalists are also depicted as being patriotic.

Kitch, Carolyn (2003), 'Mourning in America: Ritual, Redemption, and Recovery in News Narrative after September 11', *Journalism Studies*, 4(2), 213–24.
This article analyses the coverage of the events of September 11 in 20 issues of American news magazines. Kitch suggests that the news coverage contained the elements of a funeral ritual, creating a forum for national mourning and playing a central role in civil religion. Journalists make sense of even 'senseless' news events by placing them within a broader, cultural grand narrative of resilience and progress.

Knott, K. (1983), 'Conventional religion and common religion in the media', transcript of a talk given at the IBA Religious Broadcasting Consultation, April 1983, Religious Research Paper 9, University of Leeds.
This is an article-length summary of a 1982–1983 research project focusing on religious references in British mainstream media.

Kodrich, K. (2005), 'Media, Religion, and Politics in Nicaragua: How an Independent Press Threatened the Catholic Church', *Journal of Media and Religion* 4(3), 117–36.
A study focusing on newspaper *La Prensa*'s religious reporting and the power struggle between the paper and the Catholic Church in Nicaragua.

Martin, J., Trammell, K.D., Landers, D., Valois, J.M., T. Bailey (2006), 'Journalism and the Debate Over Origins: Newspaper Coverage of Intelligent Design', *Journal of Media and Religion* 5(1), 49–61.
A content analysis of almost 600 newspaper articles on Intelligent Design (ID). Results suggest that ID was largely portrayed as a religious (as opposed to a scientific) movement. Coverage also was predominantly sceptical of ID's scientific legitimacy.

McCune, C.A. (2003), 'Framing Reality: Shaping the News Coverage of 1996 Tennessee Debate on Teaching Evolution', *Journal of Media and Religion* 2(1), 5–28.

> An analysis on how public controversy over teaching evolution was framed in press coverage and how each side interacted with the news media.

Meer, N. (2006), 'Get Off Your Knees: Print media public intellectuals and Muslims in Britain', *Journalism Studies* 7(1), 35–59.

> This article examines perceptions of British Muslims deployed by 'print media public intellectuals' (PMPI). The findings suggest that PMPI argumentation ranges from an overt hostility to a qualified discrimination, and that there is a convergence between these two positions in their anti-Muslim sentiment and desire to regulate the lives of ethnic Others.

Meer, N., Dwyer, C. and Modood, T. (2010), 'Beyond "Angry Muslims"? Reporting Muslim Voices in the British Press', *Journal of Media and Religion* 9(4), 216–31.

> The article investigates the significance of how a variety of self-consciously Muslim actors have become increasingly discernible in public and media discourses in Britain. It shows how there is an observable variety of Muslim perspectives within news reporting itself, and that this marks a positive contrast with the more limited range of argumentation at an earlier period in the emergence of British Muslim identities in the late 1980s at the time of the Rushdie affair.

Moore, R.C. (2003), 'Religion and Topoi in the News: An Analysis of "Unsecular Media" Hypothesis', *Journal of Media and Religion* 2(1), 49–64.

> The article examines the news coverage of Jesse Jackson's marital infidelity to determine the extent to which the theme of hypocrisy was employed and whether this employment supported or challenged a religious (as opposed to secular) worldview. This draws upon the thesis put forward in Silk (1998).

Moore, R.C. (2008), 'Secular Spirituality/Mundane Media: One Newspaper's In-depth Coverage of Buddhism', *Journal of Media and Religion* 7(4), 231–55.

> This article continues testing and developing Mark Silk's ideas about "unsecular media" by analysing media coverage of the Dalai Lama's visit to the United States.

Poole, E. and Taira, T. (forthcoming), 'Researching Religion in British Newspapers and Television', in L. Woodhead (ed.), *Innovative Methods in the Study of Religion: Research in Practice*, Oxford: Oxford University Press.

> This article examines methodological issues in researching religious references in British mainstream media. It addresses some of the practical problems in longitudinal and comparative study of religion in the media.

Stout, D. and J.M. Buddenbaum (2008), 'Approaches to the Study of Media and Religion', *Religion* 38: 226–32.

> This article is a reflection of the past research and future prospects of the study of media and religion. It highlights three areas: the idea that media creates multiple places of worship, the study of religious audiences, and media criticism.

Underwood, D. (2006), 'The Problem with Paul: Seeds of Culture Wars and the Dilemma for Journalists', *Journal of Media and Religion* 5(2), 71–90.

> In this article Underwood suggests that journalists cannot expect to understand the dissension among conservative and liberal Christians, as well as the broader divisions between Christians and non-Christians, without examining Paul as a major source of the double-mindedness that characterises Christianity's outlook on the questions of modern life.

Valenzano III, J. and L. Menegatos (2008), 'Benedict the Bifurcated: Secular and Sacred Framing of the Pope and Turkey', *Journal of Media and Religion* 7(4), 207–30.

> The authors argue that the unique audience of the *Turkish Daily News (TDN)*, a national English-language daily newspaper in Turkey, drove the newspaper's framing of its coverage of the Pope's visit to Turkey. It contends that the *TDN* helped readers balance the sacred and secular tensions surrounding Pope Benedict and his visit by emphasising the Pope's role as a political official over his role as a religious leader and the political invitation to visit Turkey over the religious invitation.

Viney, R. (1999), 'Religious Broadcasting on UK Television: policy, public perception and programmes', *Cultural Trends* 36: 4–28.

> An examination of religious broadcasting, policy and programming on UK television in the 1990s. Later developments have rather confirmed than refuted the trends highlighted by this analysis.

Other cited references

Al-Hussaini, M., 'Occupy: the fault line between St Paul's and the Corporation of London'. Online: http://www.guardian.co.uk/commentisfree/belief/2011/nov/28/occupy-st-pauls-occupy-london (accessed 1 December 2011).

Allen, S., *News Culture*, 3rd edn (Maidenhead: Open University Press, 2010).

Anderson, J.W. (2003), 'New Media, New Publics: Reconfiguring the Public Sphere of Islam', *Social Research* 70 (3), 887–906.

Ashcroft, D., 'Christian Aid embraces Social Media to help Fund Raising', KMP Digitata, 20 August 2010. http://kmp.co.uk/2010/08/christian-aid-embraces-social-media-to-help-fund-raising/ (accessed 12 August 2011).

Bantz, C.R., 'News Organisations: Conflict as a Crafted Cultural Norm', *Communication*, 8 (1985), pp. 225–44.

Bartholomew, R. (ed.), *Bartholomew's Notes on Religion*, http://barthsnotes. wordpress.com/ (accessed 12 August 2011).

Barthes, R., *The Semiotic Challenge*, trans. Richard Howard (Berkeley, CA: University of California Press, 1989), p. 89.

Berger, P. (1968), 'A Bleak Outlook Seen for Religion', *The New York Times*, 25 February 1968, 3.

Blair, T. (2010), 'British Media have a dangerous ignorance of faith', *Church Times*, 30 July 2010: http://www.churchtimes.co.uk/content.asp?id=98376

Bradney, A. (2010), 'Some Sceptical Thoughts about the Academic Analysis of Law and Religion in the United Kingdom', in N. Doe and R. Sandberg (eds), *Law and Religion: New Horizons*, Leuven: Peeters, 2010.

Census 2001 for England and Wales: http://www.ons.gov.uk/ons/guide-method/ census/census-2001/index.html (accessed 14 December 2011)

'Church of England is "living in the past", says BBC's head of religion', the *Daily Telegraph*: http://www.telegraph.co.uk/news/newstopics/religion/7174716/ Church-of-England-is-living-in-the-past-says-BBCs-head-of-religion.html (accessed 12 August 2011).

Clark, A. and O. Lelkes (2008), 'Deliver Us From Evil: Religion as Insurance', the Royal Economic Society's Annual Conference, 17–19 March 2008.

Clifford, L., *'Thought for the Day': Beyond the God-of-the-Slots*, London: Ekklesia, July 2010.

Cohen, B., *The Press and Foreign Policy* (Princeton University Press, 1963).

Critical Religion, University of Stirling, http://www.criticalreligion.stir.ac.uk/ in collaboration with *Ekklesia*, http://www.criticalreligion.stir.ac.uk/blog/ ekklesia/ (accessed 12 August 2011).

Currie, R., Gilbert, A. and L. Horsley, *Churches and Church-Goers: Patterns of Church Growth in the British Isles since 1700* (Oxford: Clarendon Press, 1977).

Davis, F., Stankeviciute, J., Ebbutt, D. and Kaggwa, R., *The Ground of Justice, The Report of a Pastoral Research Enquiry into the Needs of Migrants in London's Catholic Community* (Cambridge: Hügel Institute, 2007).

de Certeau, M., *The Practice of Everyday Life*, trans. Steven Rendall (Berkeley, CA: University of California Press, 1984).

Eldridge, J. (ed.), *Getting the Message: News, Truth and Power* (London: Routledge, 1994).

Eldridge, J. (ed.), *News Content Language and Visuals: Glasgow University Media Reader, Vol. 1.* (London: Routledge, 1995).

Fowler, R., *Language in the News: Discourse and Ideology in the Press* (London: Routledge, 1991).

'Dietrich Bonhoeffer (1906–1945)', Boston Collaborative Encyclopedia of Western Theology http://people.bu.edu/wwildman/bce/bonhoeffer.htm (accessed 12 August 2011).

Ford, J., 'Most-watched Television Events through History', http://technology. ezine1.com/most-watched-television-events-through-history-77369aee7e8.html

Galtung, J., and M. Ruge ,'Structuring and Selecting News', *The Manufacture of News*, S. Cohen and J. Young (eds) (London: 1973).

Gledhill, R., Articles of Faith', at: http://ruthgledhill.blogspot.com/ (accessed 12 August 2011).

Gledhill, R. (2007), 'Religion's death has been widely exaggerated, *The Times*, 22 October.

Grabowicz, P., 'The Transition to Digital Journalism', Knight Digital Media Centre, Berkeley Graduate School of Journalism, California, USA. http://multimedia.journalism.berkeley.edu/tutorials/digital-transform/web-20/ (accessed 12 August 2011).

Hill, M. (2001), 'Judicial Approaches to Religious Disputes', in R. O'Dair and A. Lewis (eds), *Law and Religion*. Oxford: Oxford University Press.

Hill, M. and Sandberg, R. (2007), 'Is Nothing Sacred? Clashing Symbols in a Secular World', *Public Law* 488.

Hollis, L., *The Phoenix: St Paul's Cathedral and the Men who Made Modern London* (London: Weidenfeld and Nicolson, 2008).

Holmes, N. (2010), 'Religious television: A background paper', Church of England General Synod: Private Member's Motion. Unpublished paper.

Jenkins, B., *Better Journalism in the Digital Age* (Dunfermline: Carnegie Trust, 2012).

Keegan, J. et al., *The Eye of War: Words and Photographs from the Front Line* (London: Weidenfeld & Nicolson, 2003).

Killing the Buddha, http://killingthebuddha.com/ (accessed 12 August 2011).

Knott, K. and J. Mitchell, 'The Changing Faces of Media and Religion', in Linda Woodhead and Rebecca Cato (eds), *Religion and Change in Modern Britain* (London and New York: Routledge, 2012), c. pp. 243–64.

Lichter, S., Rothman, R.S., and L. Lichter, *The Media Elite: America's New Power-brokers* (Bethesda, MD: Adler & Adler, 1986).
    Lynch, G. (ed.), *Between Sacred and Profance: Researching Religion and Popular Culture* (London and New York: I.B.Tauris, 2007).

Lynch, J., *Debates in Peace Journalism* (Sydney: Sydney University Press, 2008).

Marr, A., *My Trade: A Short History of British Journalism* (London: Macmillan, 2004).

Menski, W., 'Law, Religion and Culture in Multicultural Britain', in R. Mehdi et al. (eds), *Law and Religion in Multicultural Societies* (Copenhagen: DJOF Publishing, 2008).

Mitchell, J., *Visually Speaking: Radio and the Renaissance of Preaching* (Edinburgh: T&T Clark, 1999).

Moore K., Mason P. and J. Lewis, *Images of Islam in the UK: The Representation of British Muslims in the National Print News Media 2000–2008* (Cardiff: Cardiff University and Channel 4, 2008). Also available online: http://www.cardiff.ac.uk/jomec/research/researchgroups/journalismstudies/fundedprojects/2008islamophobia.html (accessed 1 December 2011).

Naughton, J., 'Live with the WikiLeakable world or shut down the net. It's your choice', the *Guardian*, 6 December 2010.

Neuman, W.R., et al., *Common Knowledge: News and the Construction of Political Meaning* (Chicago: University of Chicago Press, 1992).

Philo, G. (ed.), *Industry, Economy, War and Politics: Glasgow University Media Reader, Vol. 2.* (London: Routledge, 1995).

Pugh, J.C., *Religionless Christianity: Dietrich Bonhoeffer in Troubled Times* (London: T&T Clark / Continuum, 2009).

Rushdie, S., *Haroun and the Sea of Stories* (London: Granta, 1990).

van Ginneken, J., *Understanding Global News: A Critical Introduction* (London, Thousand Oaks and New Delhi: Sage, 1998), p. 66.

http://www.guardian.co.uk/commentisfree/cifamerica/2010/dec/06/western-democracies-must-live-with-leaks (accessed 14 December 2011).

Religion Dispatches, http://www.religiondispatches.org/ (accessed 12 August 2011).

Sacks, J. (2000), 'Faith communities and the renewal of civil society', June 2000: http://www.ccfwebsite.com/archives/Dr_Jonathan_Sacks_the_Chief_Rabbi_calls_for_faith_communities_to_renew_civil_society.pdf

Schlesinger, P., *Putting Reality Together* (London: Routledge, 1987).

Shoemaker, P.J., and Reese, S.D., *Mediating the Message – Theories of Influence on Mass Media Content* (Longman: New York, 1991).

Shah, P. (2009), 'Transforming to Accommodate? Reflections on the Shari'a Debate in Britain', in Grillo et al. (eds), *Legal Practice and Cultural Diversity* (Aldershot, Ashgate).

Sightings, University of Chicago Divinity School, http://divinity.uchicago.edu/martycenter/publications/sightings/ (accessed 12 August 2011).

Simpson, J., *Strange Places, Questionable People* (London: Pan Books, 1998 [2008]).

Simpson, J., *Unreliable Sources: How the Twentieth Century was Reported* (London: Macmillan, 2010).

Smith, M.N., 'Democratizing Knowledge', in *Humanities*, September/October 2005, Vol. 26, No.5.

Start the Week, Monday 5 April 2010, BBC Radio 4, http://www.bbc.co.uk/programmes/b00rrhyd

Thompson, M. (2008), *Faith, Morality and the Media*, *Theos* Annual Lecture, 14 October 2008.

Tommasi, M., '50 Definitions of Social Media', *The Social Media Guide*, http://thesocialmediaguide.com/social_media/50-definitions-of-social-media (accessed 12 August 2011).

Towler, R., *Homo Religiosus: Sociological Problems in the Study of Religion* (London: Constable, 1974).

Traber, M., 'Communication Ethics' (Ch. 18), in George Gerbner, Hamid Mowlana and Karle Nordenstreng, 'The Global Media Debate: Its rise, fall and renewal' (New Jersey: Ablex, 1993).

Warman, M., 'Young people "bored" with social media', *Daily Telegraph*, 15 August 2011. http://www.telegraph.co.uk/technology/social-media/8702509/Young-people-bored-with-social-media.html (accessed 14 December 2011).

Westminster Declaration of Christian Conscience 2010. http://www.westminster 2010.org.uk/declaration/ (accessed 30 October 2010).

Wolfe, K.M., *The Churches and the British Broadcasting Corporation 1922– 1956: The Politics of Broadcast Religion* (London: SCM, 1984).

Williams, R. (2008), 'Civil and Religious Law in England: a Religious Perspective', 7 February 2008, the foundation lecture at the Royal Courts of Justice: http:// www.archbishopofcanterbury.org/1575 (accessed 14 December 2011).

'Williams tries to defuse row over sharia law but refuses to apologise', the *Independent*, 12 February 2008, http://www.independent.co.uk/news/uk/ home-news/williams-tries-to-defuse-row-over-sharia-law-but-refuses-to- apologise-781009.html

'Williams criticises Irish Catholic Church "credibility"', 3 April 2010, http://news. bbc.co.uk/1/hi/8601381.stm (accessed 14 December 2011).

Winston, D. (ed.), *The Oxford Handbook on Religion and the American News Media* (Oxford: Oxford University Press, forthcoming 2012).

Winston, D., *Heartland Religion: The American News Media and the Reagan Revolution* (Oxford: Oxford University Press, forthcoming 2013).

Select Webography

BBC Online: Religion and Ethics
http://www.bbc.co.uk/religion/

BeliefNet (Current Affairs and Commentary)
http://beliefnet.com/*CESNUR – Centro Studi sulle Nuove Religioni*

Center for Studies on New Religions (NRMs), based in Italy.
http://www.cesnur.org/*Crosswalk* (News, current affairs and opinions from evangelical Christian perspective)

The Center for Media Literacy
http://www.medialit.org/

Ekklesia
http://www.ekklesia.co.uk/

Guardian: Comment is Free
http://www.guardian.co.uk/commentisfree

The Muslim Weekly
http://www.themuslimweekly.com/NewsPaper.aspx

The International Study Commission on Media, Religion, and Culture
http://www.iscmrc.org/

The International Christian Media Commission
http://www.icmc.org/

Journal of Religion and Film
http://avalon.unomaha.edu/jrf/

Journal of Religion and Popular Culture
http://www.usask.ca/relst/jrpc/index.html

Online Religion Journalism (USA)
http://www.toad.net/~andrews/jreligion.html*On Religion (News Service)*
http://www.onreligion.com/*The Pauline Center for Media Studies*
http://www.daughtersofstpaul.com/mediastudies/mediastudiescenter.html

Public Faith: The Centre for Theology and Public Issues Blog
http://centrefortheologyandpublicissues.wordpress.com/

Speaking of Faith (Minnesota Public Radio, USA)
http://speakingoffaith.publicradio.org/*WorldWide Faith News (News archive from
    range of denominations)*
http://www.wfn.org/*Religion Watch (News Service)*
http://www.religionwatch.com/*New Mexico Media Literacy Project*
http://www.nmmlp.org/

The Revealer (New York University Center for Religion and Media Journal)
http://www.therevealer.org/

*Religion and Ethics Newsweekly (Site connected with PBS's Religion and Ethics
    programme)*
http://www.thirteen.org/religionandethics/home.html
http://www.pbs.org/wnet/religionandethics/calendar.html

Religion in the News (Organised by Mark Silk)
http://www.trincoll.edu/depts/csrpl/RIN.htm

Religion News from Around the World
http://www.omsakthi.org/religion_news.html

Religion News from Yahoo!
http://fullcoverage.yahoo.com/Full_Coverage/World/Religion_News/

Religion News Service (USA)
http://www.religionnews.com/

Religion Review (From World News Network)
http://religionreview.com/

Religion Newswriters Association
http://www.religionwriters.com/

Resource Center for Cyberculture Studies
http://www.com.washington.edu/rccs/

Resource Center for Media, Religion and Culture
http://www.colorado.edu/Journalism/mcm/mrc/

Ruth Gledhill's Articles of Faith Blog
http://ruthgledhill.blogspot.com/

Theos: The Public Theology Think Tank
http://www.theosthinktank.co.uk/

World Association for Christian Communication
http://www.wacc.org.uk/

Index

Lightning Source UK Ltd.
Milton Keynes UK
UKOW06f0311150916

283002UK00014B/315/P